A History of Schenectady (New York) During the Revolution

TO WHICH IS APPENDED
A CONTRIBUTION TO THE INDIVIDUAL RECORDS
OF THE INHABITANTS OF THE SCHENECTADY
DISTRICT DURING THAT PERIOD

WILLIS T. HANSON, JR., A.M.

HERITAGE BOOKS
2020

HERITAGE BOOKS
AN IMPRINT OF HERITAGE BOOKS, INC.

Books, CDs, and more—Worldwide

For our listing of thousands of titles see our website
at
www.HeritageBooks.com

A Facsimile Reprint
Published 2020 by
HERITAGE BOOKS, INC.
Publishing Division
5810 Ruatan Street
Berwyn Heights, Md. 20740

Originally published July 1916
One Thousand Copies Printed from Type

Copyright © 1916 Willis T. Hanson, Jr.

— Publisher's Notice —
In reprints such as this, it is often not possible to remove blemishes from the original. We feel the contents of this book warrant its reissue despite these blemishes and hope you will agree and read it with pleasure.

International Standard Book Number
Paperbound: 978-0-7884-1587-6

TO MY MOTHER
THIS WORK
IS AFFECTIONATELY DEDICATED

PREFATORY NOTE

The history of Schenectady during the troublesome times of the Revolution is so closely linked with the affairs of the whole Mohawk Valley, and with the tides of the Border Wars that laid waste the surrounding country almost to her gates, that, in dealing with the history of the one, one must necessarily touch to a large extent upon the history of the other.

INTRODUCTION

While in the title of this work I have made a distinction between the town of Schenectady and the Schenectady District, which included both the present townships of Glenville and Rotterdam and because of its proximity to the district, for military organization, Princetown, and while I have laid stress for the most part on the activities of the town proper, it will be seen that by reason of the men of the district sharing as they did with the inhabitants of the town the burden of civil and military service and the creation of the activities to which the following pages relate, the history of the town in reality becomes the history of the district.

In gathering material for this work I have been struck with the scarcity of available manuscript sources of information.

In the minutes of the various Committees of Safety which rightly form the base upon which the history of the early years of the war is built, wide gaps appear and the only manuscript records of these boards now known to exist are those covering the period from January 15, 1777, to February 17, 1778, deposited in the Library of Congress (Force Collection), which, being wrongly labeled and catalogued, were discovered by the writer only by the merest chance.

Judge Sanders, writing in 1879, had before him a record book of one hundred and sixty-two closely written pages covering the minutes of the first Board and its successors, but unfortunately he has given us but a few scattered extracts of the valuable and interesting data which it contained. Judge Yates, writing some twenty-three years later, intimates that he also had access to these records, but more unfortunately still, instead of making use of the rare opportunity afforded, such passages as he has given us are identical with those transcribed by Judge Sanders.

Fortunately for posterity, before the record book became irrevocably lost it came to the attention of one who with considerable labor and expense has given us, in a little magazine which he called the American Antiquarian and Quarterly Genealogical Record (note 4, p. 18), the minutes from the first meeting of the Board on May 6, 1775, to and including the minutes of the meeting of May 27, 1776.

While, without a doubt, many of the records of our early days were destroyed in the fire that in 1819 swept the lower part of the town, it is mainly to negligence, carelessness and a lack of appreciation of historical value that we owe our present lack of manuscript sources of information.

Papers found in old trunks and boxes stored away in the garrets of houses dating back to the early days are constantly coming to light to bear their testimony to the truths of the past. That there are many more such trunks and boxes in many more such garrets is not an unreasonable supposition, and that we may not find ourselves guilty of that negligence that has been responsible for the loss of so much valuable data in the past it becomes our duty to make available for posterity such pertinent matter as we may chance upon, either by depositing it with libraries and societies formed for the safe keeping of such material or by calling it to the attention of some historian whose interest in his subject should be an assurance of a proper use being made of it.

WILLIS T. HANSON, JR.

CHAPTER I

THE VALLEY OF THE MOHAWK

Due to its unique geographical position, New York, in those early times when the rivers and lakes afforded practically the only highways of importance, was rightly felt to be the key to the American continent, and from its infancy hostile nations contested its possession.

Among those factors which gave New York her strategical prominence the Mohawk River played no small part, for by its means alike were accessible the lands to the westward, through the only valley pass piercing the Appalachian Range; the Great Lakes, through the all but intermingling of its headwaters with the streams flowing northward into them, and the Atlantic seacoast, through the Hudson River.

It was the early realization of the importance of the Mohawk River that led the Iroquois Confederacy to stretch its dominion throughout the Valley, thus enabling its warriors to maintain that supremacy over far distant tribes[1] which for so many years they enjoyed.

With the coming of the white man in greater numbers, to the importance of the Mohawk River from a

---

[1] At the era of their highest military supremacy, about the year 1660, the Iroquois, in their warlike expeditions, ranged unresisted from New England to the Mississippi, and from the St. Lawrence to the Tennessee. Lewis H. Morgan.

military standpoint was added a commercial value increasing with the demands upon it until the opening of the Erie Canal transferred the traffic to that channel. The Old Iroquois Trail[2] in its turn gave way to the stage road, and this in its turn to the railroad; the successors in each case, however, following the well-defined line of early travel.

Along these lines of communication the early pioneers, for the most part, established their homes, until on the eve of the Revolution the population of the Mohawk Valley may be roughly estimated as totaling ten thousand souls.

To the westward the settlements extended in a narrow belt as far as the present town of German Flats, settled and owned as far as Canajoharie in the main by the Dutch, many of them descendants of the first settlers of Schenectady or emigrants from it, and beyond Canajoharie by the Palatines;[3] northward to a short distance beyond Johnstown, where had settled many Irish and Scotch-Highlanders[4] following Sir

---

[2] Proceeding from the site of Albany, the central trail entered the lands now covered by the city of Schenectady by the ravine through which the railroad now passes and crossed the Mohawk at a ford where now stands the Scotia bridge. From this fording place two trails passed up the river one on either side. Lewis H. Morgan.

[3] In 1723 a large tract of land was purchased from the Indians to be later confirmed by letters patent from the King. To this tract soon came many of those Palatine Germans who had in 1711 settled at Schoharie and who had been led to change their place of residence because of difficulties arising over their titles. Accessions to the settlement were made from time to time until at the period of the Revolution it embraced one of the most prosperous sections of Tryon County.

[4] They had been induced to immigrate by Sir William Johnson and were settled as tenants on his estates in various parts of the Kingsboro Tract.

William Johnson;[5] southward to the headwaters of the Susquehanna, settled mainly by Scotch-Irish,[6] and in the valley of the Schoharie to some seven miles beyond Middleburg, settled also by Palatine Germans.[7]

From among the English, Irish and Scotch-Highlanders mainly were recruited the Tories, while from the ranks of the Dutch and Palatines and from the Scotch-Irish came the men to whom we owe Oriskany and upon whom fell the burdens of resisting the repeated raids of Indian and Tory that swept the Valley with a fury that was paralleled in no other section of the Colonies during the whole war.

[5] Sir William Johnson came to the Mohawk Valley in 1738, as the agent of his uncle, Sir Peter Warren. He founded a settlement which he called Warren's Bush and remained there five years. He then removed to a tract of land near Amsterdam which he had acquired in 1741 and upon which he had already erected the stone house, still standing, known as Fort Johnson. He removed to Johnson Hall, Johnstown, in 1763.

[6] In 1741 several families, induced to emigrate from Londonderry, N. H., settled on the Lindesay Patent.

[7] This was the original Palatine settlement, dating back to 1711, from which those who had settled at Stone Arabia had removed.

CHAPTER II

SCHENECTADY

The approximately twenty-four hundred souls who, in 1773, composed the population[1] of Schenectady, were chiefly of Low Dutch origin. Among them, however, were numbered some Irish and not a few English,[2] for there had been many immigrants from New England, while British regulars and New England militia had for nearly a century garrisoned[3] the fort, and discharged soldiers mixing with the population had married Dutch wives and become settlers. The English element had moreover been augmented[4] from time to time by those who came direct from their

[1] Colonel Henry B. Livingston, in his manuscript journal of the Canadian expedition, places the number of houses in Schenectady in 1775 as three hundred. This is the same number as noted by Richard Smith in 1769. The Marquis de Chastelleux states that eight people were the average number residing in one house. The writer is inclined to believe that the estimate of Jabez Maud Fisher of four hundred houses in 1773 is too high and he has consequently determined the population of the town proper at this period on the basis of three hundred houses.

[2] Reverend William Andrews, rector of St. George's Church, reported to the Society for the Propagation of the Gospel on March 15, 1771, that "about 80 grown up persons" regularly attended his church.

[3] This was mostly previous to 1754. After the close of the Old French War few troops were stationed here. Jonathan Pearson.

[4] Daniel Campbell came to Schenectady in 1754, John Duncan in 1755, Alexander Campbell in 1762, while the later well-known firm of Phyn & Ellice was in business in 1768.

native land to take up their residence here because of the mercantile advantages offered.

Commercially, Schenectady was admirably situated, for through it ran the Great Highway leading westward and here became navigable the Mohawk River.

From its first settlement Schenectady had been primarily a trading community and early it became an important and flourishing town, a transfer point for the products of the West to be carried by wagon to Albany, or shipments of supplies from the older settlements to be borne westward by boat.

"According to our conjecture," wrote[5] Richard Smith, who visited Schenectady in 1769, "the Town counts about 300 Dwelling Houses besides Out Houses, standing in 3 Principal Streets[6] nearly East and West; these are crossed by 4 or 5 other Streets.[7] Few of the Buildings are contiguous," continues the Journal, "some of them are constructed in the old Dutch Taste[8] generally of Wood but sometimes of Brick, and there may be 6 or 7 elegant Mansions[9]

---

[5] Richard Smith, A Tour of Four Great Rivers, p. 22.

[6] Front Street, Brewer's or Niskayuna (now Union) Street, and the old road to Albany (now Albany Street).

[7] The Vrooman map of 1768 shows streets corresponding to the following of today: Washington Avenue (then Lion, afterwards Washington Street), Ferry Street, Church Street, Water Street, Mill Lane, Center Street, Jefferson Street, and North Street.

[8] The old Abraham Yates house, built about 1730, now No. 109 Union Street, is an excellent example of the Dutch style of architecture.

[9] Possibly he refers to the old Campbell mansion, now standing on the northeast corner of State and Church Streets; the John Glen mansion, now No. 58 Washington Avenue, or the old Ten Eyck mansion on the northeast corner of Governor's Lane and Front Street, at one time the residence of Governor Joseph C. Yates. These houses have all been remodeled.

without including a large Dutch Church[10] with a Town Cloc, a Presbyterian Meeting House[11] and a neat English Church[12] now finishing off, containing a particular Pew for Sir William Johnson[13] adorned with a handsome Canopy supported by Pilasters. There are no Wharves but a public Landing or Two at the Ends of the Streets where the Batteaux bring the Peltry and wheat from above. These Batteaux which are built here[14] are very large, each end sharp so that they may be rowed either way. The townspeople are supplyed altogether with Beef[15] and Pork from

[10] The Dutch Reformed Church, erected in 1734 and demolished in 1814, stood on the site of the present church, the corner of Union and Church Streets.

[11] This seems to have been a rented "meeting house" the location of which cannot now be ascertained. It was not until October 12, 1769, that a lot was purchased for the erection of a permanent house of worship. The building, completed by the end of the year 1773, had a steeple and turret for a bell on which the members of St. George's looked with envious eyes, their church having neither.

[12] St. George's, the erection of which was commenced in 1759.

[13] Sir William not only personally contributed liberally to the fund for the erection of the church, but obtained many contributions from his friends throughout the Colonies.

[14] Boat building was for many years one of the principal industries of Schenectady, nearly all the boats used on the Mohawk being built here. The yards were along the river front extending from the present Scotia bridge to North Street. The batteaux were adopted as substitutes for the bark canoes, which were too light to bear the increasing loads of merchandise. They were built of white pine boards, and were from twenty to twenty-five feet long by three and a half wide in the center, capable of carrying from two to five tons. The batteaux were generally manned by three or four men and propelled by poles, with the auxiliary of ropes pulled by men on shore when being forced over the rapids in the river. Several batteaux generally traveled together so that the batteaumen could lend aid to one another. These batteaux were in general use until 1797, when, with the completion of the enterprise known as the Inland Lock Navigation Company, they gave way to the larger Durham boats.

[15] This sold at 5d. and 6d. per pound. Richard Smith.

New England, most of the Meadows being used for Wheat, Peas and other Grain; however there are certain choice Grass Meadows about the Place and yet at the End we entered, the Sandy Pine Land approaches within 300 Yards of the Buildings."

Jabez Maud Fisher, the son of a wealthy Philadelphia shipowner, who came through Schenectady some four years later, places[16] the number of houses at four hundred. He makes special note of the "vast deal of fine Meadow and arable ground in the neighborhood," of the "very considerable and profitable trade carried on with the Indians," and further adds that "there are several 100 boats go from this place to Niagara[17] and some to Detroit[18] loaded with dry and wet goods."

The town was surrounded by a stockade of upright pickets in the shape of a parallelogram having two gates, one opening to the east and one to the north.[19] This stockade was flanked[20] at intervals by redoubts or blockhouses and at the period of which we write enclosed[21] an area bounded on the north and west

[16] A manuscript copy of his journal is in the possession of the Herkimer County Historical Society.

[17] The route taken was up the Mohawk to near Fort Stanwix (Rome), where was a carry to the waters of Wood Creek; through Oneida Lake into the Oswego River and to Oswego on Lake Ontario. From Oswego to Niagara the merchandise was sometimes conveyed in the same boats and sometimes in sloops.

[18] Reverend William Andrews reported that his church was better attended in the winter than in the summer, for when the Mohawk was open several of his congregation who were Indian traders or batteaumen proceeded in their boats to "Fort Detroit and even to Mishillimackanac in sloop which [was] reckoned upward of 1000 miles from [Schenectady]." In making this trip a further carry was necessary around the falls at Niagara to Chippewa.

[19] The Sexagenary, p. 12.

[20] Documents Relating to the Colonial History of New York, X, 677.

[21] Jonathan Pearson, History of the Schenectady Patent, p. 306.

by the river, on the south by a line starting at the river and running twenty-eight feet south of State Street southeasterly to the present location of the New York Central depot, and on the east by a line from this point intersecting with the river at a point not far from the foot of North Street.

In the center of an open space (two hundred and sixty-four by two hundred feet), at the junction of Front, Ferry and Green Streets, stood the fort, the south wall extending across Ferry Street three feet south of the north corner of the present rectory of St. George's Church.[22] This fort was erected in 1735, and was built half of masonry and half of hewn timbers piled one upon the other above the masonry[23] to a height of twenty feet.[24] It was capable of holding from two to three hundred men.[25] The four curtains, which, by the way, contained no loopholes through which to fire the few cannon[26] of which the town boasted, were about seventy-six feet long each and the four bastions or blockhouses which stood at the corners were about twenty-four feet square.[27] The fort was not encircled by a ditch, as was sometimes customary, and its entrance was through a large swing gate raised like a drawbridge.[28]

Both the stockades and the fort were, at the begin-

---

[22] *Ibid.*, p. 318.
[23] Documents Relating to the Colonial History of New York, X, 677.
[24] Jonathan Pearson, History of the Schenectady Patent, p. 318, note.
[25] Documents Relating to the Colonial History of New York, X, 677.
[26] The two largest came to be known as the "Lady Washington" and the "Long Nine Pounder." These guns were placed in the streets so as to command the gates. Jonathan Pearson.
[27] Jonathan Pearson, History of the Schenectady Patent, p. 316.
[28] Documents Relating to the Colonial History of New York, X, 677.

ning of the Revolution, wholly out of repair,[29] having been suffered to go into decay during the period of peace following the close of the French and Indian War.

While it seems unbelievable that during the stirring times of 1776 any means of defense, however meager, would be deliberately removed,—unless, perhaps, it had reached such a stage of decay as to be rendered useless or in order that more adequate protection might replace it,—there is evidence[30] to show that during this year the "Old Fort" was removed. Whether or not such was the case the writer cannot definitely ascertain, but he is rather inclined to hold the opinion[31] that the fort was permitted to remain until after the war. This opinion is based upon the statements[32] of certain soldiers who are quite positive in their assertions that the defenses of Schenectady included a fortress, which with the other works was guarded during the entire period of the war.

The fact that on June 23, 1780, an act[33] was passed by the Legislature enabling the inhabitants of Sche-

[29] Documents Relating to the Colonial History of New York, VIII, 451.

[30] Jonathan Pearson, History of the Schenectady Patent, p. 318, note.

[31] This opinion is shared by Professor Pearson who, although he makes little point of it, states (History of the Schenectady Patent, p. 332) that "after the close of the Revolutionary War the defenses of the village were never repaired, or renewed:—the *old* fort was removed and the land sold."

[32] "This place [Schenectady] was surrounded with pickets and had a fortress and other works of defense which were guarded during the whole war." Pension Office Records, John Henry R 4891.

"This place [Schenectady] was during [the] war surrounded with pickets and blockhouses and had a fortress and other works of defense were constantly erecting during [the] war." Pension Office Records, Bartholomew Clute S 12499.

[33] Public Papers of George Clinton, V, 886.

nectady to erect a fortress does not preclude the possibility of the old fort having been retained, for indeed the limited facilities for defense offered by this fort would quite justify the more extensive picket fort[34] suggested by Governor Clinton, which was subsequently[35] erected.

[34] *Ibid.*
[35] Work was probably started soon after the act was passed. There were on the east side of the picket fort (Pension Office Records, James Barhydt S 12948) seven redoubts (Pension Office Records, Wessel Cornu W 1029. Public Papers of George Clinton, VI, 715) which were used as guardhouses. Eighty-four men composed the guard, twelve being assigned to each redoubt (Pension Office Records, Wessel Cornu W 1029).

CHAPTER III

THE RISE OF THE REVOLUTIONARY MOVEMENT

In conjunction with the wave of protest against the Stamp Act and other measures of Great Britain thought to be unconstitutional and oppressive, secret organizations known as the Sons of Liberty sprang up throughout the Colonies. It is interesting to note that those who afterward became Whig and Tory were equally instrumental in the forming of these bodies. At their inception, the tendencies of these associations were for the most part not revolutionary. They "attempted no change of government,—only a preservation of the Constitution."[1]

In March, 1766, in compliance with a request from the New York Association, an organization of the Sons of Liberty was formed in Albany. While its members exhibited "the highest esteem of his most sacred Majesty, King George the Third," and swore to "bear true Allegiance to him and his Royal house forever," they nevertheless resolved that they would "Venture [their] Lives and fortunes, Effectually to

---

[1] Letter from the New York Sons of Liberty to the Albany Association, April 3, 1766. The American Historian and Quarterly Genealogical Record, No. 4, p. 148.

prevent the Stamp Act from Ever taking place in [the] City or Province."[2]

Following the organization of the Albany Sons of Liberty, their Committee of Correspondence dispatched the following letter[3] to their friends in Schenectady:

Gentlemen:

Agreeable to the general sense of the Friends of Liberty over all the Colonies, and the particular instance of the Committee at New York, we earnestly request You to advise with the respectable body of the Inhabitants of the Town of Schenectady, that they form themselves, after the example of their Brethren, and appoint a Committee for Regulations and Correspondence with us, and this, and the other Provinces as there may be occasion; and that as soon as formed You give us notice, that we may transmit to you the several Associations, and other papers of importance we have from them, and from time to time thro' them from the other Colonies. We think You will readily conceive the necessity of this measure, when You consider how general it is thro' all the Colonies, and that the design is no more than the most effectual consolidation of the best of Systems, of which we can neither be too jealous nor too careful.

(Signed) FREEDOM.

By Order of the Committee of the Sons of Liberty in Albany.

---

[2] Constitution of the Albany Sons of Liberty. The American Historian and Quarterly Genealogical Record, No. 4, p. 152. The original manuscript was at one time among the papers in the old Sanders House, Scotia. The writer has reason to believe that it is now in a private collection in Albany.

[3] The American Historian and Quarterly Genealogical Record, No. 4, p. 153.

While the original constitution of the Sons of Liberty of Albany subscribed to by ninety-four of its members is still in existence, together with several letters written by their Committee of Regulation and Correspondence, there is available not the least evidence to show that an organization was ever formed in Schenectady.

As time went on differences of opinion arose regarding the controversy with the Mother Country, and by 1770 two parties, Whig and Loyalist, were fairly well defined, each with its political organization and each subdivided into liberals and conservatives. The contest at this time "was not one between those who favored and those who opposed the acts of the English government—for both parties opposed them—but was over the form which that opposition should take."[4]

The Loyalist party helped to call the Continental Congress; although the proposal came first from the Sons of Liberty, the moderate Loyalist looked not unfavorably upon this body and even the extremists hoped for some good from it.

The First Continental Congress, which met at Philadelphia on September 5, 1774, was merely a group of committees with no technical authority, assembled with the idea of advising with each other regarding the public welfare. It did not intentionally meet as a revolutionary body, yet as something like a state of war existed in part of the country, in the absence of any formally constituted government "it took the reins" and almost immediately, to the horror

[4] Alexander Clarence Flick, Loyalism in New York, p. 22.

of the Loyalists, became the "instrument for the promotion of revolution and independence."[5]

In proportion as Congress drifted toward radicalism and assumed powers not delegated to it, it was opposed by the Loyalists and enthusiastically applauded by the Sons of Liberty, who now became the chief supporters of the revolutionary movement.

The Loyalists, while they were opposed to revolution, were not satisfied with the pretensions of Parliament. They believed it their duty to propose a solution of the problem and they did not believe that this solution could be effected through despotic committees enforcing laws made at Philadelphia. Their opposition to Congress and its recommendations was soon felt in every section of New York.

In the Mohawk Valley the esteem in which Sir William Johnson, His Majesty's Commissioner of Indian Affairs, was held, with his tact and good judgment, did much to hold the radical revolutionary element in check. In him was placed the confidence and faith of the people, and rightly, too, for Sir William had seen the clouds gathering and while he stood loyally by the King we have reason[6] to believe that he saw justice in the demands of the colonists and that he was not entirely out of sympathy with their attitude.

The Dutch of Schenectady, Whig sympathizers almost to a man, appear to have been quite content to sit on their "stoops" smoking their pipes in silence

---

[5] *Ibid.*, p. 25.
[6] William L. Stone, The Life and Times of Sir William Johnson, Bart., II, 369. William W. Campbell, Annals of Tryon County, pp. 29-30.

and watch the course of events.⁷ The armed interference of British soldiery had had no place in their lives; they were staunch friends of Sir William, for there were many who had served as officers under him in the Colonial Wars, and there was scarcely a Dutch family but that had been represented in his companies, while some had been honored with grants of land and others had held official positions under the Crown.

Following the death of Sir William Johnson in July, 1774, affairs in the Valley underwent a decided change. Sir John Johnson,⁸ his son, came into possession of his estates and Colonel Guy Johnson,⁹ his son-in-law, was appointed to succeed him as His Majesty's Superintendent of Indian Affairs. Neither Sir John nor Guy Johnson had the slightest sympathy¹⁰ with the cause of the Colonies, nor did either possess the tact of Sir William. From the first their actions were antagonistic rather than conciliatory.

With the restraining influence of Sir William removed, the revolutionary movement rapidly gained adherents throughout the Valley. Although Colonel

---

⁷ It is a matter of great regret that no source of information has been found available to warrant recording in more detail the trend of public opinion in Schenectady at this time.

⁸ Sir John Johnson was born November 5, 1742, and died January 4, 1830. He had spent considerable time in England and at the age of twenty-three had been knighted. On the death of Sir William he had refused to accept the office of Superintendent of Indian Affairs and this position had therefore been given to Colonel Guy Johnson.

⁹ Colonel Guy Johnson was a nephew of Sir William. He had acted for some time as his private secretary and had married Mary, the younger of his uncle's two daughters. Colonel Johnson resided at Guy Park one mile and a half east of Fort Johnson, the mansion house having been built for him by Sir William in 1766.

¹⁰ Both were of the aristocracy and felt only the wrongs of their own order. Douglas Campbell.

Johnson made every endeavor to check the rising tide of opposition to the British Crown, so rapidly did this opposition spring up that in one month after Sir William's death the Palatine patriots openly declared for Congress and soon the settlers in Canajoharie and German Flats were almost unanimous for "the undeniable privilege of being taxed only with their own consent."[11]

[11] Minutes of the Tryon County Committee of Safety (first meeting), August 27, 1774. Tryon County was the first in New York to organize its committee.

CHAPTER IV

THE SCHENECTADY COMMITTEE OF SAFETY[1] AND THE FIRST MILITIA COMPANIES

The First Provincial Congress, a Whig body, called because the Loyalist assembly had refused to approve the acts of Congress, was the first revolutionary body in New York. Immediately this body assumed all governing powers and to it was intrusted the enforcement of the Articles of Association signed by the Continental Congress on October 20, 1774.

The necessity of further localizing the execution of orders given by the Provincial Congress soon called into being county, and under them district, committees.

Although a Committee of Correspondence representing Albany County was organized in November,[2] 1774, it does not appear that any unusual activities engaged the attention of this body until May of the following year, when in view of the various accounts that were received "of the extraordinary commotions both in the Province of Massachusetts and at New York,"[3] it was felt "indispensably necessary" that

[1] These committees were quite as frequently known as Committees of Correspondence.

[2] A meeting, probably the first, was held on November 23.

[3] The Records of the Albany Committee of Safety. These records may be further cited as the source of subsequent matter in this chapter pertinent to the Albany Committee.

the sense of the townspeople be taken as to what line of conduct should be pursued at that critical juncture.

Under the direction of a subcommittee a meeting of the citizens was therefore called, and at this meeting, held on the afternoon of May 1, the following questions were placed before the people:

Are you willing to co-operate with our Brethren in New York, and the several Colonies on the Continent in their opposition to the Ministerial Plan now prosecuting against us?

Are you willing to appoint Persons to be (conjointly with others to be appointed by the several Districts in this County) a Committee of Safety, Protection and Correspondence with full power to Transact all such matters as they shall conceive may tend to the weal of the American Cause?

Following an affirmative decision on the questions at issue, the meeting at once proceeded to elect their Committee of Safety.

The matter of district committees seems to have been taken up almost immediately, and on May[4] 6 a meeting of the "freeholders and Inhabitants of the Township of Schenectady" was held, and as mem-

[4] The Records of the Schenectady Committee of Safety. The minutes covering the period from the first meeting until May 27, 1776, are to be found in the American Historian and Quarterly Genealogical Record, Vol. I, Nos. 1-4. These minutes form the source from which much of the material covering this period has been obtained.

The American Historian and Quarterly Genealogical Record, "edited by the Historical Society" and published by Mr. E. Z. Carpenter under a Schenectady imprint, is now practically unknown. Indirectly, from the publisher, the writer has learned the history of this little magazine. There was no "Historical Society" as indicated on the title-page of the publication and Mr. Carpenter had no associates in the enterprise. He was sole editor, proprietor and printer, setting his own type and using a hand press which he still has. The numbers were given to friends as printed, and but seventy-five copies of each were issued.

bers of a committee to represent their district were
selected the following:[5]

Reinier Mynderse,	John Sanders,
James Wilson,	Abraham Oothout,
Hugh Mitchell,	Tobias Ten Eyck,
Henry Glen,	John Roseboom,
Harmanus Wendell,	Christopher Yates.

The committee chosen met for organization on the
ninth, at the home[6] of William White. Christopher
Yates was elected chairman of the Board and Hugh
Mitchell, clerk. John Sanders and Tobias Ten Eyck
immediately refused to serve and their places were
later[7] filled by the election of Cornelius Cuyler and
Jacobus Teller.

The Schenectady Committee, organized as a subcommittee of that of Albany County,[8] regularly sent
delegates[9] to its conferences. Soon it became the
principal[10] organ of local government with duties
wide and important, for not only were its members
to attend to the raising of such troops and funds as

[5] The revolutionary records of these men and of those residents of
the Schenectady District subsequently referred to will be found in the
Appendix.

[6] Where now stands the house known as No. 9 North Church Street.
Subsequent meetings of the Committee were for some time held here.

[7] At a public meeting held on May 27.

[8] In Albany County eighteen districts elected one hundred and fifty-
four members of the County Committee. Alexander Clarence Flick.

[9] The entire Schenectady Board attended the first meeting of the
Albany Committee held after its organization. At subsequent meetings
two members generally constituted the representation.

[10] While these bodies acted quite independently in minor matters,
there was always a marked respect shown for orders or suggestions
from higher authorities and matters of major importance were referred
to them.

should be required from the district, all details of military organization and later the regulation of prices to be charged for commodities, but they were also required to seize and secure all who were believed to hold sentiments unfriendly to the cause of the Colonies and, until the appointment of the Commissioners for the Detecting and Defeating of Conspiracies,[11] to act as judges in cases of the trials of persons charged with treason against the State. All expenses incurred by the Committee were chargeable to the County Committee, and membership in subsequent organizations was determined as in the first by popular election,—the elections being held at intervals of six months and the chairman and clerk in each case selected by the Committee itself.

It is interesting to note that the activities of the Schenectady Committee were not confined to internal affairs alone. Much sympathy seems to have been evinced for their friends in New England, and in August (1775) Cornelius Cuyler was appointed to receive donation wheat for the poor of Boston, while by December 18, £73 N. Y. C. had been raised for their relief. It is interesting to note, too, the petty annoyances to which, during the early period of the war, members of the Committee were subjected by those politically opposed. There were constantly being brought before the Board at this time those who had spoken disparagingly of certain of its members, and on one occasion there was ordered to appear one George Ramsey who was strongly suspected of having

[11] Much detailed information regarding these boards may be found in the Introduction to the Minutes of the Commissioners for Detecting and Defeating Conspiracies in the State of New York, and in Loyalism in New York.

been concerned in putting tar and feathers on several of their doors the night before.

On May 24 the first measures looking toward the defense of the township were taken, for at the meeting of the Committee of Safety on that day it was voted[12] to purchase three hundred and thirty-eight pounds of powder, then in the possession of Daniel Campbell and stored in Albany, at three shillings per pound, and to immediately post "advertisements" in the most public places calling a meeting of the inhabitants on the twenty-seventh for the purpose of informing the Board how they were provided with arms and ammunition.

At the public meeting on the twenty-seventh it was unanimously agreed to accept a resolution passed by the Committee the day previous, calling for the raising of three companies of minute men,[13] two in the town and one in the Westina[14]—each company to consist of one captain, two lieutenants, four sergeants, three corporals, a drum, and fifty privates, and the

[12] This action was taken for fear "of the evil Consequences that [might] attend [its] falling in the hands of [their] Enemys." A subsequent resolution of the Committee appointed John Post and John G. Lansing custodians of this powder and empowered them to sell it to any of the inhabitants of the township at a price of "3s. 9d. per pound, 3s. 10d. by the half pound, 4s. by the quarter." No powder was, however, to be disposed of outside the district without an order from the Committee.

[13] Under the militia law of July 18, 1775, it was designated that one fourth part of the militia of every county was to consist of minute men who were "to be ready on the shortest Notice to march to any Place when their Assistance [was] required for the Defense of their own or a neighboring Colony."

[14] The Westina (Woestyne), or the Wilderness, seems to have applied alike to the land on the north side of the Mohawk now known as Glenville and to the land lying opposite on the south side now known as Rotterdam.

meeting further requested that the Committee appoint the officers for these companies.

The Committee consented to act upon the request of the meeting and the following selection was at once made:

First Company,
- Captain, Jellis J. Fonda.
- First lieutenant, Andrew Van Patten.
- Second lieutenant, Myndert A. Wemple.

Second Company,
- Captain, Cornelius Van Dyck.
- First lieutenant, John Mynderse.
- Second lieutenant, Gerrit Veeder.

Third Company,
- Captain, John Van Patten.
- First lieutenant, Cornelius Van Slyck.
- Second lieutenant, Myndert R. Wemple.

CHAPTER V

SCHENECTADY RAISES A COMPANY FOR THE DEFENSE OF TICONDEROGA

Ethan Allen, with his one hundred and fifty undisciplined troops known as the "Green Mountain Boys," had taken possession of Fort Ticonderoga on May 10, and on the next day Crown Point had been occupied by another detachment under Seth Warner. These unexpected victories had given great impetus to the American cause. Albany at once dispatched two companies to the forts to assist in retaining possession of the large number of cannon and other military stores that had been captured, and on the twenty-ninth, in consequence of a request from the Committee of Safety at Albany, the Schenectady Committee voted to raise one company[1] for service at Ticonderoga.

[1] The scale of pay allowed for the services of the men enlisting was as follows:

	£	s.	d.	
Captain, per month	6	0	0	
Lieutenant, per month	4	0	0	
Ensign, per month	3	0	0	
Sergeant, per month	2	8	0	"All Lawfull money
Corporal, per month	2	4	0	of New England."
Drummer, per month	2	4	0	
Fifer, per month	2	4	0	
Private, per month	2	0	0	

Each soldier enlisting was required to sign "the association recommended by the Honorable, the Continental Congress."

24   HISTORY OF SCHENECTADY

To Cornelius Van Dyck was given the command of this company and the authority[2] for making the necessary enlistments. Benjamin Hilton was appointed lieutenant and Cornelius Van Slyck ensign. Hilton at once refused to serve and Van Slyck was therefore promoted to take his place, while the vacancy was filled by the appointment of John G. Lansing as ensign.

On the day following the one on which it was voted to raise the company the Committee at Schenectady reported[3] to the Albany Committee that although they had been successful in raising a few men they were without arms with which to equip them. To this letter the Albany Committee replied[4] that they were well pleased with the readiness shown in raising men for "the new intended Continental Service," and they further expressed the hope that the Committee would have a company "in compleat order ready for marching on the first Notice," adding that a quantity of arms then under "Reparation" would be in good order in two or three days and that with these "such of the Forces of the County as [should] first go up [would] be supplied."

The men as enlisted were boarded[5] about town and to each recruit was given a ribbon,[6] evidently to

[2] His commission from the Provincial Congress, together with the commissions of the other officers of his company, was given on July 6.
[3] The Records of the Albany Committee of Safety, May 31, 1775.
[4] Ibid.
[5] Those first enlisting were boarded at the houses of John Welsh and Robert Martin, who were paid "at the rate of one shilling, N. Y. Currency, per day, per man," for their board and lodging.
[6] On December 20, 1775, the Committee authorized a payment of seventeen shillings to John Roseboom "for Ribbons bought for Captain Van Dyck's Recruits."

denote, in lieu of a uniform, that the wearer was a soldier in the Continental service.

On June[7] 9, word was received from the Albany Committee that it would be some little time before the company would be called upon for service. The Committee, moved perhaps by a desire to economize, certainly by no sense of justice, the more so as they further decreed that the members of the company should be required to spend two days each week in learning the military exercise, resolved that the men who had already enlisted be allowed neither provision nor billeting money until their services were required and that those to whom the arrangements were unsatisfactory should be paid off and discharged.

It was not until June[8] 17 that the commissary at Albany was authorized to issue fifty guns for the use of Captain Van Dyck's company, and it would appear from an original enlistment roll[9] still extant that it was not until the receipt of this equipment that Captain Van Dyck really endeavored to secure a full quota for his company.

Enlistments, however, were slow, as between June 19 and August 7 the names of but thirty-two men were secured, each in his turn volunteering "to preserve, if possible, the just liberties of America and to keep and defend the important Port of Ticandaroga in conjunction with [their] brethren of New England," and at the same time promising "by the ties of religion, honor and love of [their] country to obey such orders

---

[7] On June 7 the Albany Committee seriously debated the advisability of disbanding the few soldiers already enlisted, but finally resolved that the company be continued.

[8] The Records of the Albany Committee of Safety.

[9] This roll is in the possession of the writer.

as the Capt. [should] from time to time direct and command."[10]

On July 13 orders were finally received for the company to march to Lake George.[11] Both Captain Van Dyck and Lieutenant Van Slyck were absent from town recruiting at the time the instructions were received and the Committee therefore decided to order the company to march on the morrow under the command of Lieutenant Lansing.[12] Upon being drawn up and acquainted with the resolve of the Committee, the men absolutely refused to march save under the command of their captain, and as the only means of solving the problem "an express" was immediately ordered dispatched requesting Captain Van Dyck to return at once, while to General Schuyler[13] was sent a letter advising him of the reason for the delay.

[10] So reads the enlistment roll.

[11] On June 22 the Committee furnished twenty wagons "on the public credit" to carry provisions to this place.

[12] On July 10 he had been recommended to the Provincial Congress to fill the position of first lieutenant in the recruiting service.

[13] He was in command of the Northern Department.

CHAPTER VI

THE CONTINENTAL LINE, THE MILITIA AND THE ORGANIZATION OF THE SCHENECTADY BATTALION

On June 28, 1775, under a resolution of the Provincial Congress, was formed the New York Continental Line, consisting of four regiments of infantry and one company of artillery.

Philip Schuyler had already been appointed to the command of the Northern Department of New York, and Washington had taken command of the disorganized forces around Boston.

On the formation of the Continental Line many of the men throughout the Valley hastened at once to enlist. So short, however, was the term of enlistment (six months) and so scattered and inadequate are the records that it is impossible to trace either the names or the service performed by these early patriots.

To supplement the regular army, provision was made for the raising of state militia, and as it is in connection with the militia that we shall record the major part of the war activities performed by the men of Schenectady, some consideration[1] of this branch of the service may not be without interest.

[1] The material used in this connection is based for the most part upon statements of Schenectady soldiers found in the records of the Pension Office.

In the matter of recruiting, the names of the able-bodied men were (with few exceptions) enrolled in their respective localities, and from the lists so compiled companies were formed. Service was generally by draft, and members of any one company, except where the whole regiment was called out, rarely served under the officers of the company to which they belonged; both privates and officers being selected by ballot, some from one company, others from another, whenever called upon to take part in any tour or expedition. On such expeditions a detachment of militia was generally placed under the command of but one officer and when the detachment was small such an officer was not always a commissioned one.[2]

When a detachment of militia left home the men were required to provide themselves with a given number of days' provisions. Those who were too poor thus to provide themselves drew provisions from the quartermaster, commissary or other proper officer nearest to their place of residence. When stationed at posts and garrisons where there were Continental stores, the militia drew rations from these stores; but when there were no such stores at hand, as for instance when they were engaged in ranging the woods or serving in scouting expeditions, they obtained provisions as and wherever they could find them, being on such occasions furnished with authority to do so.[3]

The duties required of the militia were varied.

[2] Pension Office Records, Daniel Kittle W 21528. Pension Office Records, William Corl W 22736.

[3] Permission to purchase seems first to have been asked, but in cases of refusal provisions were taken by force. James Barhydt mentions (Pension Office Records S 12948) an instance which happened on a certain expedition to Harpersfield. A man refused to give up a sheep required for the detail, whereupon it was confiscated, and the man later

They acted as guards for Tory prisoners or supplies in transportation, served to apprehend Tories, or in reliefs on the frontier and at the option of their officers could be called upon to perform either garrison, field or fatigue duty.[4] They were not, however, required to serve outside the State, and periods for which they were drafted were usually of short duration, although the militia were liable for and often performed more extended duties.[5] Active service over, the men returned to their homes, to take up again their daily occupations—no note in most cases made of the part they played and all record of individual service forever lost.

Upon the militia little reliance was placed by the staff officers of the regular army and this not without some justification. The average militiaman was arrogant, insolent and for the most part totally devoid of any idea of discipline. He knew his rights and quite freely asserted them. At a critical point in a campaign he would not infrequently return home to harvest his crops and quite as frequently flatly refuse to serve when ordered out on an alarm.

This attitude on the part of the militiamen should not be too severely condemned nor must it be assumed that their grievances were without foundation. Their pay was small and difficult to obtain when earned; food and clothing were equally scarce; much was expected of them and a distant alarm often meant

---

sent to Hartford a prisoner, having been found guilty of disaffection upon trial by the Committee at Schenectady.

[4] Pension Office Records, Simon J. Van Antwerp S 28924.

[5] When the tours were of long duration three or four draftings often took place, one squad relieving another. Pension Office Records, Daniel Kittle W 21528.

leaving their wives and children exposed to the raids of the enemy.

It will be a matter of interest to note in the following pages that although on several occasions the men of Schenectady displayed much the same attitude as the "average militiaman," much more frequently they answered the call to arms with alacrity and performed services which are justly commendable.

On September 2, 1775, agreeable to a request from the Committee of Safety, a meeting of all the militia of the town of Schenectady was held at the Dutch Church for the purpose of forming companies in accordance with the plans of the Continental and Provincial Congresses.[6]

At this meeting the three companies already formed were reorganized and two additional companies raised. Jellis J. Fonda[7] and John Van Patten[8] were retained

---

[6] The Minutes of the Schenectady Committee of Safety.

[7] Captain Fonda served until the end of the war. The other officers in his company were:

First lieutenant, Andrew Van Patten. Reappointed June 20, 1778.

Second lieutenant, Myndert A. Wemple. Reappointed June 20, 1778. Promoted to rank of first lieutenant February 25, 1780, and assigned to Captain Mynderse's company. His office was filled by the promotion of Nicholas Yates.

Ensign, Nicholas Yates. Reappointed June 20, 1778, and promoted to the rank of second lieutenant February 25, 1780. His office was filled by the appointment of Lawrence Vrooman.

[8] Captain Van Patten resigned his commission toward the close of the war. The other officers in his company were:

First lieutenant, Cornelius Mebie. The name of Teunis Swart appears as holding this office June 20, 1778.

Second lieutenant, Simon F. Van Patten. The name of Philip Vedder appears as holding this office June 20, 1778.

Ensign, Daniel Toll. Reappointed June 20, 1778.

This company was recruited in the Westina and during the war this section, an especially exposed one, was constantly patrolled by its members. This company also garrisoned the dwelling-house of Teunis

as captains; John Mynderse,[9] who had originally been selected as a lieutenant in Captain Van Dyck's company, was promoted to the rank of captain; and to the command of the new companies were elected Abraham Wemple[10] and Thomas Wasson.[11]

Swart, who on June 20, 1778, was serving as a lieutenant under Captain Van Patten. His house was located about four and a half miles above Schenectady on the north side of the river almost on its bank; it was built of brick, was picketed in and had as an armament a small field piece fixed in a porthole and a quantity of small arms, and it was to this "fort" that the inhabitants were accustomed to resort for protection in case of alarms. There were undoubtedly a great many of these so-called forts, *i.e.*, dwelling-houses in which some means of defense was provided, scattered throughout this section. One that is well remembered by many of the older generation as being a supposed relic of the Revolutionary period was the "Old Fort" located in Scotia, a few hundred feet north of the present Vley Road, at a point about the same distance west of Halcyon Street. A few years ago the foundations of what was supposedly a watch- or blockhouse were unearthed near the river at the "Hoek" not far from Ulrich's. In the space included by the foundations were found many cannon balls.

[9] Captain Mynderse served until the end of the war. The other officers in his company were:

First lieutenant, Gerrit N. Veeder. He entered the Continental service as a captain in the spring of 1776. The office was held by Lawrence Mynderse June 20, 1778, and by Myndert A. Wemple February 25, 1780.

Second lieutenant, Solomon Pendleton. He entered the Continental service some time before October, 1777. On June 20, 1778, the office was held by James H. or Jacobus Peek.

Ensign, Lawrence Mynderse. On his promotion to the rank of first lieutenant the office was filled by the appointment of Abraham Truax.

[10] Abraham Wemple was subsequently commissioned colonel. The other officers appointed for his company were:

First lieutenant, Thomas Brower Banker, subsequently commissioned captain.

Second lieutenant, Abraham Swits, subsequently commissioned first major.

Ensign, John B. Vrooman, subsequently commissioned first lieutenant.

[11] Captain Wasson served until the end of the war. The other officers in his company were:

First lieutenant, John Little. John Thornton was promoted to fill this office on February 25, 1780, Little having removed from the beat.

The companies of Captains Fonda and Mynderse retained their classification as minute men and as such served until the spring of 1777, when they were incorporated with the regular militia. The motto of these companies as noted on their flags was "Liberty or Death," and because of the color of the uniforms worn by their members Captain Mynderse's company was known as "The Blues" and Captain Fonda's as "The Greens."[12]

At the direction of Congress commissions as field officers of the Schenectady militia (later known as the 2d Albany County) were, on October 20, issued as follows:[13]

Colonel, Abraham Wemple.[14]
Lieutenant-colonel, Jacob Schermerhorn.[15]
First major, Abraham Swits.[16]
Second major, Nicholas P. Veeder.[17]

Second lieutenant, John Thornton. Promoted to rank of first lieutenant, February 25, 1780, and his office filled by the appointment of William Moore.

Ensign, Jacob Sullivan. Alexander Crawford was appointed to fill this office on February 25, 1780, Sullivan having died.

Captain Wasson's company was recruited at Currybush, now the town of Princetown. On June 12, 1776, the Committees at Schoharie and Schenectady "prayed the advice" of the Albany Committee as to whether this company should belong to the Schenectady battalion or to that of Schoharie. It was decided that it should remain a part of the Schenectady regiment.

[12] Pension Office Records, Jellis J. Fonda.

[13] The Minutes of the Schenectady Committee of Safety.

[14] He held this office until near the close of the war, when he resigned and Abraham Oothout was promoted to fill his place.

[15] He refused to accept the commission and on January 13, 1776, Christopher Yates was appointed in his stead.

[16] He held this office until the close of the war.

[17] He refused to accept the commission and on January 13, 1776, Myndert M. Wemple was appointed in his stead.

THE SCHENECTADY BATTALION

Adjutant, Aaron N. Van Patten.[18]
Quartermaster, John Peek.[19]

At a meeting of the Schenectady Committee on January 26, 1776, it was voted to prepare a list of all the male inhabitants not already in the militia, in order to organize further companies. Following the preparation of the list those whose names appeared on it were required to meet on February 10 for organization and to choose their officers.

Three companies were thus formed and subsequently the following officers were chosen:[20]

First Company,
- Captain, Thomas Brower Banker.
- First lieutenant, John B. Vrooman.
- Second lieutenant, Aaron S. Vedder.
- Ensign, Benjamin Young.[21]

Second Company,
- Captain, Henry Glen.[22]
- First lieutenant, John B. Marselis.[23]
- Second lieutenant, Nicholas Barhydt.
- Ensign, Cornelius Z. Van Santvoord.

[18] He refused to accept the commission and on February 10, 1776, John Van Driesen was appointed in his stead.

[19] He resigned his commission on December 9, and on January 13, 1776, John Post was appointed in his stead.

[20] The Minutes of the Schenectady Committee of Safety.

[21] The name of Freeman Schermerhorn appears as holding this office, June 20, 1778.

[22] He probably did not serve actively as captain. Jacob Schermerhorn was also elected to the office but refused to serve, and at a subsequent meeting of the company the captaincy was voted to Abraham Oothout.

[23] He served as first lieutenant until August, 1776, when he was

Third Company,
- Captain, Ahasueras Marselis.[24]
- First lieutenant, Jesse Van Slyck.[25]
- Second lieutenant, William Stevens.
- Ensign, Abraham Van Eps.[26]

transferred to Bradt's Rangers and the office filled by the appointment of John Roseboom.

[24] He probably did not serve actively as captain.

[25] He was promoted to the rank of captain. The other officers of his company recorded as of June 20, 1778, were as follows:

First lieutenant, Walter Jacob Vrooman.
Second lieutenant, Francis Vedder.
Ensign, Jellis Abraham Fonda.

[26] He was appointed a captain some time previous to the summer of 1777. The other officers of his company recorded as of June 20, 1778, were as follows:

First lieutenant, Jellis Yates.
Second lieutenant, Philip Van Vorst, Jr.
Ensign, Aaron I. Van Antwerpen. The name of John Vedder appears as holding this office, February 25, 1780.

CHAPTER VII

THE INDIANS. RUMORS REGARDING THE JOHNSONS AND COLONEL GUY'S SUBSEQUENT DEPARTURE FROM THE VALLEY

Both the colonists and the Mother Country had been quick to realize the important part to be played by the Confederacy of the Six Nations[1] should their differences lead to a clash of arms. As early as 1774 efforts were made in behalf of the colonists, through the Stockbridge Indians, to secure the sympathies of the Mohawks, while to Reverend Samuel Kirkland[2] was intrusted the matter of winning[3] over the Oneidas. In behalf of England Colonel Johnson, acting under orders, had sought to hamper the work

[1] Their number in 1773 is estimated as twelve thousand five hundred. (Unnamed authority. Quoted United States Census. 1890.)

[2] He was born at Norwich, Connecticut, December 1, 1741, and died February 28, 1808. In 1764, with the approval of Sir William Johnson, he took up his residence among the Senecas as a missionary and in 1766 settled at Oneida. He performed valuable services as an interpreter, acted as a chaplain in the army during the Revolution and in 1793 founded Hamilton-Oneida Academy, the germ of Hamilton College.

[3] On June 23, 1775, Kirkland appeared before the Schenectady Committee with five Oneida Indians and requested that some member of the Board accompany them to Albany, whither they were bound. John Roseboom was appointed for this service and on the return of the Indians to Schenectady a few days later the Committee voted to give them some presents to show their "friendly disposition" and to entertain them while in town at the house of William White.

of Kirkland and to retain the friendship of the Indians.

Scarcely had the Committee of Safety at Schenectady been formed when rumors[4] began to be freely circulated to the effect that Colonel Johnson, in abuse of his office as Indian Superintendent, was desirous of bringing about an Indian uprising with a view of "cutting off" those who opposed him and that he was laying plans to this end.

So persistent were these rumors that Colonel Johnson, fearing the consequences were he to permit them to go unrefuted, placed[5] the matter before the Schenectady Committee on May[6] 18, thus stating his position:

Gentlemen: We have, for some days past, heard of many threats from the public, that give us reason to apprehend that the persons or properties of gentlemen of the first consequence, both with respect to station and property, would have been insulted in this county, and myself in particular,

[4] On May 20 the Committee received a letter stating that the bearer "had heard Colonel Guy Johnson desire some Indians to rise in arms and Cut off the Inhabitants" and on the twenty-second it was reported on good authority that one Mr. Fletcher, a schoolmaster in the town, had said that Colonel Johnson "would come down the river with five thousand Indians and cut [them] all off" and that he had further stated "that it would be right and if he had it in his Power he would do the same for [they] were all rebels." Mr. Fletcher seems to have very wisely left town after indulging in these remarks, as he could not later be located by the Committee.

[5] Jeptha R. Simms, Frontiersmen of New York, I, 494.

[6] On May 20, Colonel Johnson dispatched a second letter to the Committees of Albany and Schenectady representing the danger he believed himself to be in of being seized and imprisoned "either by the New Englanders or some persons in or about the city of Albany or town of Schenectady," as the result of the "ridiculous and malicious report that [he] intend[ed] to make the Indians destroy the inhabitants." William L. Stone, Life of Joseph Brant, I, 67-69.

under color of a gross and notorious falsehood, uttered by some worthless scoundrels, respecting my intentions as Superintendent of Indian affairs. To gentlemen of sense and moderation these malicious, ill-founded charges ought to be self-evidently false, as my duty is to promote peace, and my office of the highest importance to the trade and frontiers; but as these reports are daily increasing, it becomes me, both as a subject and a man, to disavow them, and until I can find out and chastise the infamous author, to assure the public of their mistake, and to acquaint them that it has rendered it my duty for self-preservation, so necessary, that I have taken precaution to give a very hot and disagreeable reception to any persons who shall invade my retreat; at the same time I have no intention to disturb those who choose to permit me the honest exercise of my reason and the duties of my office; and requesting that you will immediately cause this to be made public to the Albany Committee.

I remain, Gent'n, your very humble serv't,

G. JOHNSON.

Much, however, as Colonel Johnson sought to check it, the current of opinion continued to increase in its hostility to him. The gossip of the day abounded in stories, false or otherwise, circulated for the benefit of one side or the other. One, to the effect that the person of Colonel Johnson was in danger of being seized and their supply of powder thereby cut off, evidently spread with a view of inciting the Indians against the colonists, so well succeeded in its purpose that on May 20 Little Abram, a chief of the Lower Castle of Mohawks, in behalf of the Indians, thus appealed[7] to the magistrates and committees at Albany and Schenectady:

[7] The original of the speech as interpreted by Reverend Samuel Kirkland is to be found among the Trumbull Papers in the possession of the Massachusetts Historical Society, XXVII, 243.

Brothers—

Our present situation is very disagreeable and alarming, what we never expected, therefore desire to know what is designed by the reports that are spread amongst us. We hear that Companies and Troops are coming from one quarter to another to molest us, Particularly from New England to apprehend and take away by Violence our Superintendent and extinguish our Council Fire, for what reason we know not—

Brothers—

We desire you would inform us, if you know of any such design on foot either by the New England People or in your Vicinity and not deceive us in this Matter for the Consequences will be important and extensive—

Brothers—

We shall support and defend our Superintendent and not see our Council Fire extinguished—

We have no Inclination or purpose of interfering in the Dispute between Old England and Boston; the white People may settle their own Quarrels between themselves; we shall never meddle in those matters, or be the Aggressors, if we are let alone. We have for a long time lived in peace with one another and due wish ever to continue so. But should our Superintendent be taken from us, we dread the Consequences, the whole Confederacy would resist it, and all their Allies, and as reports now are, we should not know where to find our Enemies; the innocent might fall with the Guilty. We are so desirous of maintaining Peace that we are unwilling the Six Nations should know the bad Report spread amongst us & threats given out—

Brothers—

We desire you will satisfy us as to your knowledge of the foundation of those reports, and what your News are and not Deceive us in a matter of so much Importance—

Signed Abram Chief.

In answer to the appeal of Little Abram, at a conference of the Indians called at Guy Park on May 25, a committee[8] composed of delegates from Albany and Tryon[9] counties declared[10] to the Indians in the presence of Colonel Johnson that the reports concerning intended harm to their superintendent were false. They declared further that they hoped the report in regard to the powder was false also, and assured the Indians that on their return they would inform their "old and wise men" of the report and use every endeavor, if it were so, to prevent any recurrence in the future.

The Indians on their part again expressed themselves as being peaceably disposed toward the inhabitants, but made it quite plain that if their supplies of powder which they obtained from their superintendent were cut off, they would surely distrust them.

The Indians who attended the conference were mostly Mohawks, and as the Western Indians who were invited to attend were not represented, the council was soon adjourned with a view of meeting later at Crosby's Manor near German Flats. This council was never held. Colonel Johnson remained but a short time at Crosby's Manor and then proceeded westward to Fort Stanwix,[11] accompanied not only

---

[8] Christopher Yates and John Roseboom were appointed to represent the Schenectady Committee.

[9] Tryon County was taken from Albany County in 1772 and named in honor of William Tryon, then governor of the province. It included all the colonial settlements west and southwest of Schenectady, and was divided into five districts,—Mohawk, Canajoharie, Palatine, German Flats and Kingsland.

[10] Trumbull Papers, XXVII, 246.

[11] This fort, begun in 1758 by Brigadier-General John Stanwix of the British Army, was situated within the boundaries of the present vil-

by his family and some five hundred retainers who had left Guy Park with him, but also by a large body of Mohawk Indians from the Upper Castle. The stay at Fort Stanwix was but a brief one, Colonel Johnson and his followers proceeding almost at once to Ontario, where a council of the Western Indians was convened.

Thus far no act of open hostility had been committed by Colonel Johnson, although his movements were viewed with the greatest suspicion by the settlers. While the council was being held at Ontario the whole Valley was again thrown into alarm by rumors that reached the Tryon County Committee on good authority that "Col. [Guy] Johnson was ready with eight or nine hundred Indians to make an invasion of the Country, that the Indians were to be under the Command of Joseph Brant[12] and Walter Butler[13] and that they were to fall on the inhabitants below the little falls in order to divide the people in two parts."[14]

The cause for this alarm seemed the more real as Sir John Johnson still remained at Johnstown, surrounded by a large body of loyal followers.

---

lage of Rome, N. Y. It was occupied in June, 1776, by Colonel Elias Dayton and at this time the name was changed to Fort Schuyler.

[12] Joseph Brant (Thayendanegea), a full-blooded Mohawk of the Bear clan, was born in 1742 and died November 24, 1807. He was a brother-in-law of Sir William Johnson, Sir William having married his sister Molly. Early he became an active Loyalist and later rendered valuable services to the British Government, under which he held a colonel's commission.

[13] The celebrated Tory of the Valley, whose oft-mentioned deeds of cruelty render his name abhorred to this day.

[14] Letter from the Tryon County Committee to the Committees at Albany and Schenectady, July 13, 1775. Washington Papers, Library of Congress.

The Tryon County Committee wrote[15] to the Albany and Schenectady Committees on July 13, placing the matter before them, stating that they had every reason to believe the reports true, and further that they feared that all their enemies in the county would appear in arms as soon as the Indians approached. "Our ammunition is so scant," continued the letter, "that we cannot furnish three hundred men so as to be able to make a stand against so great a number. In these deplorable circumstances we look to you for Assistance both in men and ammunition to save this County from slaughter and desolation."

It will be remembered that Captain Van Dyck's company was on July 13 under orders to march to Lake George.

Immediately upon its receipt the letter from the Tryon County Committee had been forwarded[16] by the Schenectady Committee (who first received it) to the Committee at Albany who at once dispatched it by "an express" to General Schuyler, who was then at Saratoga, with the suggestion[17] that if he thought it advisable he should countermand his former orders and permit the company to march to the relief of their friends to the westward.

On the fourteenth General Schuyler's answer was received. "The letter you have enclosed," it read,[18] "is of a truly alarming nature and requires the most immediate and vigorous efforts to counteract the meditated evil, And I would advise that not only Capt. Van Dyck and his company but also such others as

---

[15] *Ibid.*
[16] The Records of the Albany Committee of Safety.
[17] *Ibid.*
[18] *Ibid.*

you can possibly get should immediately March into Tryon County with the Albany and Schenectady Militia who should also be requested to march to the relief of that County. You will please to supply Capt. Van Dyck's Company with ammunition[19] and send all you can spare to the Inhabitants of Tryon County."

Whatever may have been the plan of the Johnsons, the one feared was not carried out. Colonel Guy returned to Oswego from Ontario, succeeded in winning a few more Indians to the British cause, and then proceeded with his followers to Canada.

[19] The Albany Committee had but three hundred pounds of powder in store. Of this they sent one hundred and fifty pounds to the Tryon County Committee, charging them for it at the rate of five shillings per pound, and twenty-five pounds to the Committee at Schenectady for the use of Captain Van Dyck's company. (The Records of the Albany Committee of Safety.) The Schenectady Committee was without powder (*ibid.*) but forwarded three hundred pounds of lead at forty shillings ($5) per cwt. (The Minutes of the Tryon County Committee of Safety, July 15, 1775.)

CHAPTER VIII

EFFORTS ON THE PART OF THE COLONISTS TO HOLD THE INDIANS IN A POSITION OF NEUTRALITY AND THE FRICTION WITH SIR JOHN JOHNSON

To counteract the influence of Colonel Johnson, the Tryon County Committee, on June 29, met with the sachems of the Oneida and Tuscarora tribes. At this meeting[1] were present delegates from Albany and Schenectady[2] and in the chair was Nicholas Herkimer. Mutual speeches[3] were made, friendship and confidence with the two nations renewed, with a promise from the latter, if possible, to bring the rest of the Six Nations to unite with them in measures of peace.[4]

The Indians expressed themselves as greatly pleased with the kindness and generosity manifested toward them and recommended that "the gate of Fort Stanwix be shut, that nothing might pass or

[1] This was a "Meeting Extraordinary" of the Committee held at the house of Frederick Bellinger in the German Flats District.
[2] Hugh Mitchell and Abraham Oothout.
[3] Some of the speeches may be found in Stone's Life of Joseph Brant and Campbell's Annals of Tryon County.
[4] The Minutes of the Tryon County Committee of Safety, June 29, 1775.

repass to hurt the country.'"⁵ A like recommendation was made⁶ to the Tryon Committee on July 3, by the associated settlers at Fort Stanwix, who represented their dangerous situation due to their exposed position, and it was immediately resolved that the matter be brought to the attention of the Schenectady Committee that they might if so inclined⁷ send one hundred men to the post.

With a view of using still further means of keeping the Indians in a position of neutrality, Congress on July 12 established an Indian Department with three subdivisions—Northern, Middle and Southern. Major-General Philip Schuyler was appointed one of the five commissioners of the Northern Department, and under the direction of this body a second conference⁸ with the Indians was held at Albany in August.⁹

About five hundred Indians attended this conference. Presents to the amount of one hundred and fifty pounds worth of goods were distributed and, while the Council was not wholly representative, the

---

⁵ *Ibid.*

⁶ The Minutes of the Tryon County Committee of Safety, July 3, 1775.

⁷ Other than bringing the matter to the attention of the Albany Committee no action appears to have been taken by the Schenectady Committee, they ''being unable to afford any assistance.''

⁸ On August 19, a letter was received by the Schenectady Committee from Turbot Francis, another of the commissioners of the Northern Department, requesting that no rum or strong liquor be sold to the Indians as they passed through the town on their way to the Council. Upon receipt of the letter the instructions were immediately acted upon, ''the Crier being sent Round the Town'' to give the necessary warning.

⁹ The Council commenced its sittings on the twenty-third and was the last Indian council ever held in Albany. The proceedings of the Council may be found in Stone's Life of Joseph Brant, I, 430-457.

Indians solemnly agreed not to take up arms for either side.

Toward the end of July a more serious clash than had yet occurred took place between Sir John Johnson and his Whig neighbors. Alexander White,[10] the sheriff of Tryon County, had imprisoned John Fonda,[11] much to the displeasure of the Whigs, who, some one hundred strong, went[12] to the jail[13] and forced his release. Following this the mob attempted to take the sheriff, shots were exchanged and White subsequently sought the protection of Sir John Johnson.

"Expecting that an attempt would be made to retake Fonda," wrote[14] Christopher Yates[15] to the Albany and Schenectady Committees on July 22, "we have collected together about 5 or 600 men to protect Fonda and take the Sheriff prisoner. We have wrote to Sir John Johnson, Bart. and requested him to deliver the sheriff to us, or that we would take him by force.

---

[10] He was the first sheriff of Tryon County and had held office since March 16, 1772. He was a bitter partisan and very unpopular with his Whig neighbors because of his Tory opinions freely expressed.

[11] Fonda was a man of some prominence. He had been arrested for striking with a hoe one Thomas Hunt, a servant of White's, following a quarrel brought about by reason of Hunt's having trespassed on Fonda's land after he had been warned against so doing.

[12] Letter of Christopher P. Yates, July 22, 1775. The Records of the Albany Committee of Safety.

[13] This jail is the one still standing in the city of Johnstown.

[14] The Records of the Albany Committee of Safety.

[15] Christopher P. Yates, one of the most active of the Tryon County Committee and a deputy to the first and third Provincial Congresses. He held a captain's commission in 1774 and was commissary of General Herkimer's brigade. He served as a volunteer in the Canadian expedition and in 1776 was a major in the 1st New York Line.

"The Gent. we sent up being John Frey[16] and Anthony Van Veghten[17] inform us that Sir John has got about 400 men in Johnstown and has fortified his house in such a manner that it is not possible for us to take the sheriff out of the house with small arms and Sir John declared to Messrs. Frey and Van Veghten that he would protect the sheriff so long as he remained in his house.

"As the sheriff gives us a great deal of trouble Insulting us on every occasion and bids us open defiance we are therefore now determined to have him, and as we understand that their are field pieces in Schenectady we request you would send us a couple with all the implements necessary."

The letter from Christopher Yates came first to the Schenectady Committee, who immediately forwarded[18] it to the Albany Committee "by the Mohok's Express[19] viz: Jno. Newkirk & Wm. Snook," with an enclosure[20] stating that the Board was of the opinion that it was necessary that something be done in the matter at once, the more so because if their friends who were then gathered together were permitted to return home without having accomplished the desired end the moral effect would be very bad.

---

[16] Major John Frey was a prime mover in organizing the Tryon County Committee of Safety. He was commissioned a captain by the Provincial Congress June 28, 1775, and elected sheriff after the deposition of Alexander White. He was wounded at Oriskany and taken prisoner to Canada, where he remained until October 28, 1778.

[17] Anthony Van Vechten, adjutant in Colonel Klock's regiment.

[18] The Minutes of the Schenectady Committee of Safety, July 22, 1775.

[19] These "expresses" were sometimes fleet runners or men on horseback. In this case they appear to have been two Mohawk Indians.

[20] The Records of the Albany Committee of Safety.

While they expressed their admiration of the spirit shown by their friends in Tryon County, the members of the Albany Committee were not wholly in accord with their seemingly hasty action, and fearing possibly that in the excitement of the moment the Committee at Schenectady might be led to take some action which they might later have cause to regret, it was resolved that a letter suggesting caution be sent them.

"It is more than probable [that the] sheriff has repeatedly been imprudent and perhaps insulting," read[21] the letter in part, "but let our enemies never have cause to upbraid us for infringing on the laws and Constitution which we are studiously endeavoring to preserve against Parliamentary encroachment.

"It gives us pain that we on this head differ in sentiments with our Brethren to the westward but we flatter ourselves in the expectation that when they will suffer passion and Resentment to subside that they will agree with us in these observations."

The letter further suggested that a committee proceed at once to Johnstown for the purpose of "healing the unhappy and distressing differences," and agreeable to this suggestion Henry Glen and Harmanus Wendell were subsequently chosen to represent the Schenectady Committee.

On the next day (July 23) John Fonda reported to the Schenectady Committee that Sheriff White had left[22] Johnstown, presumably for Canada, and on the twenty-ninth the Albany Committee reported[23] to

[21] *Ibid.*
[22] He was afterward captured and imprisoned at Albany, to be finally, in 1783, banished by the Committee.
[23] The Records of the Albany Committee of Safety.

48   HISTORY OF SCHENECTADY

General Schuyler that not only was the unhappy dispute with Sir John amicably settled, he agreeing to take no further active part in the dispute between Great Britain and the American Colonies, but that the apprehension of the inhabitants of Tryon County respecting the Indians was entirely removed.

In spite of his promises, however, Sir John Johnson continued to cause trouble throughout the remainder of the summer and autumn of 1775, and in December the Continental Congress resolved to send General Schuyler to Tryon County under orders to secure the arms and stores of the Tories and "to apprehend their chiefs."[24]

On January 13, 1776, word of the intended expedition was received by the Schenectady Committee, the letter[25] containing a request that the Board send immediately to Albany "a company of 60 men completely armed, with proper officers to command them and four days provisions." Orders[26] were at once given to the officers of the "minute" companies to have the necessary men ready for the march, with further instructions to include besides the number required any who wished to go as volunteers, and on the next day[27] the expedition set out for Albany in sleds, there to join the militia already assembled.

In order that the Indians might not be alarmed at seeing troops in the Valley (this being a direct violation of the treaty entered into with them at Albany the previous autumn, whereby it was solemnly agreed

[24] The Journals of the American Congress.
[25] The Minutes of the Schenectady Committee of Safety.
[26] *Ibid.*
[27] *Ibid.*

that the Mohawk River should be open for trade, that no troops should be sent into those parts and that Sir John should remain unmolested), General Schuyler dispatched[28] a messenger to the Lower Mohawk Castle[29] to explain that he was marching to Johnstown in order to ascertain the condition of affairs.

Without waiting for the return of his messenger General Schuyler went forward. At Schenectady he was met by a delegation of the Mohawks under Little Abram, who reported[30] in substance that the coming of an armed force had alarmed the Indians and that the delegation wished to be present at any interview that might take place between General Schuyler and Sir John in order that they too might know the true state of affairs.

At the request of the Indians General Schuyler wrote[31] to Sir John Johnson from Schenectady on the sixteenth, requesting Sir John to meet him at any place between Schenectady and Johnstown, whither he would set out on the following day.

On the seventeenth General Schuyler, his force constantly increasing until it numbered nearly three thousand men, had proceeded some sixteen miles beyond Schenectady before the meeting with Sir John took place. Sir John asked until the evening of the next day to consider the proposals placed before him by General Schuyler and his request being granted he returned to Johnstown. It was not until the eleventh hour that

---

[28] William L. Stone, Life of Joseph Brant, I, 121.

[29] The Mohawks of the Lower Castle had not gone with Colonel Johnson.

[30] The speech of Little Abram is given in Stone's Life of Joseph Brant, I, 123-132.

[31] William L. Stone, Life of Joseph Brant, I, 132-133.

the terms proposed[32] were acceded to, and on Sir John's agreement to surrender all his arms and military stores and to use his influence to induce all the Loyalists in the county to do the same, he was released on parole.

Reports that Sir John was acting in violation of his parole, and continued rumors of Indian uprisings finally caused General Schuyler to order his arrest and in May (1776) Colonel Dayton[33] was dispatched to Johnstown for the purpose, without avail, however, as, forewarned of the approach of the troops, Sir John had taken alarm and with a large number of followers hastily departed for Canada.

[32] The correspondence passing between General Schuyler and Sir John Johnson is given in Stone's Life of Joseph Brant, I, 133-141.

[33] Colonel Elias Dayton, then colonel of the 3d New Jersey.

CHAPTER IX

THE CANADIAN EXPEDITION

To the garrisoning of Ticonderoga and Crown Point, Congress had consented after much hesitation, believing that such an act of offensive warfare would further remove the chances of conciliation for which many still hoped.

Events, however, moved rapidly during the summer of 1775, and before fall Congress was laying plans for an invasion of Canada. Their decision was influenced by the knowledge that the Canadians were but lukewarm in their attitude toward the British Crown and by the memory of the French and Indian raids by way of Canada that had terrorized the northern provinces for over a century and a half. With Canada in hostile hands and without the co-operation of its inhabitants it was felt that no perfect unification of the Colonies could be effected.

Contingent upon the transportation of the army and its supplies destined for the Canadian campaign arose the necessity of boats on Lake George and Lake Champlain, together with necessary barracks and storehouses at the former place. To meet this demand the services of available carpenters were eagerly sought. From Schenectady, Jacob Vrooman, Michael (or Claus) Veeder and Tacarus Van der Bogart were, in September, appointed overseers or captains and under them enlisted[1] not a few of their fellow townsmen; the companies thus formed remaining on duty at the Lakes for practically the rest of the year.[2]

Captain Van Dyck, assigned to the 2d New York Line, had finally left Schenectady with his men late in August or early in September, the company marching to Ticonderoga, thence to Crown Point, and after having performed guard duty for a short period at the latter place, proceeding to the Isle Aux Noix,[3] later forming part of the detachment that reduced Chamblee[4] and seeing active service at the siege[5] of St. John's.[6]

Late in December the whole of Colonel Wemple's regiment stood a draft, about every seventh man being chosen for service. The troops thus selected marched to Fort Edward, then to Skenesborough, whence, news having been received of the death of Montgomery and of the failure to take Quebec, they were, after remaining some time at the fort, ordered home.[7]

Early in February, in response to a request[8] from the Committee at Albany, Harmanus Wendell and

[1] The services of these men, as in fact of all artisans in the Continental service, should not be depreciated for it must be remembered that they as well as the militiamen were jeopardizing their liberties. When workmen were enlisted in the service, the master workmen placed in command of the companies as overseers held corresponding army ranks.

[2] Pension Office Records, Simon J. Van Antwerp S 28924; Adam Conde; Jacob P. Clute; Christopher Peek W 16371.

[3] At the northern extremity of Lake Champlain.

[4] Chamblee was captured by the American troops on October 20, 1775.

[5] Fort St. John's was taken in November.

[6] Pension Office Records, Peter Warren Cain W 16525.

[7] Pension Office Records, Frederick Weller S 14816.

[8] The Minutes of the Schenectady Committee of Safety.

Abraham Wemple were appointed[9] by the Schenectady Committee "to take the sense of the people" in order to ascertain how many sleds could be counted upon from the district for the use of the troops then on their way to reinforce the remnant of the American army encamped before Quebec.

The letter[10] from the Albany Committee contained the further request that the consideration of the Schenectady Board be given to the appointment of necessary officers to command such additional troops as it might be called upon to raise in the district, and in compliance with this request it was decided[11] to recommend for appointment the following:

Captain,	John A. Bradt.
First lieutenant,	Solomon Pendleton.
Second lieutenant,	David Bates.
Ensign,	Christopher Peek.[12]

Captain Bradt, who was absent from town at the time his appointment was made, was still absent on April 10, when under the direction of the Committee the proposed company was being formed, and as it was felt that the filling of the office of captain could not "with propriety" be longer delayed, the command was given to Gerrit S. Veeder, much to the displeasure of the other officers, who immediately appeared before the Board and resigned their commissions, stating that their action was prompted by reason of

---
[9] *Ibid.*
[10] *Ibid.*
[11] *Ibid.*
[12] He resigned his commission on March 11, 1776, because of his father's displeasure with him for having accepted it and Ephraim Snow was appointed to his place.

the men being mutinous and dissatisfied with the selection of the Committee.[13] The differences were, however, almost immediately adjusted,[14] their commissions being returned to the officers by the Board upon request, but with a word of caution regarding their future behavior, and the company numbering thirty-eight men (officers excluded) was assigned[15] to the regiment of Colonel Cornelius D. Wynkoop.

With the approach of spring, to the multiplicity of other affairs was added the necessity of again taking up the building operations at the Lakes which had been suspended at the beginning of the winter. Many artisans from Schenectady were again engaged[16] for this work and early in March repaired to their assigned posts, continuing their work of constructing

[13] The Minutes of the Schenectady Committee of Safety.
[14] *Ibid.*
[15] Pension Office Records, Gerrit S. Veeder S 7792. Archives of the State of New York, p. 98.
[16] There is in the possession of the author an original agreement dated March 1, 1776, signed by Philip Schuyler as party of the first part and by thirty-eight of the townspeople, who, as parties of the second part, agreed to "immediately repair to Fort George, Tyconderoga, or such other place in the provinces of New York or Quebec, as Gen. Schuyler [should] direct, and there employ themselves in building and constructing such and so many batteaus or other vessels or buildings" as should be directed, and on the following terms: that they were "to begin their work at sunrise and continue at it till sunset (excepting one hour for breakfast and one and one-half hour for dinner). That each of them was to find and provide necessary tools and implements for the construction of the said work," and that each should receive over and above his wages "one pound and one-quarter of a pound of pork, and one-half pound of flour per day, four pints of peas per week, one pint of milasses per week, and half a pint of rum per day."
A company of fatigue men under Captain John Clute was also enlisted at about this time. This company served at Saratoga, Fort Miller, Albany and Stillwater, remaining on duty until January 1, 1777. Pension Office Records, John Corl S 15263.

barracks, storehouses and gunboats for the army until well into the fall.[17]

The ravages of smallpox, which had broken out in the American camp during the winter, added to the scarcity of food and proper equipment, had by spring rendered half the troops unfit for duty. Schuyler communicated[18] this deplorable state of affairs to the Albany Committee on May 15, urging that they collect as many wagons as possible to transport provisions to Lake George, to be later forwarded to the army. This communication was sent later to the Schenectady Committee, who at once "made public by advertisement" their resolve "that no waggons be employed in carrying any goods or stores up or down between Schenectady and Albany for ten days unless they were going into the public service."[19] Myndert M. Wemple was further employed as a committee of one to engage every available wagon for the service.

Arnold meanwhile, stubbornly contesting his ground, slowly retreated from Canada, and on July 3 his mere skeleton of an army, presenting a most pitiable picture, arrived at Crown Point, where it had been determined to make a final stand.

Due to Arnold's foresight of the year before the strength of the American flotilla, meager though it was, was sufficient to retain the control of Lake Champlain, and it was to the overpowering of this flotilla, the strength of which the Americans were meanwhile making every endeavor to increase, that

---

[17] Pension Office Records, Joseph Peek W 2568; Benjamin Van Vleck R 10897; Albert L. Vedder S 11840; Simon J. Van Antwerp S 28924; Adam Conde.
[18] The Minutes of the Schenectady Committee of Safety.
[19] Ibid.

Sir Guy Carleton, the British commander, turned his attention, moving forward early in October with everything in readiness, and on the tenth entering into the three days' engagement that ended in the complete accomplishment of his purpose. The way to Crown Point was now open and towards this fortress Carleton at once proceeded,[20] only to find on his arrival that the works had been abandoned and that the Americans had fallen back on Ticonderoga.

The season was now well advanced, and deeming it unwise on this account to hazard a campaign that might be prolonged, Carleton did not press his advantage but withdrew his forces to Canada and there went into winter quarters.

Although so disastrously defeated, the first American navy had gloriously served its purpose, for it had necessitated a delay in the British advance just long enough to save the American forces an engagement, which, with Howe in possession of New York, might have accomplished in 1776 what Burgoyne failed to accomplish the next year.

[20] At about this time a company drafted in Schenectady was on duty at Skenesborough and Fort Ann guarding boats and ammunition. Pension Office Records, Nicholas Barhydt; J. Wemple S 23490; Bartholomew Schermerhorn S 17078.

CHAPTER X

THE ACTIVITIES OF LOCAL WHIG AND LOYALIST

On May 18, 1775, the Albany Committee had resolved[1] that all who refused to give up arms for the American cause or sold either arms or supplies to "inimical persons" should be held up to the public as enemies of their country. Later any one who refused public service, and on March 6, 1776, every "non-associator,"[2] was placed in the same category. Upon the militia acting under orders from the Committees[3] of Safety devolved the duty of apprehending those against whom complaint had been entered.

These complaints and subsequent arrests were

[1] The Minutes of the Albany Committee of Safety.

[2] On February 6, 1776, the Schenectady Committee resolved that inasmuch as "a number of the inhabitants of [the] Township was from home at the time the General Association was handed about to be signed, consequently had not an opportunity at that time, and by carelessness [had] neglected doing it since," and that inasmuch as they were "willing to give all those who [were] friendly to the American cause an opportunity of Evincing their sentiments to their neighbors . . . that the association paper be again opened, and that all who [were] inclined] to sign it [might] have an opportunity by applying to the Chairman of [the] Committee." The Minutes of the Schenectady Committee of Safety.

[3] With the establishment of the state government, the passing of laws to deal with the Tories and the appointing of committees to enforce these laws the powers of the local committees gradually waned and their activities ceased.

incited by a variety of causes: aiding the enemy in any way;[4] associating[5] or corresponding with Tories; refusing to sign the Association or violating its provisions; denouncing or refusing to obey congresses and committees; writing[6] or speaking[7] against the American cause; rejecting[8] Continental money or drinking[9] the King's health, and even mere suspicion was not infrequently deemed sufficient to justify a man's seizure.[10]

[4] Alexander Campbell was sent a prisoner to Connecticut for having warned Sir John Johnson of his danger.

[5] John Duncan owed his recommendation as "a dangerous person" and subsequent arrest to the fact that enemies of the American cause were supposed to meet not infrequently at his house.

[6] On January 14, 1776, Benjamin Hilton was brought before the Committee for writing a letter to Sheriff White "containing some expressions very unfriendly to the American cause." The Minutes of the Schenectady Committee of Safety.

[7] On January 31, 1776, George Ramsey was brought before the Committee on the complaint of William Murray because "said Ramsay called him a Tratore and a Rebel, and asked him if he was not ashamed to fight against his king." On February 8, Joseph Kingsley was committed to the Albany jail for making use of "unwarrantable expressions." The Minutes of the Schenectady Committee of Safety.

[8] At the meeting of the Schenectady Committee on July 31, 1777, a resolution was brought in by a subcommittee "concerning John Sanders and Daniel Campbell with respect to their refusing the Continental Currency in payment and in general for all Persons guilty of the same crime." Sanders was subsequently delivered over to the State Committee of Safety at Kingston. The Minutes of the Schenectady Committee of Safety.

[9] On August 6, 1777, John Gregg was committed to the Albany jail upon the evidence of John A. Bradt and William Moore, who swore "on the holy Evangelists of Almighty God" that they were present when said John Gregg drank "a Health to King George the third and success to him in all his proceedings." The Minutes of the Schenectady Committee of Safety.

[10] On May 13, 1777, the Schenectady Committee resolved that inasmuch as they looked upon certain persons (ten in number whose names are mentioned) as "dangerous," "their names should be given in to

To Albany[11] as a concentration center to await their final disposition were transferred the greater part of those arrested in this section, and by December, 1775, so crowded was the jail there that the Committee was obliged to provide additional quarters and secure an extra jailer.[12]

While, as was natural with the spirit of the times, not a few Loyalists suffered not only indignities[13] and loss of property[14] but also sustained sentences on somewhat questionable testimony,[15] mob action was universally condemned[16] by the Whig authorities and an honest effort for the most part appears to have been made by the Committees to give the accused ones fair trials.[17] In Albany County it was permitted the accused not only to produce witnesses to corroborate his testimony and establish his innocence, but to demand that his accuser appear also.[18]

The nature of the individual case appears to have governed the imposed sentence of convicted Loyal-

the field officers." All were subsequently arrested. The Minutes of the Schenectady Committee of Safety.

[11] The Minutes of the Albany and Schenectady Committees of Safety.

[12] The Minutes of the Albany Committee of Safety.

[13] On July 14, 1775, the Schenectady Committee was informed "that Serjeant Welsh, with a party of men, had gone to Currey Bush and brought in Simon Vedder to town in a riotous manner." The Minutes of the Schenectady Committee of Safety.

[14] In 1776, because of his action in warning Sir John Johnson (note 4, above), a mob burned the storehouse of Alexander Campbell at Schoharie and later destroyed "his store at Schenectady with goods and merchandise burning at the same time eight loads of hay and poisoning two milch cows." Loyalists' Papers.

[15] The Minutes of the Albany Committee of Safety.

[16] Alexander Clarance Flick, Loyalism in New York.

[17] The Minutes of the Albany and Schenectady Committees of Safety. Alexander Clarence Flick, Loyalism in New York.

[18] The Minutes of the Albany Committee of Safety.

ists rather than any uniform mode of procedure followed by the Committees; some were placed in confinement,[19] others were released on parole or bond[20] or simply disarmed,[21] some were exiled to neighboring states[22] or sent within the enemies' lines,[23] many were forced to sign the Association or take the Oath of Allegiance and nearly all were required to carry certificates of character[24] and, when leaving the county for any reason, to obtain permission from the proper authorities.[25] All expenses incurred by Loyalists either in their trials, imprisonment or banishment were charged against them.[26]

[19] The Minutes of the Albany and Schenectady Committees of Safety.

[20] John Duncan on December 19, 1776, was ordered confined to the limits of his farm and required to give a bond of £500 for his good behavior and the carrying out of the order. The acceptance of bonds by the Commissioners of Conspiracies was quite frequent.

[21] The treatment accorded some was even more lenient. On August 28, 1777, one John Moneer was summoned before the Committee to answer the charge of being an ''inimical'' person. Moneer alleged that he had come to Schenectady for the sake of his health, as he received much benefit from the air here. Upon hearing his testimony the Committee immediately resolved that he be permitted to remain ''for his health.'' The Minutes of the Schenectady Committee of Safety.

[22] Alexander Campbell was one of these (note 4, above). He was later released on parole.

[23] Daniel Campbell, James Ellice and others were under orders to remove, but at the last moment were permitted to stay on their signing the Oath of Allegiance. Alexander Campbell, John Doty (the rector of St. George's) and John Stuart (the Indian minister at Fort Hunter who was confined at Schenectady), were sent to Canada.

[24] These certificates were refused to those who had not signed the Association.

[25] The Minutes of the Schenectady Committee of Safety.

[26] In the case of Kingsley and Ramsey (note 7, above), Kingsley was charged twenty shillings for a sled and two men to carry him to Albany. This he absolutely refused to pay and the Committee therefore ordered that he be given until nine o'clock on the following Monday to pay and that if the account was not settled at that time he was to be again

Throughout New York the Loyalists were exceptionally strong and numerous, and although they had neither organized nor taken up arms as soon as their Whig neighbors, it was not long before Tory plots were everywhere unearthed.

While in Schenectady not a few influential and wealthy citizens were of English sympathies, the Committee of Safety appears to have experienced little trouble from them as compared with the annoyance caused by the Tories[27] in the outlying districts who constantly threatened the Whig settlers in their exposed positions in the Westina and at the Aalplaats.

The failure of the campaign against Canada, the success of the British around New York and the anticipation of an early advance on the part of the King's troops from the north added many recruits to the Loyalist party, and in spite of the various measures adopted for their suppression, so obnoxious did they become throughout Albany County during the summer of 1776, when threats were even made to raise the English flag,[28] that two companies of State Rangers were ordered formed for their apprehension, and in August, John A. Bradt of Schenectady

committed to the Albany jail, there to remain until the amount was paid, together with what charges might arise on account of his second confinement. Ramsey was charged sixteen shillings, which amount he promised to pay. The Minutes of the Schenectady Committee of Safety.

[27] One that caused the Whigs no end of annoyance was the famous Joseph Bettis. "He and his associates did great injury to the American cause by communicating intelligence to the enemy, and gave the country great uneasiness and trouble for two or three years. Spies and detached parties were again and again sent in pursuit of them but without success." [Pension Office Records, Adam Van Patten S 17168.] He was at last taken and hung in Albany.

[28] American Archives, 4th Series, V, 343, 345.

was commissioned a captain and given a warrant by Congress for the raising of one[29] of these companies.

The increasing activities on the part of the Tories, the continuing unfavorable news from the north and, as we have seen, the fears regarding Sir John Johnson, brought with them the necessity of increased vigilance on the part of the Schenectady Committee. Steps were early taken looking towards the conservation of the town's resources,[30] those known to hold Tory sentiments were more closely watched, guards were placed on both sides of the river to prevent the passing either up or down of persons who were not known to be friends of the American cause,[31] and for "fear of broils," because of the number of strangers that thronged the town the watches were ordered doubled.[32] The stockades were strengthened, the work being done by members of the militia,[33] and for the better accommodation of the troops passing through or to be later quartered here, General Washington, on September 23, 1776, at the instance of the Committee, was approached[34] through General Schuyler regarding the erection of barracks.

[29] The original roll of this company is in the possession of the author.

[30] On December 29, 1775, the Committee resolved to apply to the magistrates to use their authority in putting a stop to the customary firing of guns on New Year's Day, believing that such a custom was attended with an unnecessary waste of powder. The Minutes of the Schenectady Committee of Safety.

[31] This action was directly connected with the affairs at Johnstown and the precaution was taken that no news of the intended expedition against the Tories in that quarter might precede it.

[32] The Minutes of the Schenectady Committee of Safety, January 14, 1776.

[33] When not on guard duty or out on expeditions members of the militia were often employed in this work.

[34] Washington Papers, Library of Congress.

The site chosen for their erection was the southwest corner of Union and Lafayette Streets,³⁵ and by November 6 the construction of a building containing accommodations for six hundred men was well under way.³⁶

³⁵ Jonathan Pearson, History of the Schenectady Patent, p. 318, note. On the present site of the German Methodist Church. Lafayette Street had not, of course, been cut through.

³⁶ Philip Schuyler to Congress. Orderly Book of the Northern Army, p. 168.

CHAPTER XI

THE PLAN FOR THE CAMPAIGN OF 1777.
FURTHER ACTIVITIES OF INDIAN AND
TORY. THE SCHENECTADY COMMIT-
TEE ESTABLISHES A WATCH.
THE DIFFICULTIES OF
PROCURING WAGONS
AND MEN

During the winter (1776-1777) General John Burgoyne, who had been serving under General Carleton, sailed for England to lay before the Ministry a plan of campaign for the following year, the easily successful accomplishment of which he confidently believed would end the war. The plan as proposed and accepted was for the main British army to move southward up Lake Champlain; a second army under Lieutenant-Colonel Barry St. Leger to move eastward by way of Oswego down the Mohawk, and a third force under Sir Henry Clinton to move northward up the Hudson—the three forces concentrating on Albany. Thus a division of the Colonies would be effected and from their central position the combined British forces could easily crush in turn each isolated section.

The effect on the Indians of the withdrawal of the American forces from Canada had been very soon apparent.[1] General Schuyler, redoubling his efforts to hold them in a position of neutrality, had in July (1776) called a council[2] at German Flats, the outcome of which was on the whole satisfactory, or enough so to cause him to feel[3] that although he could count for active support upon none save the Oneidas, the Indians would not engage against the colonists.

General Schuyler's hopes were, however, not to be realized, for with the coming of spring came news of matters that were transpiring of dire import to the settlers of the Valley. Joseph Brant had joined a rapidly increasing body of Indians at Oghwaga, where the British flag had been raised, leaving little doubt as to their probable course of action.[4]

Throughout Cherry Valley the alarm spread rapidly, nor were the rumors of Indian and Tory raids confined to that section alone, for on April 11, word[5] was brought to the Schenectady Committee that a number of Tories residing in the vicinity of Clifton Park had left to join a band of Indians and that they were "to come to destroy the people that lived thereabout in about three days time." For the apprehension of the enemy and the protection of the patriots Colonel Wemple was applied to for a detail of militia, while to the Ballston and Albany Committees were dis-

[1] "Our misfortunes in Canada have made them [the Indians] somewhat assuming," wrote Schuyler to John Trumbull on July 31. Trumbull Papers, XXV, 109.

[2] On July 11 the Albany Committee sent a request to the Committee at Schenectady that "they furnish as many of their Troop of Horse as possible to join General Schuyler," who was to set off on the morrow for German Flats. The Minutes of the Albany Committee of Safety.

[3] Trumbull Papers, XXV, 109-113.

[4] Francis Whiting Halsey, The Old New York Frontier.

[5] The Minutes of the Schenectady Committee of Safety.

patched letters asking that they forward detachments to meet the Schenectady militia at Wilson's Mill, Ballston, at noon of the following day. These letters contained a further admonition that they "be sure and not take a man but what was a friend to the States."[6]

With the necessity of increased diligence the Committee of Safety at Schenectady determined upon the establishment of a regular watch,[7] and on April 13 the following resolution was therefore passed:[8] "that all persons in this Town, above the Age of sixteen years, shall watch, and that their be a watch Established of One Officer & Eleven men, that such watch begins at 9 O Clock, in the Evening & Continues Till Daylight Next Morning, that the persons ordered to watch be warned by the Town Major Appointed for that Purpose, & that the said Town Major attends the watch Every Evening at Ten O Clock to see if they all Appear, & Take an Account of all persons not attending the watch, which List he is to give in to the Chairman of this Committee & such Person or Persons so Neglecting of if warned shall forfit a fine not Exceeding Twelve pence which shall be recovered by a Warrent of the Chairman of this Committee."

At the meeting on the nineteenth the following rules and orders covering the watch were issued:[9]

[6] *Ibid.*

[7] This was by virtue of a resolve of the Continental Congress of August 22, 1775. On November 2, 1778, a state law required the establishment of a regular watch in certain counties, of which Albany was one. In the city of Albany and town of Schenectady clergymen alone were exempted from service.

[8] The Minutes of the Schenectady Committee of Safety.

[9] *Ibid.*

1. The wach are to meet at 9 OClock every Evening and whoever belongs to the wach and does not appear before ten OClock Shall be Judged fineable.

2d. Two men belonging to the wach to go round true all the Streets in the town once every hour.

3. A Centry to be fixed in the Box on the top of the wach house[10] to be released once every hour.

4. As the wach house will once more be made Convenient and in repair it is Expected that the wach will not abuse the same as has been Customare it is resolved that if any thing Shall be broke or put out of order that the officer of the wach when the same happens shall be Liable to pay the Damages.

At this same meeting it was further resolved:

that the town wach be very delegent in apprehending all Negroes that may be found to run on the Street after ten OClock that if they take any of them up to confine them in the wach house till next morning and then their owners may releas them on paying three Shillings to the watch for Each Negro or Els they are to receive thirty Lashes on their naked back and also that the said wach be very Delegent in apprehending such places that Negroes may be combined together and take them in Confiniment and inflict the above punishment on them, and the owner of such house where such Negroes may be found together Shall pay a fine of forty Shillings to the Officer of the wach, which fine Shall be recovered by warrent from the Chairman of this or any future Committee.

At the meeting of the Committee on April 24 a letter[11] was received from the Albany Committee

[10] This was probably the old Dutch Church which stood at the intersection of State, Church and Water Streets and which, after the new church was erected, was turned into a guard- and watchhouse and so used for many years.

[11] The Minutes of the Schenectady Committee of Safety.

requesting the furnishing of twenty wagons for service between Albany and Lake George, and a detail of forty-four men for garrison duty. Steps were immediately taken to comply with the request, and after having conferred with the field officers present at the meeting Colonel Wemple ordered the men allotted for duty warned to appear properly equipped at his home the next morning at eight o'clock. The matter of collecting wagons, however, presented difficulties which were not to be overcome and of this the Albany Committee was at once thus advised:[12]

In regard of the Weagons you requested us to send, we had received a Letter from Col. Lewis A few Days before Desiring our assistance in Procuring a Number of wagons out of our Distract, as they were much wanted we accordingly tryed all in our Power to git waggons, but the season of the year being such at Present that our waggoners (as they Chiefly all Raise their own Grain) cant Possibly Leave home. We made shift to git Eleven on Promising they should only do one trip to Lake George and then Return home again. We Accordingly sent them to Col. Lewis acquainting him of our Promise to said Waggoners. On Receiving your Letter we made another Tryal true the hole Distract thinking that by warning the Militia to go on Duty, it would induce Several Rather to go with a waggon than on other Duty, but have not been able to git more than five Waggons which we now send Down. If they will not anser the Present Demand from our Distract then we Expect your further advice in this mater.

In answer to the summons for service but twenty-two men, including officers, appeared as ordered. These immediately set out, to be followed later by

[12] *Ibid.*

eight more, who, because they lived out of town, had received no proper warning.

The fact that so many had failed to obey their orders was at once reported to the Committee by Colonel Wemple. It was thereupon resolved[13] "that those person that [had] neglected to appear, having been duly [warned should] be emedeately fined for ten Shillings Each And be warned again to appear at the Captains Dore on monday [at] 8 OClock in the morning acquipt to go on garison duty as before and if they or any of them [neglected] to appear then they [should] be fined for twenty Shillings Each and ordered again to appear the same day [at] One OClock in the afternoon which if they [neglected] again they [were] to be Sent to Close Confiniment."

The threats of fines and of close confinement seem to have availed little, for on the twenty-eighth the Committee decided[14] that inasmuch as "it [appeared] that those people that [had] refused to go on Duty [could not] be made willing by fining them, and [that as they had] no proper president before [them] what Should be done . . . further," it was best that the matter be placed before the Albany Committee for their advice.

The detachment that had set out marched under Lieutenant Van Slyck to Albany, to Saratoga, where they joined some four hundred of the Vermont militia under Colonel Seth Warner, thence to Jessups Patent by way of Fort Edward.[15] The object of the expedition was to capture one John Morrell, a Tory

[13] *Ibid.*
[14] *Ibid.*
[15] Pension Office Records, Frederick Weller S 14816; Bartholomew Schermerhorn S 17078.

who was busily engaged in enlisting men for the British cause, and to disperse a considerable number of Tories who had already gathered and there erected a blockhouse.[16] When the American troops arrived they found that the enemy had scattered the day before, but not until they had destroyed their fortifications.[17]

[16] Pension Office Records, Cornelius Williams W 18456; Christopher Ward.
[17] Pension Office Records, Christopher Ward.

CHAPTER XII

THE CAMPAIGN OF 1777

On May 5 General Burgoyne returned to Quebec, and four days later the command of the approximately eight thousand troops assigned for the suppression of the rebellion was transferred to him.

On June 29 Burgoyne arrived at Crown Point and on July 1 his forces appeared before Ticonderoga, which post was abandoned by the American forces on July 6.

At the news of the British advance on Ticonderoga General Ten Broeck[1] ordered[2] Major Swits to march[3] with all of the Schenectady militia to Fort Edward, much to the anxiety of a number of the inhabitants of Schenectady, who appeared[4] before the Committee on July 9 with petitions that they be ordered to stay in town "on account of the alarming news from the westward." General Ten Broeck was appealed to regarding the matter and in the afternoon an answer

---

[1] Abraham Ten Broeck. He was in command of the brigade to which Colonel Wemple's regiment was joined.

[2] The Minutes of the Schenectady Committee of Safety.

[3] Details of Schenectady militia were already on duty, a company having been mustered here in May. Pension Office Records, Jacob Lyport S 13813; Elias Rosa W 17546.

[4] The Minutes of the Schenectady Committee of Safety.

to the Committee's letter was received ordering[5] the militia to march[6] without delay.

On July 30 General Burgoyne advanced to Fort Edward, and the American forces fell back upon Stillwater.

With the troops under General Schuyler that had thus far so successfully disputed the advance of the British was a detachment of Schenectady militia under Lieutenant-Colonel Christopher Yates. This detachment was detailed for fatigue duty and under a strong guard had been busily engaged in felling trees and in otherwise rendering impenetrable the comparative wilderness that lay between Skenesborough and Fort Edward.[7]

With the further advance of the British, discouragement and alarm spread rapidly. All the militia that could be collected throughout Albany County had been sent to the army.[8] They had already been for some time in the service and it was reported that they intended soon to return to remove their families to a place of greater safety.[9] Albany was in a state of panic and "the appearance of a few of the enemie's troops on the Mohawk River," it was felt, "would

---

[5] *Ibid.*

[6] Quite a considerable number of men appear to have marched as ordered. These detachments remained with the Northern Army until the defeat of General Burgoyne, many of them seeing active service in the various battles fought during the retreat and in the battle of Bemis Heights. Pension Office Records, John Corl S 15263; Bartholomew Schermerhorn S 17078; Adam Van Patten S 17168; Nicholas P. Van Vranken S 17170; David Sacia W 17768; George Staley N 19123.

[7] Pension Office Records, Simon J. Vrooman W 6370.

[8] Public Papers of George Clinton, II, 210.

[9] *Ibid.*, p. 201.

immediately make the inhabitants lay down their arms.''[10]

Schenectady presented a no less gloomy picture. "We are sorry," wrote[11] Reinier Mynderse in behalf of the Committee to General Schuyler on August 5, "to be under the Necessity of informing you of the disagreeable Situation of our Affairs in this place at present. The inhabitants in General seem much dejected. Since the Loss of Tyconderoga many of them who formerly seemed warm in the Interest of the Country are now quite cool, or rather inclined to the other side. We believe this change of Sentiment in many of them to be greatly owing to the bad counsel and advice, they daily receive from disaffected Persons who begin to be pretty numerous amongst us. We are unable to take any measures to prevent their spreading Influence, or any thing else for want of a few Troops to support us. A few days ago we issued a warrant to impress a number of waggons to go and relieve those who have been a considerable time in the Service, but the Constables returned without getting one for want of force to put the warrant into execution.[12] We beg you will take our case into consideration, and if you can spare them, send about sixty men with good Officer to remain with us some time."

On August 3 the forces under St. Leger,[13] proceeding in accordance with the formulated plan, arrived

[10] *Ibid.*, p. 210.
[11] *Ibid.*, p. 187.
[12] The unsuccessful efforts of the Schenectady Committee are detailed in its minutes.
[13] St. Leger's second in command was Sir John Johnson.

before Fort Stanwix. Rumor that Fort Stanwix was under siege seems to have reached Schenectady even before the siege actually commenced, for Colonel Goose Van Schaick writing from here to General Schuyler on the fourth mentions it as "a common report."[14] Van Schaick, with "near one hundred Continental troops, men and boys," was at the time on his way to German Flats, where, under Nicholas Herkimer, the Tryon County militia had gathered, and was endeavoring to prevail upon members of the Schenectady militia[15] to join the expedition as volunteers; without avail, however, for "I find to my great surprise," he adds in the same letter, "that not a man will go with me, either from this place or Scoharie."

As soon as news was brought of the actual investment of Fort Stanwix General Herkimer advanced to its relief, encamping on August 5 to await reinforcements about eight miles to the east of the fort. Any delay was, however, displeasing to his officers and on the morning of the sixth, irritated by their impatience and insinuations, General Herkimer finally, against his better judgment, gave the order for the advance which subsequently terminated in the ambuscade and slaughter known as the battle of Oriskany.

The siege of Fort Stanwix was soon renewed, to be continued until August 22, when news of the

[14] Public Papers of George Clinton, II, 169.
[15] One half of them were then under orders to march to German Flats but refused to go because of the dangers to which their families might be subjected from Tory depredations.

approach of the troops[16] under Benedict Arnold caused St. Leger[17] to withdraw hastily.

The Tories in the vicinity of Schenectady had seized upon the cooling of the patriotic spirit as an opportunity to renew their activities. On August 10 it was reported[18] to the Committee of Safety that a number of them had actually "disarmed some of the inhabitants that were on guard and that they had assembled to the number of 300."

The remaining militia were already under orders from General Schuyler to join the main army, but on the report of the Tory raid it was immediately resolved[19] by the Committee "that they be detained in Town, and that a Watch of 25 Men be kept up Day and Night."

The report that another raid was imminent was brought to the Committee on the next day, and in the afternoon Jacob Schermerhorn, who had been sent out on scout duty, reported[20] to the Board "that on

[16] Abraham I. Van Eps states (Pension Office Records W 25831) that he performed eight days' service under Captain Van Eps "when the Schenectady militia marched to Oriskany." Cornelius Bradt states (Pension Office Records W 18649) that while serving under Colonel Christopher Yates he went "with Major Arnold's division up the Mohawk Valley." While these references are rather meager, it appears evident that some of the Schenectady militia marched to the relief of Fort Stanwix.

The 2d New York Line, under orders to march for the same purpose, sailed in sloops from Fishkill to Albany but had occasion to proceed no further than Schenectady. *Magazine of American History*, December, 1881.

[17] Authorities have expressed the opinion that to St. Leger was assigned the most important part of the program with the most inadequate means of carrying it out.

[18] The Minutes of the Schenectady Committee of Safety.

[19] *Ibid.*

[20] *Ibid.*

the 10th inst at Night [the Tories] lay at the House of a Thoms Morall and in the Morning went to one Nicholas Van Patten." A detail of Continental troops, who were in town, under Captain Childs and a number of the militia under Major Swits were immediately dispatched for the capture of the Tories, and on the twelfth turned over to the Committee eleven prisoners who had been taken with their arms and accoutrements.[21]

The news of the successful outcome of General Arnold's relief expedition, whereby General Burgoyne was deprived of the hope of reinforcements, coupled with the news of the defeat of Colonel Baum at Bennington, depriving him of much needed supplies, wrought a complete change in public opinion. The attitude of the Tories became less threatening and in answer to the call from the Continental Congress regulars and militia hastened to join the rapidly increasing forces at Van Schaick's Island, whence the American army had fallen back after the first entrenchments at Stillwater, and it was at this time[22] that many[23] more of the Schenectady militia

[21] *Ibid.*
[22] Pension Office Records, John J. Van Eps; John DeGraff S 15090; Andrew Bearup W 16188; Peter Warren Cain W 16525; Samuel Kennedy W 20317.

Official orders for all those not already in actual service to join the army under General Gates were sent to General Ten Broeck by Governor Clinton on September 18.

[23] That all the available men did not go, however, is shown from the fact that when, on October 16, the Albany Committee reported that "the enemy were coming up the North River with a number of ships," the Schenectady Board, in compliance with their request "to send down the Militia immediately," at once ordered that the request be complied with. The Minutes of the Schenectady Committee of Safety.

joined[24] the ranks to remain with the army until the culmination of the campaign[25] in the surrender of Burgoyne.[26]

[24] On September 25 it was reported in Schenectady that the American troops were surrounded by the British and that it was therefore "folly" for the militia to attempt to join them as they could not get through. The Minutes of the Schenectady Committee of Safety.

[25] The failure of General Howe to co-operate with Burgoyne laid him open to severe criticism. It is now known, however (Life of William, Earl of Shelburne, I, 358 et seq.), that through the carelessness of Lord George Germaine the proper orders were never forwarded to him.

[26] After the surrender of General Burgoyne a detachment of Schenectady militia under Colonel Wemple was detailed for guard duty and escorted General Poor's brigade part way to Esopus. They did not, however, complete the journey, but were ordered home after a few days' service. Pension Office Records, John J. Van Eps.

CHAPTER XIII

THE WINTER OF 1777-1778. A TORY PLOT. SCHENECTADY DECLARES A GRIEVANCE

The winter of 1777-1778 seems on the whole to have passed quietly in Schenectady, although about the middle of December the town was visited by a disastrous fire which caused considerable suffering to several families, for the relief of whom committees were appointed to solicit contributions throughout the Schenectady District, the city of Albany and Tryon County.[1]

The attention of the Committee of Safety was for the most part given over to the settling of petty disputes arising among the townspeople, to the hearing of charges brought against those considered unfriendly to the patriot cause and to the relief of the distressed condition which early in the winter had prevailed throughout the district, due to the scarcity of salt necessary for the proper preparation of the winter's supply of meat.[2]

Details of the militia[3] stood guard at the pickets in

---

[1] The Minutes of the Schenectady Committee of Safety.
[2] *Ibid.*
[3] The return of General Ten Broeck's brigade, dated February 19, 1778, credits Colonel Wemple's regiment with four hundred men, of whom thirty-three were officers. Public Papers of George Clinton, II, 780.

THE WINTER OF 1777-1778

their regular turns and further protection was afforded the town by the presence[4] of a detachment of Colonel Van Schaick's regiment which was garrisoned here.

Although the activities of the Tories had received somewhat of a check by reason of the success of the American arms the previous fall, they did not long remain inactive and late in the winter rumors of a plot wide in its scope reached the state authorities.[5]

That agents connected with the conspiracy were working among the many "disaffected persons," who were now included among the inhabitants of Schenectady, was early suspected, and the Marquis de Lafayette who had been sent to make a personal investigation reported[6] to the Albany Committee on March 3 that the suspicions were "very far from groundless." "A soldier who I think is a Spy," continues the report, "has been taken up and examined by me Yesterday. It has been impossible to obtain a true Confession from that Man, but I can however assure you that there is a Conspiracy and an important one. Major Carleton, General's own Nephew, was some days ago disguised in this Town and making preparations—two parties are gone on after him but I question much if they will be successful."

Dissatisfaction it would seem was at this time quite as prevalent in Schenectady as disaffection. Many of the townspeople felt that they had just causes for complaint against the treatment accorded them by the authorities and on March 20 in the hopes that

[4] Public Papers of George Clinton, III, 108.
[5] Ibid., II, 248 et seq.
[6] Ibid., p. 852.

through their intercession redress might be obtained, the whole matter was placed before the Committee of Safety in the form of the following petition[7] signed by fifty-five of the inhabitants, which number included not a few of the more prominent militia officers:

Gentlemen, We the Inhabitants of this town & Distract beg leave to Lay before you a state of Grievences which (in our opinions) we have Just cause to Complain of, and as you are appointed by us to the Care and management of the public affairs in this District, It is through your Means we Look for and Expect Redress.

In the first place you know that a Barracks[8] was Built Here for the Reception of Such Troops as might be ordered Here from time to time, in order that the Inhabitants Should be free from the Trouble and expence of Having them billited on them; that notwithstanding this, Last fall the Barrecks was converted into an Hospital[9] and the troops to be quartered here was billeted on us, which have been Both troublesom and finding them with firewood attended with a Great deal of Expence, which we have not had the Least allowance for but hope you will indevour to procure us a proper Consederation for it.

Secondly, the director of the Hospital appointed a Commisary,[10] and under him a Number of other officers for that

[7] Ibid., III, 63.
[8] See chapter X, pp. 62-63.
[9] A burying ground was in the rear about halfway between Union and Liberty Streets. From this burying ground in November, 1854, were exhumed the remains of fifty-seven American soldiers. These remains were reinterred in Vale Cemetery with military honors in August, 1859, and the spot where they rest is marked by an imposing monument erected by the citizens of Schenectady.
[10] John Duncan. On October 27, 1777, the townspeople had petitioned for his removal and on November 7 the Schenectady Committee was advised of his resignation. The Minutes of the Schenectady Committee of Safety.

Department, who are a part disafacted persons to the States, which we look to be both Verry ungenerous and unjust to appoint Enemys to the Country to posts of profits while so many true friends are in want of bread; and altho the Sick have been entirely removed from the hospital Some Consederable time ago, a Doctor Commesarry, Deputy Commessary and their attendents are still keep in pay, which we look upon to be intirely a waste of the public money, and as we Expect to Bear a part of the public Expence we Cannot help Complaining of this abuse and hope that they may be Emediately Discharged.

Thirdly, that Great partiallity hath hetherto Been Shewen to the Inhabitants of Albany, apointing them in preference to us to posts and places in the public Service, tho the far greatest parte of the Citizens of Albany are in Some public posts, there is only three Inhabitants of this Town Imployed in public Services (Exclusive of Soldiers); That they not Settesfyed with filling all the posts in Albany with their own friends but have Sent a Commisary and Commisary's Clark here to act, while we are Confident we have people Enough Capable to fill Such places.

That Upon all Ocations when the Melitia is Called out, we have Sent three men to the field for one that the City of Albany have done, they being Chiefly Exempt By the public Employment they hold; and we have been obliged to do their duty; this we look upon to be unjust and must beg Leave to tell you that we Expect a more Equatable Distribution of public offices will be made; That we at all times are willing to do our part of the public Service, providing we Can Keep Some proportion of the public Benefit, and unless we can have that, we disvice you will not call on us for any further Services, but on those who are filling their pockets while many of us are in Dainger of Suffering for want.

Fourthly, that one[11] of the three Gentlemen in this town imployed in the public Service, hold no less than four posts

---

[11] Henry Glen is probably the one referred to.

viz A.D. Quarter Master General, D.Commisary, D.Barrack Master, D.Forrage Master, which we look upon to be unjust for so many posts to be given to one man while so many are in want and have none at all.

Gentlemen These are the Grevences we at present Complain of and in full assurance that they will be redressed as far as in your superior Judgment they ought and in your power to procure we Remain.

Gentlemen with the Greatest Respect your most humble Sarvants.

The petition was forwarded[12] to Governor Clinton on the twenty-fourth and some three weeks later his answer was received. "Be pleased to assure them," he wrote[13] in part, "that as far as I have anything to do in the Distribution of Offices, the People of the Town of Schenectady shall equally participate with the People of Albany, or of any other part of the State, and that my Orders shall never charge them with more than their due Proportion of Military Duty. As to the appointments in the Continental Line, in which tho' there may have been Partiality, it is out of my Power to correct it, but as to any abuses which have been committed by the Staff of the army on proper Complaint & Proof the Persons injured will be redressed and the Offenders punished."

[12] Public Papers of George Clinton, III, 78.
[13] *Ibid*, p. 165.

CHAPTER XIV

THE DECISION OF THE INDIANS. THE RAIDS OF 1778

Although the Indians had taken a more or less prominent part on the side of the British in the military movements of the year 1777, it was hoped that they might still be induced to assume a position of neutrality, and with this in view a council was held at Johnstown on March 9, 1778, under the direction of the Northern Department. So far as obtaining pledges was concerned the meeting was without avail, the only word from the Senecas, who did not even send a representative, being a message[1] affecting great surprise "that while [their] tomahawks were sticking in their heads, their wounds bleeding, and their eyes streaming with tears for the loss[2] of their friends at German Flats the commissioners should think of inviting them to a treaty." And so it was brought about that prompted by a desire for personal vengeance the Indians, with the exception of the Oneidas and a few Tuscaroras, now definitely cast their lot with the British, soon to commence, with the co-operation of the Tories, that border warfare which in the next five years was to bring desolation to many a once fertile and prosperous section.

[1] William L. Stone, Life of Joseph Brant, I, 305.
[2] The Indian loss at Oriskany was about one hundred men, of whom thirty-six were Senecas.

While in the raids that were to follow the action of the Indians was prompted by one motive, another of real strategic value seems to have governed the movements of their allies, for these border campaigns bear a direct relation to the main conflict inasmuch as it was hoped that to repel them Continental forces would be diverted,[3] thereby weakening more important points.

Although since the opening of spring[4] the frontiers had been in a constant state of alarm in anticipation[5] of Indian and Tory raids, it was not until May 30 that the culmination of the first movement in force occurred. On that day Joseph Brant, at the head of a force of from three hundred to four hundred men, attacked the little settlement of Cobleskill.[6]

Christopher Yates writing to Colonel Wemple from Schoharie on the same day reported[7] "the people in great disorder, the buildings all destroyed." "We have this afternoon received information," continues the letter, "that a party far Superior to that of Cobuskill, or perhaps them joined with the other, are to come upon Scoharie in order to destroy the

[3] Their end in this particular was not accomplished, the defense of the frontier falling therefore almost entirely upon the militia.

[4] In March a company of artificers, enlisted in Schenectady and commanded by Jacob Vrooman as master workman, left for Saratoga, where they remained until near the first of December engaged in building barracks and batteaux and in rebuilding the mills and dwelling-house of General Schuyler, which had been burned by the British the year before. Pension Office Records, Benjamin Van Vleck R 10897.

[5] In April a detail of one hundred and twenty-five of the militia and several Indians under Colonel Abraham Wemple went out on scout duty to Beverdam to apprehend some Tories from Unadilla and elsewhere. Pension Office Records, James Barhydt S 12948.

[6] Public Papers of George Clinton, III, 377.

[7] *Ibid.*, p. 378.

whole." The news of the attack was received in Albany the next morning while the people were at church, and although application was made to General Ten Broeck for the immediate ordering out of the militia he refused to do so until church was over "for fear," he said,[8] "of frightening the Town into fits."

Accompanying the troops, who with Colonel Wemple in command, finally set out for Schoharie was a detachment of one hundred and nineteen of the Schenectady militia.[9] On June 2 Colonel Wemple reported[10] to General Ten Broeck from Schoharie that he had that morning sent a detail of one hundred and fifty men under Lieutenant-Colonel Yates to Cobleskill, but that after they had been gone some time he had received information of a large party coming down to destroy the settlement of Brakeabean and had therefore ordered them to return to the upper settlement at Schoharie where he himself would reinforce them. "If I am lucky enough to meet them [the enemy]," continues the letter, "I hope to give them a trimming." On June 6 he again reported [11] in part as follows:

I have Buried the dead at Cobuskill, which was 14 in number; found five more burnt in the ruins of the House of one Yurry Wainer, where the engagement has been; they were Butchered in a most inhuman manner; burnt 10 Houses and Barns, Horses, Cows, Sheep, etc., lay dead all over the fields.

[8] *Ibid.*, p. 379.
[9] *Ibid.*, p. 383.
[10] *Ibid.*
[11] *Ibid.*, p. 413.

With the actual appearance of the enemy the alarm on the frontiers became the more acute and to the many appeals for assistance that were forwarded to Governor Clinton there was added on June 15 the following[12] plea from the Committee at Schenectady:

Honoured Sir, The distressed situation of Tryon County, Schoharie and indeed the whole of our western Frontiers, seem to call so loud for relief that we think we should be wanting in our duty, if we did not acquaint your Excellency, of the real danger our Frontiers are in; Your Excellency may depend on it, that it is no sham to frighten the people, but a thing in real existence, for the people are flying and crowding into this town in great numbers, and by the best information the enemy are really round about there, and are determined to destroy, and burn up that whole country, and unless soon relieved we undoubtedly believe they will affect it, and the loss that will arise therefrom to the unhappy individuals of that part of the country will be nothing, in comparison to the loss of the United States, as it is one of our principal wheat countrys.

Governor Clinton replied[13] to the letter from the Committee on June 18, detailing the steps that had already been taken toward meeting the danger that threatened the settlers on the frontiers. "Considering the militia as the only force whose services I can command," he added, "more could not have been done by me for their protection."

In spite of the many urgent pleas made to the authorities for Continental troops to protect the frontiers, no effective measures had yet been taken. "If they do not come soon," wrote[14] General Ten

[12] *Ibid.*, p. 459.
[13] *Ibid.*, p. 467.
[14] *Ibid.*, p. 562.

Broeck in reporting the criticalness of the situation to Governor Clinton on July 20, following the news of Brant's raid on Springfield and Andrustown, "I dread the Consequences—it is now harvest & it is with the utmost difficulty I get the militia to turn out—the number now Ordered out (Exclusive of Col. Wemple's Regt.[15]) is ab't 700 men; about 600 were Ordered the 12th June & only ab't 220 did come. What number I shall get now is Impossible for me to tell. I shall do everything in my power."

The next movement by the enemy in force culminated early in July in the massacre of Wyoming in the valley of the Susquehanna, to be followed in the middle of September[16] by Brant's long-expected raid on German Flats. News of the disaster attending the enemy's appearance in the Mohawk Valley reached General Ten Broeck at Albany on the eighteenth, and almost immediately Colonel Wemple's regiment set out for the relief of the quarter attacked,

[15] The whole of Colonel Wemple's regiment was ordered to Schoharie on July 19. Public Papers of George Clinton, III, 563. On August 27 forty-four men from this regiment were reported as stationed there. *Ibid.*, p. 736.

[16] During the interim the available military force of Schenectady was augmented by the formation of a company of "Associated Exempts" numbering fifty men, under Captain Jacob Schermerhorn, with Isaac Glen as first lieutenant and Cornelius A. Van Slyck as second lieutenant. This company was organized under a state law which recommended that those men who had heretofore held commissions form themselves into companies, as well as those who were over fifty years of age and thereby exempt from militia duty. Public Papers of George Clinton, III, 590. Service in the Exempts was entirely voluntary and those who enrolled engaged to provide themselves with proper arms, accoutrements and ammunition, "adding a pledge that on alarm they would repair to their appointed rendezvous, and when drafts were made on the militia, they would contribute their portion of men to be commanded by their own officers."

soon to return home, however, as the enemy had on their arrival retreated too far to render pursuit by the militia advisable.[17]

On November 11 the enemy under Captain Walter Butler fell upon the settlement of Cherry Valley. The success of the attack, which had been instigated as a means of retaliation for the vigorous offensive measures instituted by the American forces the month before, resulting in the destruction of Unadilla and Oghwaga, was the more lamentable as repeated and timely warnings had been given regarding the enemy's intentions.

On receipt of the news of the attack the militia were again ordered out.[18] "Altho my Letter of the 13th and General Ten Broeck's of the 16th give no great Credit to the Militia in General," wrote[19] General Hand to Governor Clinton of the eighteenth, "I think it my Duty to acquaint your Excellency that Col. Wemple's Schenectady Militia, (a very respectable Body of Men) turned out with much Chearfulness, tho the remoteness of their Situation prevented their answering the wished for purposes."

Many of the inhabitants of Cherry Valley who were fortunate enough to have escaped from the massacre[20] with their lives, although they lost all else, at once hastened to Schenectady[21] "in a Dolefull, Lamentable, and Helpless Condition, Destitute

[17] Public Papers of George Clinton, IV, 54, 80, 82.
[18] *Ibid.*, p. 293.
[19] *Ibid.*, p. 298.
[20] A younger son who was in school at Schenectady was the only survivor of the family of Robert Wells, who, with his wife, mother, brother, sister, three children and three servants, lost his life in the massacre.
[21] Public Papers of George Clinton, IV, 334.

(many of them) of meat, money and Cloathing, Either for Back or Bed."[22] For the relief of these refugees General Hand was appealed to from Schenectady on the twenty-sixth, the petitioners humbly praying[23] that their distressed condition be given serious consideration and that some means be devised whereby they might be supplied with provisions, wood and "sufficient clothing to cover them from the inclemency of the weather."

[22] *Ibid.*, pp. 338-339.
[23] *Ibid.*, p. 339.

CHAPTER XV

STEPS TAKEN TO PROTECT THE FRONTIER. SULLIVAN'S CAMPAIGN

During the winter (1778-1779) roving bands of Indians and Tories kept the settlers on the frontiers in constant alarm.

In the spring the first active steps that had yet been taken looking toward an adequate protection of the frontiers were embodied in an act of the State Legislature which provided for the raising of a force of one thousand men[1] for this purpose. The men drafted were to continue in the service until the following January and were to be allowed the same pay and rations as the Continental army. For the force to be raised the schedule called for nineteen men[2] to be drafted from Colonel Wemple's regiment.

While the proposed force was slowly being enrolled, the Continental Congress, realizing the seriousness of the situation, decided to itself take the matter in hand, and to General Washington was given the direction of the campaign which aimed not only at checking the raids but also at the total destruction and devastation of the settlements of the raiders and the capture of as many of the enemy as possible.

---

[1] A greater part of this force was later requisitioned by Congress to fill up the regiments of the New York Continental Line.

[2] Public Papers of George Clinton, V, 167.

The plan of Sullivan's campaign as adopted called for one division under General Sullivan to proceed by way of the Susquehanna River and a second under General James Clinton to proceed up the Mohawk from Schenectady to Canajoharie, crossing to Otsego Lake, thence down the Susquehanna, the two divisions joining at Tioga Point.

Under the direction of Henry Glen work was early actively undertaken to prepare and assemble at Schenectady the necessary provisions and stores in anticipation of the arrival of Clinton's division.[3] Schenectady seems to have been chosen for the concentration of the supplies rather than Canajoharie for the reason that there were no proper storehouses at the latter place and further because it was felt that at Schenectady there would be less likelihood of their being the object of an attack on the part of the enemy.[4]

On May 28 General Clinton reported to Washington that a quantity of provision had been successfully collected, and further that there were one hundred batteaux assembled ready to be loaded on the shortest notice.[5]

While these preparations were going on, small bodies of Indians appearing simultaneously in different quarters again necessitated the calling out of the militia. General Clinton reported the matter to his brother on April 28 in part as follows:[6]

[3] Pension Office Records, David Van Derheyden W 6373.
[4] James Clinton to Washington, Albany, May 28, 1779. Washington Papers, Library of Congress.
[5] *Ibid.*
[6] Public Papers of George Clinton, IV, 771.

The alarm was general thro' the whole Country, and I believe in a few days Schenectady woud have been the Frontier of the State, if it had not been for the appearance of the Troops, which I immediately marched up, consisting of that part of Gansevoort's Regt., which was in town, and the Schenectady Militia, amounting in the whole to about two hundred, with which I proceeded as far as Johnstown, where I was joined by a number of the Tryon County Militia who turned out chearfully on the occasion.

"[As] the only method left of restoring the Inhabitants to their former Tranquility," General Clinton determined[7] to erect a blockhouse at Sacandaga. To Colonel Gansevoort[8] was intrusted the duty of carrying out the orders and a detail of the Schenectady militia was ordered out to assist in the work.[9]

On June 15 General Clinton reported[10] that the one hundred boats[11] at Schenectady had been loaded and were already on their way up the Mohawk. "I have ordered one hundred more Boats to be had in readiness immediately," continues the report, "as the Genl. has ordered me to embark all the Troops, and take no P. Horses."

Under the direction of the Committee of Safety and under the command of Lieutenant-Colonel Yates

[7] *Ibid.* This had been suggested to Governor Clinton by Jellis Fonda. Public Papers of George Clinton, IV, 670.

[8] Colonel Peter Gansevoort of the 3d New York Line. He had been in command at Fort Stanwix when besieged by St. Leger.

[9] Pension Office Records, John B. Veeder R 10927; John DeGraff; Ephraim Bradt W 16860.

[10] Public Papers of George Clinton, V, 86.

[11] They were escorted by the 3d New York Line and a detachment under Colonel Butler.

many of the Schenectady militia were employed in the embarkation of Clinton's brigade, and not a few, as volunteers, in the conveying of the baggage and supplies of the army up the Mohawk. Some of the men also accompanied the division on its march and on fatigue duty assisted in cutting the road through to Otsego Lake and in the erection of the dam necessary to transfer the batteaux to the Susquehanna River.[12]

The devastation and havoc wrought by the American forces as they advanced through the Indian country fulfilled to the letter the instructions of Congress and yet how ineffectual were these measures in the attainment of the main object of the expedition is amply shown by the subsequent history of the frontiers. Neither were the Indians subdued nor the prime movers in their raids captured, and the blackened ruins of their homes served only to further incite them to measures of retaliation. Scarcely had Sullivan returned when reports of murders committed by roving bands of Indians were borne to the authorities, and on October 25, Colonel Van Dyck, writing from Fort Schuyler, reported[13] a plan of the "Regulars" to lay siege to that post while the Indians were in the meantime destroying "the Country down as far as Schenectady."

While the reported plan did not mature, sufficient alarm was caused to warrant the militia being kept almost constantly on duty during the fall, details from Colonel Wemple's regiment forming part of the

[12] Pension Office Records, Simon J. Vrooman W 6370; James Barhydt S 12948.
[13] Public Papers of George Clinton, V, 330.

garrison[14] of many of the forts to the westward and acting as guards for the farmers in the vicinity while they gathered their harvests.

[14] On November 19 eighty men from Colonel Wemple's regiment, ten of whom were "Exempts," were on duty at Fort Paris. Public Papers of George Clinton, V, 365. Details at Fort Hunter and Fort Plank, Pension Office Records, Daniel McMichael S 13885; Richard Van Vranken S 11623; Matthew DeGarmo S 23599. Details at Schoharie, Pension Office Records, Gerrit Schermerhorn S 14422; John DeGraff S 15090; George Passage R 7889.

CHAPTER XVI

THE MOHAWK VALLEY LAID WASTE

The enemy did not wait until spring to again commence their activities. In February, 1780, a small band effected some damage at German Flats, in March a settlement to the north of Palatine sustained a like invasion, and early in April came news of Brant's raid on Harpersfield.

Reports of minor raids, rumors of intended movements by the enemy on a large scale, actual suffering on the part of the settlers for want of provisions, depreciation in Continental currency which had by now become practically worthless, and the difficulties of affording a semblance of protection by reinforcing the meager garrisons already posted, due to the impossibility of obtaining supplies for the militia, the only force available for this service, had by May brought about a most lamentable condition on the frontiers. As a result of this condition the more remote settlements were reported as daily breaking up and Colonel Van Schaick was led to express[1] the fear that unless some speedy and effectual measures were taken to inspire the desponding people with confidence, Schenectady would in all probability soon be the frontier to the westward.

[1] To Governor Clinton, May 17, 1780. Public Papers of George Clinton, V, 715. He expressed the same view to General Washington a few days later. Washington Papers, Library of Congress.

At daybreak on the morning of May 22 the much feared attack of the enemy materialized, Sir John Johnson appearing on the Mohawk River at Tribes Hill with a strong force[2] of Indians and whites. From Tribes Hill the enemy proceeded westward "burning the Houses and Barns of the Inhabitants and putting to Death every Male capable of bearing arms."[3]

"Collo. Fisher[4] is mortally wounded," reported[5] Colonel John Harper from Johnstown on the same day, "and his two[6] Brothers killed, [and] old Mr. Douw Fonda[7] with seven others."

Of the Schenectady militia who had marched under Colonel Wemple "on the first alarm" some were almost immediately obliged to return for want of provisions.[8] The remainder, however, hastened towards Johnstown and, joined by troops from Fort

[2] Four hundred whites and two hundred Indians.
[3] Public Papers of George Clinton, V, 743.
[4] Frederick Visscher (Fisher), a colonel in the Tryon County Militia. He had removed his family to Schenectady for safety's sake a few days before. Having been brought down by a tomahawk, scalped and left for dead by the raiders he subsequently recovered consciousness and managed to escape from the burning house he had so gallantly helped to defend. With the aid of a negro slave belonging to one of the neighbors Colonel Visscher managed to reach friends, who at once sent him to Schenectady by canoe. Here he received medical attention and subsequently recovered from his wounds.
[5] Public Papers of George Clinton, V, 737.
[6] John and Harman. They with Colonel Visscher were the sole defenders of the family homestead where the attack occurred.
[7] He had removed from Schenectady and settled at Caughnawaga (Fonda) about the year 1751. An account of his murder may be found in Jeptha R. Simms, Frontiersmen of New York, II, 339.
[8] Public Papers of George Clinton, V, 744. Pension Office Records, Philip Viele R 10947.

Hunter[9] under Colonel Harper[10] and others under Colonel Volkert Vedder,[11] swelling their force to about four hundred and fifty men, determined to engage the enemy should Sir John, who had rendezvoused there, show any disposition to fight.[12]

Sir John, although his force, swelled by the addition of many Tories who had hastened to join him, now outnumbered the American troops about two to one, did not offer an engagement, but almost immediately withdrew and, eluding the troops which Governor Clinton sent to intercept him, made his way safely back to Canada.[13]

The opportunity afforded by the dispirited condition of soldiers and settlers alike had early been seized upon by the British, who with no small success endeavored through their emissaries to stir up mutinies in the ranks of the main army or induce those holding Tory sentiments to take up arms in their behalf.

Many Tories had joined Sir John Johnson during his raid, and from time to time small bands from Albany and Tryon counties left to join the enemy. That a large party so inclined were assembled at Beaverdam was reported[14] to the Schenectady Com-

---

[9] This fort stood a short distance east of the Schoharie Creek near its confluence with the Mohawk River.

[10] Colonel John Harper of the Levies.

[11] His name was spelled both Vedder and Veeder. He was lieutenant-colonel of the 5th Albany County and later of the 3d Tryon County Militia.

[12] Public Papers of George Clinton, V, 743.

[13] He took with him the family silver which had been buried at the time of his departure in 1776.

[14] Public Papers of George Clinton, VI, 30.

mittee on July 18. Colonel Vrooman[15] at Schoharie was at once apprised[16] of the fact that he might order out a detachment in an endeavor to intercept them, while in Schenectady a party was at once organized[17] for the same purpose. Although the Schenectady detachment after having marched all night arrived at the rendezvous at daybreak, they were successful in securing but three of the band who had secreted themselves in a barn, while the main body, having undoubtedly been alarmed, succeeded in making their escape.[18]

Late in July the enemy under Joseph Brant appeared in force before Fort Schuyler. This movement was probably a feint, for while the troops were hastening to the defense of the post, leaving the lower valley without adequate means of protection, Brant and his followers quietly withdrew and, advancing by way of the Unadilla and Susquehanna Rivers on August 2, fell upon Canajoharie.

The Albany and Schenectady militia, who had turned out with alacrity[19] under orders previously given, had just gone into camp at Caughnawaga[20] opposite Mr. Frey's at about eleven o'clock on the morning of the second, when they were alarmed by the heavy smoke "between John Abeails and Fort Plank about four miles distant."[21]

"Instantly I did order both Regiments to be

---

[15] Peter Vrooman, colonel of the 15th Albany County Militia.
[16] Public Papers of George Clinton, VI, 31.
[17] *Ibid.*
[18] *Ibid.*
[19] *Ibid.*, p. 79.
[20] Now Fonda, Montgomery County.
[21] Public Papers of George Clinton, VI, 80.

formed," reported[22] Colonel Wemple in his dispatch to General Ten Broeck, "& proceed against the Enemy, who were at that time in their full Carear and tho our Numbers were not equal, yet I can assure you I should be void of Justice if I omitted mentioning their Prudence and cool behavior without Distinction to all Rancks. An Altho they had been in full march since early in the morning they came up with such Vigor that the Enemy on our approach gave way & tho in sight we had no opportunity to give them Battle they retired in the usual way."

"Such a Scean as we beheld since we left the River," reads another section of the report, "passing dead Bodies of Men & Children most cruelly murdered, is not possible to be described. I cannot ascertain at present the Number of poor Inhabitants killed and missing but believe the Loss considerable as the People were all at work in the Fields. . . . Some Persons pretend to say not less than one hundred dwelling House are burnt."

On August 21 Colonel Goose Van Schaick, writing[23] to General Washington from Albany, confirmed the details of the withdrawal of Brant from Fort Schuyler and of the attack on Canajoharie. "From thence," continued the letter, "they returned towards the susquahanna, & in a few days after made a Descent on Schohary; here they burnt twelve Houses, & have by information taken and killed a larger number of the Inhabitants than at the former place, & it is expected the remainder of Schohary will share the same fate. The Indians are seen daily

[22] *Ibid.*
[23] Washington Papers, Library of Congress.

in small parties, & take prisoners & Scalps, Schenectady is threatened & the Inhabitants are moving their effects to Albany with all dispatch seeing no appearance of support, & numbers going off to the enemy daily."

In England Riverton's Royal Gazette told of the successful progress of the expedition. "The Indians have laid waste the whole country," reads its issue[24] of September 23, "the Tory houses excepted, down to Schenectady, where some rebels are at work throwing up works to oppose the progress of the British troops and our Indian allies. The rebel women and children have retired to Albany."

[24] Franklin B. Hough, The Northern Invasion of October, 1780, p. 81.

CHAPTER XVII

THE RAIDS ON BALLSTON AND THE SCHOHARIE SETTLEMENTS

Late in August word was brought to the authorities in Albany that another raid along the Valley was being contemplated by the enemy. Sir John Johnson was reported to be in command and with the two thousand men under him was to strike first at Stone Arabia. From Schenectady scouts were kept continually out, and here General Van Rensselaer[1] took up his headquarters so that in case the accounts were found to be true he might in person collect troops to repel the invasion.[2]

On September 4 General Van Rensselaer reported[3] to Governor Clinton from Fort Rensselaer[4] that small parties of the enemy were frequently seen on the frontiers, although the reports of their intentions were still vague and uncertain. The militia were already under orders to be in readiness to march at a moment's notice as soon as the advance of the enemy was reported and on September 8 Colonel William Malcolm, under orders to march to the front,

---

[1] On June 29, 1780, the Albany militia was ordered to be divided into two brigades and to General Robert Van Rensselaer was given the command of the Second Brigade.
[2] Public Papers of George Clinton, VI, 136.
[3] *Ibid.*, p. 169.
[4] Still standing in the village of Canajoharie and used as a museum.

encamped near Albany with his brigade of State Levies[5] raised to reinforce the troops on the frontiers.

"I find but very few Persons here which manifest a Disposition to forward the Service," Colonel Malcolm wrote[6] to Washington, "although they express great Apprehensions about the Indians."

"I send forward one Regiment Tomorrow," continued the letter, "they go entirely upon the Prospect of obtaining Provisions from the Country—there is no Magazine at Schenectady[7]—not one Ration."

On October 12 word[8] reached Albany that on the eighth Sir John Johnson, Butler and Brant were at Oneida on their way to Stone Arabia and ultimately Fort Schuyler. From the north came information[9] that a second expedition under Major Christopher Carleton had already taken possession of Fort Ann and that Fort George was threatened.

On the night of October 16, the settlement of Ballston[10] was attacked. The enemy, which comprised a

[5] In August five hundred Massachusetts Levies were detailed to defend the New York frontiers and on the eleventh one hundred of them were reported in Schenectady on their way to Tryon County. On March 11, 1780, a law was passed in New York State to raise men for the same purpose. Of the twenty-nine men required from Colonel Wemple's regiment under this act twenty-two had been enrolled on August 10, twenty of whom were on duty at West Point and two at Albany.

[6] Washington Papers, Library of Congress.

[7] Schenectady had been a regular army post until the spring of 1780, but on March 16 orders were transmitted by the Board of War at Philadelphia to discontinue this post together with certain others because of the cost of maintenance. Public Papers of George Clinton, V, 697.

[8] Public Papers of George Clinton, VI, 288.

[9] *Ibid.*

[10] The sources of material used in connection with the raid on Balls-

detachment[11] from Major Carleton's division, consisted of British regulars, Tories and Indians and was under the command of Major John Munro, a former merchant of Schenectady. It is believed that the original intention of the enemy was to surprise Schenectady but that possibly due to some information obtained through their scouts they decided to proceed no further than Ballston.

A fort built of oak logs surrounded by a stockade comprised the defenses of the settlement. This fort had a few days before been garrisoned by a small detachment of Schenectady militia, and perhaps fearful lest they be unable to effect a surprise complete enough to insure its capture, this post was carefully avoided by the enemy, who instead directed their efforts to attacking some of the exposed houses. One man killed, one wounded and the capture of twenty-two prisoners whom the enemy took with them as they hastily withdrew[12] bore witness to the success of the expedition.

The approach[13] of Sir John Johnson on the Schoharie settlements was almost simultaneous with Munro's raid on Ballston, for early on the morning of the seventeenth his forces were discovered[14] pass-

---

ton are: Jeptha R. Simms, The Frontiersmen of New York, II, 413; Franklin B. Hough, The Northern Invasion of October, 1780, p. 45.

[11] About two hundred strong.

[12] On news of the raid a detachment from Schenectady set out in pursuit of the enemy. Pension Office Records, David Van Derheyden W 6373; John N. Marcellus W 26232; George Passage R 7989.

[13] It is now considered that this second invasion of Sir John Johnson was part of a well-defined plan revolving about the surrender of West Point by Benedict Arnold.

[14] Public Papers of George Clinton, VI, 303.

ing the Upper Fort.[15] No attempt was made to attack this position, the enemy, finding themselves discovered, devoting themselves instead to burning whatever buildings they came upon as they made their way toward the Middle Fort.[16] Here they met with some resistance[17] and finding that a display of their force was not sufficient to induce the garrison to capitulate, the enemy about three o'clock in the afternoon continued their march down the Valley and, passing the Lower Fort,[18] burning and pillaging as they proceeded, went into camp some six miles below.

Word of the enemy's presence at Schoharie reached Albany about noon on the seventeenth and General Van Rensselaer at once set out for Schenectady with such troops as he was able to rally for the pursuit.[19] When he arrived in Schenectady early in the evening the light of fires toward the lower end of Schoharie

[15] The Upper Fort was a one-story building enclosed by a stockade and breastwork. It stood about five miles southwest of the present village of Middleburg.

[16] The Middle Fort stood in the present village of Middleburg about one half mile northeast from the bridge. It comprised a two-story stone house owned by John Becker and was surrounded by a stockade of pickets with blockhouses mounted with small cannon on two of its angles.

[17] A detailed account of the refusal of the militia to obey the orders of Major Woolsey, the Continental commander, and the firing on the flag of truce by Timothy Murphy as the British came forward for a parley is to be found in Jeptha R. Simms, The Frontiersmen of New York, II, 424.

[18] The Lower Fort comprised a stockade with two blockhouses mounted with small cannon. This stockade surrounded the stone church now standing at Schoharie village, the home of the Schoharie County Historical Society.

[19] Minutes of the Court of Inquiry into the Conduct of Brigadier-General Van Rensselaer. Public Papers of George Clinton, VI, 692-703. These minutes are the source from which has been obtained most of the material relative to this campaign.

bore evidence of the destruction being wrought by the enemy. A conference of the principal inhabitants was at once called and with them was discussed the practicability of procuring a number of horses and wagons by the next morning in order that such of the militia as could be collected might be sent forward with greater expedition. The attempt was made during the night, but a very inadequate number was secured.

Henry Glen, the issuing commissary, was approached on the matter of furnishing rations for the troops and later reported "that there was not a Sufficiency of Provisions of the meat kind to victual the Troops for a Day & a very small Quantity of Bread." Some cattle, however, destined for the garrison at Fort Schuyler, arriving opportunely, were ordered killed and all the ovens available were pressed into service that a sufficient quantity of bread might be baked during the night.

Between nine and ten o'clock on the eighteenth the troops having received their provisions and being reinforced by members of Colonel Wemple's regiment, General Van Rensselaer left Schenectady and proceeded up the Valley, taking with him two field pieces on wheels which he had obtained at Schenectady.

On the morning of the nineteenth Colonel Brown,[20] who was in command at Fort Kayser,[21] left the post with a force of one hundred and thirty men under orders to join General Van Rensselaer. Marching south they later were surprised by Sir John John-

[20] Colonel John Brown, one of the bravest men on the frontier. He lost his life in the engagement that followed.
[21] To the north of Palatine Bridge.

son's forces proceeding in the opposite direction and, outnumbered seven to one, disastrously defeated.

General Van Rensselaer was apprised of the enemy's whereabouts and of the defeat of Colonel Brown by fugitive soldiers who had succeeded in making their escape from the field, and in the afternoon, overtaking the enemy, he forced the engagement known as the battle of Klock's Field.

That Sir John and his forces were permitted to escape has always been a matter of regret, and although General Van Rensselaer has been severely blamed[22] for his failure to at once follow up the advantage gained, the Court of Inquiry convened for the purpose of investigating his action not only wholly exonerated him, but declared that his conduct "was not only unexceptional, but such as became a good, active, faithful, prudent and spirited officer."

Not a few of the Schenectady militia marched[23] as far as Herkimer in the effort to overtake the enemy and some were detailed[24] as guards and batteaumen to bring by boat to Schenectady those of Colonel Brown's soldiers who had sustained injuries that their wounds might here be dressed under the direction[25] of Dr. Dirk Van Ingen.

On October 29 Governor Clinton wrote[26] to James Duane detailing the destruction that had been effected by the enemy. He estimated the loss at one

[22] Had Simms, Stone or Douglas Campbell had access to the Clinton Papers or to the Minutes of the Court of Inquiry their judgment would have been more favorable.
[23] Pension Office Records, Simon J. Vrooman W 6370; John Van Eps W 27862.
[24] Pension Office Records, Nicholas R. Bovie S 12275.
[25] Pension Office Records, Henry H. Peek W 9219.
[26] Public Papers of George Clinton, VI, 345.

hundred and fifty thousand bushels of wheat in addition to other grain, forage and some two hundred buildings. "Schenectady may now be said to become the limits of our western Frontier," continued the letter, "the first Object worth a new Enterprise."

The incursions of the enemy had so delayed the raising of troops intended to relieve the Levies stationed at the various posts that late in October Governor Clinton decided to order forward details of the militia for this service, promising, however, that they would be relieved as soon as possible. In accordance with this decision Colonel Wemple was ordered[27] to dispatch seventy of his regiment to Fort Rensselaer, much to the alarm of the people in Schenectady, who on the twenty-fourth petitioned Governor Clinton that the order be reconsidered.

"Whereas," reads the memorial,[28] "the present situation of this place is become a frontier Town, which we have reason to believe the Enemy aims to destroy, and which we your memorialist are a good deal concerned about, particularly when we Consider the Different Settlements round about us, if we turn our eyes to the north, we find a Settlement called Galloway, and another called Peasly, who are all enemies to the Country and even Balls Town a great part of them; To the southwest from us we have the Hellebergh, which are likewise mostly Tories, at which places the enemy may lay conceald untill they find an opportunity to destroy this place. And one half of our Regiment are joining to these Settlements.

"We, your memorialist, therefore, humbly pray that your Excellency will take our Situation in Con-

[27] *Ibid.*, p. 333.
[28] *Ibid.*

sideration and grant that our Regiment may remain at Home to defend this place. And as Balls Town is likewise exposed to great Danger of an other attack of the enemy we lying nearest to them might on occasion be a great assistance to the good people of that place."

The year was not to close without further alarm, for the militia had scarcely returned from the western frontier when they were again ordered[29] out to check a second invasion threatened from the north by forces under Major Carleton.

"Plots, Conspiracies, Conflagrations, Alarms, Burning of the City, Destruction of Schenectady, &c. &c.," wrote[30] Stephen Lush to Governor Clinton on November 7, in describing the terror reigning at Albany, "are the only Subjects of Conversation at present." Adding, in all probability not without some degree of truth, that "a chimney took Fire the other Evening and it was instantly determined [that] the enemy were in the midst of us."

[29] *Ibid.*, p. 376.
[30] *Ibid.*, p. 395.

CHAPTER XVIII

THE ONEIDAS AT SCHENECTADY

Unmoved by promises and threats alike the Oneida Indians alone of the Six Nations had continued to favor the cause of the colonists both with their influence and actual support. Because of this allegiance they had early incurred the enmity of the other tribes who, as we have seen, had ultimately decided to cast their lot with the King. The devastation effected by General Sullivan had naturally widened the breach and in the measures outlined for retaliation it was planned that the Oneidas should not escape.

On June 18, 1780, a delegation of Oneida chiefs acquainted[1] Colonel Cornelius Van Dyck, who was then in command of Fort Schuyler, of the danger that was apprehended and of the information that had given rise to the belief that their town was soon to be destroyed unless they transferred their allegiance. The threatened attack culminated in July. "[The Oneidas] too weak to make effectual resistance," wrote[2] General Schuyler to the Marquis de Lafayette on August 18, "but too firmly attached to us to submit, or take part with the enemy, prudently took shelter at Fort Schuyler the day before the arrival of the Enemy, who burnt part of their Village, siezed

[1] Public Papers of George Clinton, V, 883.
[2] Washington Papers, Library of Congress.

their Cattle, and destroyed the Crops and even pursued the fugitives as far as the fort.''

Because of the scarcity of provisions the Indians were permitted to remain at Fort Schuyler but a few days.[3] They were, however, under the direction of the authorities, transferred to Schenectady, where, supported at the expense[4] of the Government, they remained until the end of the war.

On their arrival at Schenectady the Indians, to the number of four hundred and six[5] (which included seven Caughnawagas), were ordered quartered in the barracks,[6] and to Jellis Fonda and others was given the contract of supplying them with necessary provisions. Frequent complaints soon began to be heard[7] to the effect that the Indians were suffering for want of food. General Schuyler investigated these complaints and on October 10 reported[8] that he had been advised by one of the contractors that the Indians were well supplied with provisions with the exception of corn, which it was impossible to obtain. He reported further that the contractors complained that up to this time no money had been paid on the contract and that he was given to under-

[3] Colonel Van Schaick to General Washington, July 29, 1780. Washington Papers, Library of Congress.

[4] As early as March 24, 1779, Congress empowered the commissioners in the Northern Department to supply provisions to their ''faithful friends the Oneidas.'' So low were the public funds and so inadequate the supplies for the troops that on more than one occasion both the State and Philip Schuyler personally advanced funds and supplies.

[5] Ninety-three of this number were men, fifty-four women and the balance children. The majority of the warriors probably remained with the troops. Papers of the Continental Congress, III, 551.

[6] *Ibid.*, p. 541.

[7] *Ibid.*

[8] *Ibid.*

THE ONEIDAS AT SCHENECTADY

stand that unless money was furnished further supplies would in all event not be readily forthcoming. Schuyler spoke[9] of the poverty of the Indians as being such as to render them "an affecting spectacle of distress" and added that few had clothing sufficient to render them comfortable even at that season of the year.

Because of the expense of supplying the barracks with firewood it was now proposed to remove the Indians to the neighboring woods, where they were to be quartered in huts.[10] This arrangement, moreover, would, it was felt, simplify the food problem, as the Indians would be able to replenish their stores by hunting.[11]

The plan proposed was probably tried but evidently did not meet with the success hoped for, as on December 5 James Clinton reported[12] to Washington that the Indians were again in possession of the barracks and that he was at a loss to know to what point to remove them in order to make room for Continental troops[13] who were to be quartered in Schenectady during the winter and who were soon expected to put in their appearance.

On the subsequent arrival of the Regulars the matter[14] of quarters was finally adjusted by billeting the officers with the townspeople while soldiers and Indians were required to share the barracks. As might well be imagined this arrangement was not to

---

[9] *Ibid.*
[10] *Ibid.*
[11] *Ibid.*, p. 551.
[12] Washington Papers, Library of Congress.
[13] The 2d New York Line.
[14] *Magazine of American History*, December, 1881, p. 409.

prove practical. "Disagreeable Controversys have frequently arisen between the soldiery and Indians," reported[15] General Schuyler on March 29 of the following year, "and one of the latter [has] lately been barbarously murdered and others Assaulted and dangerously wounded." Because of this friction it was found necessary to make some other provision for the Indians and under the direction of Schuyler they were again removed[16] outside the town and supplied with boards[17] with which to cover rude huts which they had already constructed.

"The Indian Village," wrote[18] the Marquis de Chastelleux, who visited Schenectady soon after the Indian encampment was established, "is nothing but an assemblage of miserable huts in the wood, along the road[19] to Albany. [Colonel Glen] took me into that of a savage du Saut Saint Louis, who had long lived at Montreal, and spoke good French. These huts are like our barracks in time of war, or those run up in vineyards, or orchards, to watch the fruit

[15] Papers of the Continental Congress, III, 547.
[16] *Ibid.*
[17] Schuyler procured these and later replaced them from his own stock, as he had no money with which to pay for them. He however expressed the hope "of being repaid at a future day, when the public treasury [was] in better condition."
[18] The Marquis de Chastelleux, Travels in North America, I, 401.
[19] Hon. E. Winslow Paige, than whom few are better versed in the early history and traditions of Schenectady, has told the writer that he has always supposed that the Oneidas lived on what used to be called "Injin" or "Engine" Hill, now Mount Pleasant, along the west edge of Cotton Factory Hollow, and that it was always a subject for discussion as to whether the name of the hill was "Injin" from the fact that the Oneidas lived there or "Engine" from the stationary engine of the Mohawk & Hudson Railroad. It is not unlikely that the Indians lived on both sides of the Hollow.

when it is ripe. All the timber consists in two uprights and one cross pole; it is covered with a matted roof, but this is well lined within by a quantity of bark. The inner space is rather below the level of the ground, and the entrance by a little sidedoor; in the middle of the hut is the fire-place, from which the smoke ascends by an opening in the roof. On each side of the fire, are raised two branches, which run the length of the hut, and serve to sleep on; these are covered with skins and bark. Beside the savage who spoke French, in this hut, there was a squah, the name given to the Indian women, who had taken him as her second, and was bringing up a child by her first husband; two old men composed the remainder of the family, which had a melancholy and poor appearance. The squah was hideous, as they all are, and her husband almost stupid, so that the charms of this society did not make me forget that the day was advancing, and that it was time to set out.''

"All that I could learn from the Colonel, or from the savages," adds the Marquis, "was that the State gives them rations of meat, and sometimes of flour; that they possess also some land, where they sow Indian corn, and go a hunting for skins, which they exchange for rum. They are sometimes employed in war, and are commended for their bravery and fidelity. Though in subjection to the Americans, they have their chiefs, to whom application is made for justice, when an Indian has committed any crime. Mr. Glen told me, that they submitted to the punishments inflicted on them; but had no idea that it was right to punish them with death, even for homicide.''

CHAPTER XIX

THE RAIDS OF 1781

With the coming of spring (1781) discouragement and apprehension grew. The continuance of the frontier posts, which had with difficulty been maintained throughout the winter because of the scarcity of provisions, was by now dependent upon the immediate furnishing of supplies which were practically unobtainable.¹ The Line troops were "in a manner naked," desertions were frequent, public credit was almost at an end, Tories were everywhere increasing in numbers and from Albany came word² that the militia were destitute of both arms and ammunition.

In the expectation that Schenectady, which had by now in a measure become a frontier town, would be an early object of attack on the part of the enemy, the magistrates and field officers on February 27 drew up a memorandum³ recommending that Gov-

---

¹ "The Troops at Schenectady, Saratoga and this Post are with the utmost difficulty supplied from Day to Day with Flour from the Wheat drawn from the Inhabitants by assessments, a mode which it is unnecessary to mention is so disagreeable to the country in general that we fear we shall not be able to draw in the small quantities now due without the interposition of the Military, but even this supply if we were now possessed of the whole would be greatly inadequate." Isaac Stoutenbergh to General Clinton. Albany, January 15, 1781. Washington Papers, Library of Congress.

² Public Papers of George Clinton, VI, 765.

³ *Ibid.*, p. 715.

ernor Clinton be acquainted with their opinion that it was necessary to reinforce the picket defenses with seven[4] blockhouses and further that they felt it incumbent upon them to apply to him for a small number of cannon, an artillery officer[5] with a sufficient number of men to work the cannon, a quantity of ammunition and an engineer to superintend the erecting of the blockhouses. The memorandum further suggested that Governor Clinton give his opinion as to how the blockhouses should be manned, whether or not the field officers and justices were invested with proper authority to appropriate private property to carry on the work of fortification and in what manner some funds could be raised to pay for ranging scouts, which it was felt would be of the greatest importance in the matter of the town's safety.

In order to satisfy himself as to the best means of reaching the desired end, Governor Clinton visited Schenectady, and on March 24 ordered[6] that work on the alterations and additions suggested by him during his visit should be proceeded with without delay, counseling that the advice of Major Nicholas Fish,[7]

[4] "One Battery at Mr. DeGraff's;
One Block House at V Eps;
One Do at Doctor Specker's;
One on Vrooman's Land;
One Do at Mr. Ab. Groet's;
One Do in Alb'y Street at the house of Isaac Merselus;
One at the back of David Frank's;
One at or near the Continental Stables.''
Public Papers of George Clinton, VI, 715.

[5] It was at this time that an artillery company of fifteen men under Captain John Crousehorn was raised in Schenectady.

[6] Public Papers of George Clinton, VI, 715.

[7] He was in command of the soldiers of the 2d New York Line stationed here.

then stationed here, should be sought in case any question should arise as to what was desired, adding that inasmuch as the prospects of obtaining cannon were not at all promising, although there were some small pieces and swivels scattered in different parts of the country near the river which it might be possible to transport to Schenectady and having made carriages eventually obtain some service from them, it were better that the "works be calculated as much as [might] be for Defence by Musquettry."[8]

Although small parties of the enemy had been reported in the Valley from time to time since early in the year, it was not until the latter part of April, when a band of eighty attacked Cherry Valley, that a raid of any importance occurred.[9]

On May 15 word[10] that an Indian hunting party to the north of Saratoga had been fired upon caused General Schuyler, to whom the incident had been reported, to recommend to General Clinton that scouts be dispatched from Schenectady without delay. A few days later an anonymous letter[11] bore the information that a party of from four to five hundred Loyalists and Indians had gone to the southwest of Albany to begin burning, that there were fifteen hundred more then at Ticonderoga for the same purpose and that Albany and Schenectady were to be their main objective points.

[8] Harmon Peters states (Pension Office Records, S 11224) that in March, 1781, he entered service as a volunteer in a company of forty-six men commanded by Walter Swits, raised to keep guard at Fort Volunteer and Fort Squash at Schenectady. The company was divided twenty-three men to each fort.
[9] Public Papers of George Clinton, VI, 811.
[10] *Ibid.*, p. 880.
[11] Washington Papers, Library of Congress.

That treason was at work and the enemy correctly informed regarding the true situation of the country was plainly evident from a British Secret Service document[12] intercepted on May 27, which among other items contained advice as to sending a force against Albany, first preparing the way by distributing handbills hinting at pardon and protection for all who might assist the British. Schenectady was described in the document as "strongly picketed all round, [having] six pieces of Ordinance, 6 pounders, [with] Block Houses preparing." "It is to be defended by the Inhabitants," continued the report, "who except about a Dozen, are for Government. There are a few of Courtlandt's Regiment here. A large Quantity of Grain stored . . . for the Use of the Troops [and] large Boats building[13] to convey heavy Metal and Shot to Fort Stanwix."

[12] *Ibid.*
[13] The batteaux were being built under the greatest difficulties because of the trouble met with in procuring boards. Henry Glen reported the matter to headquarters on July 17 as follows: "Yours of the 14th Inst. I have received and ever since have used every exertion that lay in my power to prevail on the Proprietors of the Boards to let the Public have them. They say that it is impossible, unless they receive hard money for them, or we may as well cut their Wife's and Children's throats, for it is their only support for the Necessarys of Life. As to sending soldiers or Persons to impress them, they seem to be determined not to suffer their Property to be taken from them any longer at the risque of their Lives, as they have not been paid for their Boards etc. furnished the Public for these two years past, and no prospect of their being paid yet, this is their Language and what to do in the matter I do not know. I have this Spring when Congress and the Head of the Department's credit failed, pledged my own Credit to build 16 new Boats for which I have made myself payable, and with the Expectation of receiving the Money in a few days, which I had the promise of and am daily ask'd for the Cash, and still no Money, all this I do not mind; no man longs more to make an end of the War than I do by carrying it on with Vigour, I am and always was

The anticipated attacks fortunately did not mature and soon the settlers had occasion to again take heart, for in June Colonel Marinus Willett,[14] persuaded by Governor Clinton to leave the main army in order to take command of such troops as were already in the service or to be raised for the defense of the frontiers, arrived at Fort Rensselaer to enter upon the difficult task for which he had been summoned.

The services of this efficient officer at Torlock,[15] his untiring efforts in the pursuit of the raiders whenever they appeared, his wisdom and skill in the disposition of the meager forces under his command soon justified the confidence that had been placed in him, and during the summer[16] the lower Mohawk Valley was practically free from incursion, while the

willing to pledge my Life and little Property for the support of the War but am sorry to find the Virtue and exertions of the People are lost throughout the Whole Country. The Service is neglected by those at the Helm for want of money. Why is not part of the Continent pledged to some Power to carry on the War with Vigour and borrow a sufficient Sum.'' Letter Books of Colonel Hugh Hughes. New York Historical Society.

[14] ''I am glad we have a Hero left in the room of a Montgomery that he may live and see the Pride of Britain fall, and a Glorious Peace Established for Centuries to come. It is a Brave WILLETT, I mean.'' Letter of Henry Glen, July 17, 1781. Letter Books of Colonel Hugh Hughes. New York Historical Society.

[15] Now the town of Sharon, Schoharie County. The Levies wounded in the battle at that place were sent to Schenectady for treatment.

[16] At this time details of the Schenectady militia were on garrison duty at some of the forts to the westward. Details at Fort Hunter, Pension Office Records, James Barhydt S 12948. Details at Fort Plank, Pension Office Records, Gerrit Van Eps W 2200; Daniel Kettle W 21528; John B. Veeder R 10927. Details at Schoharie, Pension Office Records, Reuben Wheaton. A company was also on duty at Claas Viele's Rifts about four miles above Schenectady where a log house served as a fort. Pension Office Records, Philip Viele R 10847; Frederick Vedder S 21547.

activity of the enemy on the frontiers was given over to raids by small detachments attended with consequences of little importance.

In September Albany was again thrown into a panic by a report[17] that the enemy were determined to burn the city. The Tories in the vicinity were again active, and in fear many people packed their valuables in order to have them conveyed to a place of greater safety.[18] It was, however, late in October before the enemy in force made their appearance in the Valley. Major Ross with a following of some four hundred and fifty Indians, Regulars and Tories, which number was augmented as he proceeded, advancing by way of Cherry Valley to the Mohawk River, on October 24 fell upon Warren's Bush.[19] On news of the attack Schenectady was at once ordered[20] reinforced, but these orders were later countermanded as word was brought that the enemy after burning Warren's Bush had retired.

Although the scene of the attack was about twenty miles to the east of Fort Rensselaer where Colonel Willett had established his headquarters, so unexpected was the attack that the enemy had ample opportunity to accomplish their purpose before Colonel Willett was able to collect forces to repel them.

Immediately upon receipt of the news of the raid

[17] On receipt of the news a company under Captain Thomas Brower Banker marched as far north as Galway but later returned to Ballston, where they remained quartered for a fortnight or so. Pension Office Records, Wessel Cornu W 1029.

[18] Public Papers of George Clinton, VII, 304.

[19] *Ibid.*, p. 443.

[20] *Ibid.*, p. 448.

Colonel Willett dispatched messengers down the Valley asking the militia to join him, while he himself at once set out in pursuit of the enemy with what forces he could collect.

Major Ross had retired to Johnstown and here on the next day (October 25) Colonel Willett forced an engagement, causing the enemy to retreat. On the evening of the twenty-eighth, having been reinforced by a band of Oneidas and the militia, which included a detachment[21] from Schenectady under Captain Jellis Fonda, Colonel Willett started in pursuit of the raiders, subsequently attacking a detail of them on the West Canada Creek, killing several, among whom was Walter Butler, and leaving the rest "to the compassion of a starving wilderness."[22] The news of the death of Butler was received in Schenectady with great rejoicing. The Whigs illuminated their houses and the Tories under threat of being mobbed were forced to do likewise.[23]

With the expedition under Major Ross closed for the year the active operations of the enemy on the frontier, and ten days before the engagement on the West Canada Creek, Cornwallis surrendered at Yorktown.

[21] This detachment was with others complimented on their behavior in General Orders. Public Papers of George Clinton, VII, 483. Other members of the militia appear to have marched to Johnstown on the alarm, but evidently a small detachment only as volunteers went as far as the West Canada Creek, the remainder being assigned to garrison duty in the neighboring forts.

[22] Colonel Willett to Governor Clinton. Public Papers of George Clinton, VII, 474.

[23] Jane Ferguson's Revolutionary Recollections. *The American Monthly Magazine,* April, 1902. Jane Ferguson was one of the survivors of the Cherry Valley massacre who sought refuge in Schenectady. She remained here until after peace was declared.

CHAPTER XX

AFTER YORKTOWN

While with the culmination of the campaign ending in the American victory at Yorktown active hostilities in the country at large were brought to an end, minor raids were to keep the frontiers in alarm for nearly a year and a half, necessitating constant watchfulness and preparedness[1] on the part of the authorities.

In June, 1782, reports[2] brought to General Washington indicated that Albany and Schenectady were to be the chief objects of another attack on the part of the enemy. While these reports were probably without foundation there may have been some connection between them and the visit which General Washington paid to Albany during the latter part of the month.

It was during this visit that Washington, on the

[1] The Act of the New York Legislature of November 17, 1781, and the Act of March 23, 1782, brought into being during the spring of 1782 the class of militia known as "Militia-Land Bounty Rights." Under this arrangement for raising fifteen hundred men for the defense of the frontiers and to fill the vacancies in the Line, the militia companies were divided into "classes" averaging fifteen men in number and each "class" was obliged to furnish one man fully equipped for service, for which it received a compensation of two hundred acres of land. The granting of lands as a bounty was necessitated because of the very great scarcity of specie.

[2] Washington Papers, Library of Congress.

invitation of the townspeople, took occasion to pay his second[3] visit to Schenectady, riding over in a carriage with General Schuyler on the thirtieth. On their arrival these two distinguished guests were received with "no little formality by the civil and military authorities and escorted some distance by a numerous procession in which [Washington] walked with his hat under his arm."[4] At the public dinner given later at the tavern of Robert Clench were assembled "a respectable number of gentlemen," and to Colonel Frederick Visscher, who was then living in Schenectady, Washington assigned the seat on his right.[5]

At some time during the day an address was publicly delivered and before Washington set out on his return to Albany he took occasion to write the following reply:[6]

To the Magistrates and Military Officers of the town of Schenectada:

Gentlemen—I request you to accept my warmest thanks for your affectionate address.

In a cause so just and righteous as ours, we have every reason to hope the Divine Providence will still continue to crown our arms with success, and finally compel our enemies

---

[3] His first visit was a hurried one soon after the commencement of the war in order to make arrangements for frontier defense. He dined and lodged at the residence of John and Henry Glen and also took tea at the residence of John Sanders. Washington again visited Schenectady in 1786 while making a tour through the country. On this occasion he was quartered at the inn of Robert Clench. Hon. John Sanders, Early History of Schenectady, p. 274.

[4] Jeptha R. Simms, The Frontiersmen of New York, II, 624.

[5] *Ibid.*

[6] *Ibid.*

to grant us that peace upon equitable terms, which we so ardently desire.

May you, and the good people of this town, in the meantime, be protected from every insidious and open foe, and may the complicated blessings of peace soon reward your arduous struggles for the establishment of the freedom and independence of our common country.

Go. WASHINGTON.

The news of the declaration of peace in 1783 was received in Schenectady amid great rejoicing and followed by a befitting celebration; a large bonfire of pine knots was built on the hill overlooking the town and hung in the midst of the flames was an effigy of Benedict Arnold.[7]

With the return of peace to the frontiers the settlers began to return to the desolation that everywhere prevailed to rebuild their homesteads and again take up their daily tasks.

For the Indians who had fought on the side of the King, deprived now of British support and not even mentioned in the treaty of peace, nothing remained but to abandon themselves to the mercy of the victors.[8]

In Schenectady the fortifications were permitted to go into decay or removed and at this time also, for the war had brought the townspeople into contact with the men and customs of the other colonies, there

---

[7] Jane Ferguson's Revolutionary Recollections. *The American Monthly Magazine*, April, 1902.

[8] Due to the influence of Washington, who advocated a liberal policy toward the Iroquois, they were not expelled from the State, where by the laws of war all their lands had been forfeited. To the Oneidas and Tuscaroras in 1785 were granted certain lands in the western part of New York, which were subsequently in 1788 purchased from them by the State.

began to disappear many of those primitive usages peculiar to the Dutch inhabitants of the town.

In the English Church (St. George's), while many of the indignities suffered by her sister churches had been escaped, desolation now prevailed. The building, dilapidated, with windows broken out, had even become the resort of the swine that roamed at will through the streets of the town.[9] Of those who had attended service before the war but a few remained,[10] upon whom, as courage revived, devolved the burden of restoring the church building and renewing parochial activities.

Soon came many from New England to the rich lands of western New York, journeying with their families in ox-cart and covered wagon or transferring to boats at Schenectady. To meet the ever increasing demands of the travelers and to facilitate the transportation of supplies there was incorporated in 1792 and completed in 1797, under the direction of General Philip Schuyler, the enterprise known as the Inland Lock Navigation Company, whereby boats of a deeper draught than the small batteaux might proceed without unloading from Schenectady to Oswego. For a quarter of a century the Mohawk was to remain a scene of commercial activity, or until 1825, when

---

[9] Jonathan Pearson, History of the Schenectady Patent, p. 396.

[10] Mr. John Doty reported in 1780 from Montreal where he had taken refuge that "his poor little flock [had] been almost dispersed and the few remaining were in the most deplorable circumstances," adding that he had "been informed by a young man, lately from Schenectady, that the congregation consisted of only twenty-seven white adults, twenty children and some blacks." The fate of the Presbyterian congregation was in all probability not unlike that of St. George's. Jonathan Pearson, History of the Schenectady Patent, p. 401.

with the completion of the Erie Canal the traffic of the Valley was transferred to that channel.

In 1795 the Academy built by the Dutch Reformed Church through the influence of Doctor Romeyn became Union College, the consummation of a movement started four years before the war cry of the Indian and crack of the rifle had ceased to resound throughout the Valley.

With these enterprises looking toward the economic, commercial and intellectual welfare of the community as well as with the political affairs of the State, early became associated many men of Schenectady, who, with distinction, had served their country throughout her struggle for independence and whose names appear quite as prominently in the history of the years following the Revolution, until each in his turn was claimed by death, as they appear in the short period covered by the war itself.

INDIVIDUAL RECORDS OF SERVICE

INDIVIDUAL RECORDS OF SERVICE

ADAMS, WILLIAM: Settled in Schenectady about 1757. His name appears as having served as a physician and on the rolls of the 2d Albany County Militia, Land Bounty Rights.

ALEXANDER, ALEXANDER: Born February 19, 1765; died September 1, 1809. His name appears on the rolls of the 2d Albany County Militia. At the commencement of the war he was but ten years of age and it is therefore probable that he saw very little active service.

ALEXANDER, ROBERT: On March 1, 1776, he signed an agreement with Philip Schuyler for service at Ticonderoga and Lake George. He is mentioned in the state treasurer's pay book as having served as a lieutenant in the 2d Albany County Militia.

ALEXANDER, SANDY: His name appears on the rolls of the 2d Albany County Militia.

AMENT, ELDERT: Died shortly before March, 1798. A merchant in 1790, living on the south corner of Union and Ferry Streets. His name appears on the rolls of the 2d Albany County Militia. On November 21, 1776, there was an Eldert Ament serving as ensign in the 5th Company, 3d New York Line. He resigned on December 23, 1778.

BANKER, THOMAS BROWER: Born in 1729; died May 25, 1807. A blacksmith by trade. He built and lived in a house on State Street at the present location of No. 224. He and his wife, Anna Mebie, are buried side by side near the State Street entrance of Vale Cemetery, their bodies having been removed from the old Dutch Reformed Church burying ground on Green Street. On October 20, 1775,

Banker was commissioned first lieutenant in the 4th Company, 2d Albany County Militia. On November 22 he received a commission as captain from the Provincial Congress and on February 10, 1776, was assigned to one of the newly organized Schenectady companies of militia. In May, 1777, he was on duty at Fort Edward. He remained there for some time, after which his company was ordered to Snookkill. He served through the campaign against Burgoyne. On June 20, 1778, he was reappointed captain, and during this year served at the Schoharie Forts and in command of a detachment under General Clinton erecting fortifications at Sacandaga. In the spring of 1779, he commanded a detachment to Beaverdam and captured seven Tories. In the summer he was in command of a detail at Schoharie and in August went with his company to Herkimer. In the fall he served at Fort Plank and Stone Arabia. In August, 1780, he went with the troops to Fort Plain after the destruction of Canajoharie and in the fall to Ballston after the raid. In September, 1781, he commanded a detachment which marched some thirty miles to the north of Schenectady "to drive back the enemy who were said to be advancing towards this place," and in October, he commanded a detachment in pursuit of Major Ross and Butler. Simms mentions an amusing incident which occurred during General Washington's visit to Schenectady in June, 1782. Washington was walking on the street in company with Captain Banker when an old negro passing removed his hat and bowed. Washington immediately returned the compliment much to the surprise of Banker, who suggested that it was not the custom of the country to notice slaves. "I cannot be less civil than a poor negro," Washington replied as they walked on.

BARCLAY, JAMES: His name appears on the rolls of the 2d Albany County Militia, Land Bounty Rights.

BARHYDT, CORNELIUS: He served as a captain of batteaumen, and in the 2d Albany County Militia.

BARHYDT, JACOB: Baptized February 9, 1753. His name appears on the rolls of the 2d Albany County Militia.

BARHYDT, JAMES: Born in Schenectady, March 28, 1762, and lived here until the year 1784. In the spring of 1778 he enrolled as a private under Captain Jesse Van Slyck, 2d Albany County Militia. He performed considerable scout and patrol duty and about June 20, 1779, as a volunteer private was assigned to a company of Rangers from Cherry Valley under Captain Robert McKean. With this company he assisted in the transportation of the stores and baggage of General Clinton's brigade; performing both guard and fatigue duty. In October, 1780, as a private under Captain Van Slyck he marched to Schoharie in pursuit of Sir John Johnson, Brant and Butler, and in October, 1781, he went to Warren's Bush in pursuit of Major Ross and was with the troops at the West Canada Creek when Butler lost his life. A pensioner.

BARHYDT, JERONE: Born in the Schenectady Township, October 28, 1764; died July 10, 1849. When called into the service he lived at the Norman's Kill. In 1779 he volunteered under Major Swits, 2d Albany County Militia, for the pursuit of Tories at the Heldebergh. In the fall of 1780 he enrolled under Captain Thomas Brower Banker and went with the troops under General Van Rensselaer in pursuit of Sir John Johnson. In the spring of 1781 he enlisted in the state troops. He served at the Middle Fort, Schoharie, and at the Upper Fort, where he took part in a battle with a party of Mohawk Indians under a Tory named Christler. After four months' service he again enlisted under Captain Banker and served to the end of the war. In the fall of 1781 he took part in the battle of Johnstown and went with the troops in pursuit of Walter Butler as far as the West Canada Creek. He performed considerable garrison duty at Schenectady and elsewhere. He received a pension which was later suspended and his widow's claim rejected.

BARHYDT, JOHN: Baptized January 7, 1739. His name appears on the rolls of the 2d Albany County Militia.

BARHYDT, LEWIS: Born in 1755; died March 7, 1829. His name appears on the rolls of the 2d Albany County Militia. In August, 1780, he was in command of the guard at Schenectady.

BARHYDT, NICHOLAS: Born November 12, 1744; died April 15, 1827. On February 10, 1776, he was elected second lieutenant in Captain Abraham Oothout's company, 2d Albany County Militia. He was spoken of as "an active, zealous and valuable officer, always ready when occasion offered to serve his country." In the fall of 1776, he took part in an expedition to Fort Edward, Fort Ann and Skenesborough, and in the summer of 1777, was with the Northern Army at Van Schaick's Island, Bemis Heights and Saratoga. On June 20, 1778, he was regularly commissioned second lieutenant, his commission being signed by Nathaniel Woodhull, president of the Provincial Congress. During the summer of 1778 he was on duty at the Schoharie Forts and in July at Fort Plain. In the spring of 1779 he again served at Fort Plain and in the fall at Stone Arabia. In the spring of 1780 he was ordered to Johnstown and there joined the forces under Colonel Gansevoort. In the fall of this same year he went on an expedition to Fort Hunter. He often commanded detachments on tours for the apprehension of Tories or on alarms when towards the end of the war the militia was frequently called out on short excursions. His name appears on the rolls of the 2d Albany County Militia, Land Bounty Rights. His widow received a pension which was, after her death, transferred to her four children.

BARHYDT, TEUNIS: His name appears on the rolls of the 2d Albany County Militia. In 1778 he was enrolled under Captain Jesse Van Slyck.

BARTLEY, DANIEL: His name appears on the rolls of the 2d Albany County Militia.

BARTLEY, MICHAEL: His name appears on the rolls of the 2d Albany County Militia.

BASTIAN, JOHN: His name appears on the rolls of the 2d Albany County Militia. He served as a private under Captain John Mynderse and as a sergeant under Captain Thomas Wasson. In 1781 he was a member of Captain John Crousehorn's company of artillery.

BATES, DAVID: On February 14, 1776, while serving as a lieutenant in the Line under Captain Gerrit S. Veeder in Colonel Cornelius D. Wynkoop's regiment, he was recommended for the office of second lieutenant in the company of Rangers to be formed under Captain John A. Bradt. He accepted this office, but on April 12 asked permission of the Committee to resign, stating that the men were mutinous and dissatisfied at Gerrit S. Veeder being appointed their captain instead of waiting for the return of Bradt. The next day Bates delivered his commission to the Committee but he was later induced to ask for its return and his request was granted with the admonition that he watch his future behavior.

BEARUP, ANDREW: He was enrolled under Captain John Mynderse, 2d Albany County Militia. In January, 1776, he took part in the expedition to Johnstown, and in the fall of 1777 in the campaign against Burgoyne. In the fall of 1779 he was on duty at Stone Arabia. He served as a batteau and fatigue man under both William Peters and Joseph Peek, and in the fall of 1780 was stationed at Saratoga. During the year 1781 or 1782 he is said to have served in the Levies under Colonel Willett. His widow received a pension.

BEARUP, JOHN: Probably from Princetown. His name appears on the rolls of the 2d Albany County Militia. In the fall of 1779 he served under Captain Abraham Oothout in an expedition to Stone Arabia, acting as a substitute for Christopher Ward. In July 1782, he went on scout duty to Harpersfield. His widow's claim for pension was rejected.

BEARUP, THOMAS: He is buried on the old Blessing farm in Princetown about three hundred feet east of the house. His name appears on the rolls of the 2d Albany County Militia.

BECKER, GERRIT: His name appears on the rolls of the 2d Albany County Militia.

BEEKMAN, JACOB: Baptized August 9, 1761; died November 4, 1817. He lived on Washington Avenue. Towards the end of the war he was appointed captain of militia to succeed Captain John Van Patten, resigned.

BERKIN, WILLIAM: Born in "Old England." On September 1, 1781, he was reported a deserter from the Levies under Colonel Willett and was described as being five feet three inches in height, brown complexion, black hair and eyes and fifty-five years of age.

BESTEDO, CLARA: On January 18, 1776, she informed the Committee of Safety that she had some intelligence to communicate relative to the proceedings at Johnstown. She was examined under oath and her information forwarded to General Schuyler, who was then on his way there.

BETH, JELLIS: Baptized August 11, 1751. His name appears on the rolls of the 2d Albany County Militia.

BETH, ROBERT: Baptized November 28, 1742. In 1777 he was serving as an ensign in Captain Abraham Oothout's company, 2d Albany County Militia, and in the fall of 1780 was on duty at Caughnawaga.

INDIVIDUAL RECORDS OF SERVICE 135

BETH, THOMAS: Baptized January 8, 1749. His name appears on the rolls of the 2d Albany County Militia and the 2d Albany County Militia, Land Bounty Rights.

BOICE (BUYS), ABRAHAM: His name appears on the rolls of the 2d Albany County Militia.

BOICE (BUYS), JAMES: His name appears on the rolls of the 2d Albany County Militia.

BOND, RICHARD: A complaint lodged against him with the Committee of Safety was dismissed on May 30, 1777, for lack of proof. His name appears on the rolls of the 2d Albany County Militia.

BONNY, ICHABOD: His name appears on the rolls of the 2d Albany County Militia, Land Bounty Rights.

BONNY, JOHN: Born in 1754; died September 3, 1832. He served in the Levies under Colonel Marinus Willett. A pensioner under the Act of June 7, 1832.

BOVIE, ABRAHAM: His name appears on the rolls of the 2d Albany County Militia.

BOVIE, ISAAC: His name appears on the rolls of the 2d Albany County Militia.

BOVIE, ISRAEL: His name appears on the rolls of the 2d Albany County Militia.

BOVIE, JACOB: Born in 1756. In March, 1776, while residing in Glenville he was pressed into the service as a teamster and required to make a trip to Montreal carrying baggage and sick soldiers. During the years 1776 and 1777 he served in Captain Abraham Van Eps's company, 2d Albany County Militia, and performed garrison duties on several occasions. In September, 1777, he marched with his company to Bemis Heights and was one of the picket guard during the battle. He served later at Ballston, Caughnawaga, Stone Arabia and the Schoharie Forts, generally on draft and under various officers.

BOVIE, NICHOLAS P.: On August 25, 1776, he enlisted in Captain John A. Bradt's company of State Rangers and also served during this year under Captain Gerrit S. Veeder. He was a familiar figure about Schenectady where he came to live several years after the Revolution. He was nicknamed "Sculpennick" or "Scalped Nick," for in July, 1777, he was shot, tomahawked and scalped by the Indians at Fort Stanwix. He was taken to the fort as dead by some of the soldiers. After recovering sufficiently to perform invalid duty, he again joined the army. His widow received a pension.

BOVIE, NICHOLAS R.: Baptized August 26, 1744. In February, 1777, he enlisted at Schenectady in a company of batteaumen under Captain Reuben Symonds. He served on the North River and Saratoga Lake assisting in transporting artillery both before and at the surrender of Burgoyne. After this service he was ordered to Fort Stanwix with clothing and provisions. In March, 1778, he again enlisted at Schenectady in a company of batteaumen under Captain Cornelius Barhydt, and was discharged December 25, 1778. He subsequently served in the regiments under Colonels Du Bois and Visscher, and after the repulse of Sir John Johnson in the fall of 1780 he was one of the guards to pilot to Schenectady a boat containing a number of the wounded. A pensioner.

BOWMAN, FREDERICK: His name appears on the rolls of the 2d Albany County Militia.

BRADFORD, JAMES: Probably from Glenville. His name appears on the rolls of the 2d Albany County Militia.

BRADT, ANDRIES: On September 26, 1776, he enlisted in Captain John A. Bradt's company of State Rangers.

BRADT, ANTHONY D.: His name appears on the rolls of the 2d Albany County Militia.

BRADT, ARENT A.: Baptized January 9, 1762; died previous to 1809. His name appears on the rolls of the 2d Albany County Militia.

BRADT, ARENT S.: Born in 1743; died February 3, 1814. Buried in Vale Cemetery. His name appears on the rolls of the 2d Albany County Militia.

BRADT, CHARLES: His name appears on the rolls of the 2d Albany County Militia.

BRADT, CORNELIUS: Born April 21, 1762; died August 16, 1814. Buried in Vale Cemetery. He was enrolled in the company of Captain Jesse Van Slyck, 2d Albany County Militia. In the summer of 1777 he served in the campaign against Burgoyne and in the spring of 1778 in an expedition to Beaverdam under Captain Thomas Brower Banker. During the summer of this same year he was on duty at the Lower Fort Schoharie and in the fall one of the garrison at Fort Plain. In October, 1781, he marched under Captain John Van Patten in pursuit of Major Ross and Butler. His widow received a pension.

BRADT, ELIAS: Baptized September 14, 1756. His name appears on the rolls of the 2d Albany County Militia.

BRADT, EPHRAIM: He was enrolled in the company of Captain Jellis J. Fonda, 2d Albany County Militia. During the summer of 1777 he served two months in the campaign against Burgoyne and in 1778 performed garrison duty at the Schoharie Forts, Fort Plain and Fort Paris. In May or June, 1779, he was with Captain Thomas Brower Banker under General Clinton, erecting fortifications at Sacandaga. From August to October, 1781, he was on guard duty at Claas Viele's Fort under Sergeant William Teller.

BRADT, FREDERICK: Baptized November 20, 1748. His name appears on the rolls of the 2d Albany County Militia, Land Bounty Rights.

BRADT, GERRIT: His name appears on the rolls of the 2d Albany County Militia.

BRADT, JACOBUS: Born in 1730; died March 26, 1801. His name appears on the rolls of the 2d Albany County Militia.

BRADT, JACOBUS S.: Baptized June 9, 1745. His name appears on the rolls of the 2d Albany County Militia.

BRADT, JOHN A.: Baptized March 22, 1741. A silversmith. On July 10, 1775, he was recommended to the Provincial Congress for the office of captain in the recruiting service. On February 13, 1776, while absent on a trading expedition to Canada he was favorably considered by the Committee of Safety for the captaincy of a troop to be raised in the district. When approached by two members of the Board regarding the possibility of his accepting the office his wife stated that "she did not know when her husband would be home and that for her part she did not approve of his going into the army, though he always did as he pleased. She was of the opinion that he would not accept the commission [and] that he was ill used last year in that respect." This report evidently did not discourage the Board, for on the same day (February 14) he was assigned the captaincy in case the organization of the company could wait until his return. On April 10 Bradt had not yet returned and it was therefore decided to appoint Gerrit S. Veeder in his place. On May 7 he was elected a member of the third Committee of Safety, and on August 10 commissioned by the Provincial Congress captain of a company of State Rangers for service in apprehending Tories in Albany County. On October 26 he commanded a detachment for service at Coxsackie and on October 30 marched with his company to Tryon County under orders to report to Colonel Goose Van Schaick. From December 16, 1776, to January 15, 1777, he was stationed with his company at Fort Constitution and in January he petitioned Congress as the men complained that such duty was contrary to their terms of enlistment. On March 27 the company was ordered discharged. On April 19, he was granted a tavern license by the Committee of Safety. On May 20 the election of a new Board was held at his home.

BRADT, JOHN S.: Born September 16, 1754; died October 19, 1804. His name appears on the rolls of the 2d Albany County Militia.

BRADT, MINDERT: Born in 1752; died June 7, 1806. A blacksmith. Buried in Vale Cemetery. His name appears on the rolls of the 2d Albany County Militia.

BRADT, SAMUEL: Born August 22, 1715; died August 3, 1799. He served in the 2d Albany County Militia previous to July 8, 1777, on which date he was relieved from further duty as being "disordered in mind and in a bad state of health."

BRADT, SAMUEL S.: Baptized April 10, 1737. His name appears on the rolls of the 2d Albany County Militia.

BRAGHAM, JOHN: Baptized October 16, 1743; died in 1820. He is buried on the Michael Brougham farm (now owned by Henry Raeger) in Princetown. The graveyard is about three hundred feet east of the house on the south bank of the creek. His name appears on the rolls of the 2d Albany County Militia.

BRAGHAM, JOSEPH: Baptized May 5, 1734. His name appears on the rolls of the 2d Albany County Militia.

BRAGHAM, SIMON: Baptized June 14, 1718; died before 1786. His name appears on the rolls of the 2d Albany County Militia.

BROACHIM, JOHN: A farmer. On July 23, 1780, he was sent under arrest to Albany as being connected with a plot to join the enemy or supplying them with provisions. On August 10 he was released on bail.

BROWER, HENDRIC: Born October 15, 1731; died December 11, 1801. His name appears on the rolls of the 2d Albany County Militia and the 2d Albany County Militia, Land Bounty Rights.

BROWER, RICHARD: His name appears on the rolls of the 2d Albany County Militia.

BROWN, ABRAHAM: His name appears on the rolls of the 2d Albany County Militia.

BROWN, JOHN: Enlisted from Schenectady under Captain John Graham, 1st New York Line.

BURNHAM, WILLIAM: Born in 1760; died January 9, 1822. He served as a private in the Connecticut Line. A pensioner under the Act of March 18, 1818.

BURNS, ARENT: His name appears on the rolls of the 2d Albany County Militia.

BURNS, DAVID: His name appears on the rolls of the 2d Albany County Militia.

CAHILL, JOHN: Born in 1745; died March 1, 1822. On November 17, 1776, he enlisted for the war and was assigned to the 8th Company, 1st New York Line. He deserted on October 10, 1780.

CAIN, BARENT: His name appears on the rolls of the 2d Albany County Militia.

CAIN, PETER WARREN: Born in Warren's Bush, March 2, 1750. During the Revolution and after he lived in Glenville. In the spring of 1775 he enlisted for one month under Captain John Van Patten, 2d Albany County Militia. He then enlisted under Captain Cornelius Van Dyck in the New York Line, and served for nine months. He marched to Ticonderoga, Crown Point and the Isle Aux Noix. He was with the detachment that reduced Chamblee and fought at the siege of St. John's. In January, 1776, he took part in the expedition to Johnstown, and on his return mounted guard at Teunis Swart's Fort. In the fall of 1777 he served twenty-five days with the Northern Army as orderly sergeant under Captain John Van Patten. Previous and subsequent to this service he volunteered in the company of batteaumen under Myndert Wemple and was employed in transporting supplies on the Hudson and Mohawk Rivers. He performed various garrison and fatigue duties and went on several tours for the apprehension of Tories. In 1780 he was stationed at the Highlands, in a fatigue company under Captain William James, and in October, 1781, was in the battle of Johnstown, marching with the detachment in pursuit of the enemy to the West Canada Creek. A pensioner under the Act of June 7, 1832.

CAMPBELL, ALEXANDER: A native of Scotland. He settled in Schenectady in 1762, later removed to Schoharie, but was again a resident of Schenectady on June 3, 1775, under orders never to return to Schoharie. In 1776 it being ascertained that he had warned Sir John Johnson of his danger, a mob burned his storehouse at Schoharie and later destroyed his store at Schenectady with goods and merchandise, "burning at the same time eight loads of hay and poisoning two milch cows." He was subsequently sent a prisoner to Connecticut, but on December 3 was permitted to return home on parole. In May, 1777, he was recommended to the field officers as "a dangerous person," and on May 3 was arrested to be taken to Albany but was released on his oath that he would take up arms in defense of the country in case of any invasion. On September 7, 1778, he refused to take the Oath of Allegiance, and requested permission of the Commissioners of Conspiracies to remove to Canada with his family. This request was granted and he was ordered to prepare himself to be removed on the shortest notice. He probably acted as a spy on various occasions, as his petition to the British Government for remuneration contains an item of £15 13s., cash paid to sundry expenses in obtaining information of the situation of the Continental Army for Generals Burgoyne and Fraser.

CAMPBELL, DANIEL: Born September 19, 1730; died August 16, 1802. He came to Schenectady some time in the year 1754. He commenced business as an Indian trader with a pack on his back and at the commencement of the war was reputed to have amassed a considerable fortune. He lived in the house now known as 101 State Street, which was erected for him in 1762. He was an intimate friend of Sir William Johnson and in 1771 was one of the judges of the Court of Common Pleas for Albany County. On August 5, 1775, he was granted a permit by the Committee of Safety to go to Canada on private business. On April 17, 1776, he was refused a recommendation from the Board for permission to obtain a pass from General Schuyler "to forward goods up the country." In May, 1777, he was recommended to the field officers as "a dangerous person." On May 22 he voluntarily took an oath that he would take up arms in defense of the country in case of any invasion. On July 30 he was ordered arrested and to appear before the State Committee for refusing to receive Continental currency in payment of a debt. On May 1, 1778, he was brought before the Commissioners of Conspiracies "for speaking words that in the opinion of the Board might have a dangerous tendency and prove detrimental to the liberties of America." He was released on bail and on June 14, was cited to appear before the Committee to render satisfaction touching his conduct conformable to the Act regarding persons of a neutral and equivocal character. On July 17 he refused to take the Oath of Allegiance and was ordered to hold himself in readiness to be removed within the enemy's lines. On July 29 he requested a temporary suspension of the proceedings and on August 1 declared his readiness to take the Oath, but was not permitted to do so as the Act did not permit of the Oath being administered to one who had already refused to take it. He was ordered to be ready for removal on the fourteenth. On May 19, 1779, the Oath was administered to him in accordance with the provisions of the amended Act. His name appears on the rolls of the 2d Albany County Militia.

CAMPBELL, KENNETH: Born in 1743. On January 23, 1777, he enlisted for the war and was assigned to Captain Henry Tiebout's company, 3d New York Line. He was later transferred to the company of Captain George Sytez. He was in Fort Stanwix when besieged, at the battles of White Plains and Monmouth and at the surrender of Cornwallis. A pensioner under the Act of March 18, 1818.

CANOOT, JOHN: On March 4, 1776, he was appointed an overseer of batteaumen by the Schenectady Committee of Safety for service at Lake George.

CARLEY, JOSEPH: Born in 1762; died April 23, 1842. On May 6, 1779, he was drafted for nine months' service and assigned to Captain John F. Hamtramck's company, 5th New York Line. He served in Sullivan's expedition against the Indians. At the expiration of the period for which he was drafted, in January, 1780, he enlisted for the war under Captain Henry Du Bois. He remained in this company until the winter of 1783, when he was transferred to Captain Hamtramck's company of light infantry connected with the same regiment. At the close of the war he was honorably discharged and given a badge of merit. A pensioner under the Act of March 18, 1818.

CARTWRIGHT, HENRY: His name appears on the rolls of the 2d Albany County Militia.

CARTWRIGHT, JOHN: His name appears on the rolls of the 2d Albany County Militia.

CASSADA (or CASSETY), JOHN: He was enrolled in the company of Captain Jellis J. Fonda, 2d Albany County Militia, entering service some time in 1776. He served two months in the campaign against Burgoyne. In 1778 he was on duty near German Flats with State troops or Levies, and in the same year served at the Schoharie Forts and at Fort Plain. In the fall of 1781 he marched with the troops in pursuit of Major Ross and Butler. His widow received a pension.

CATLET, THOMAS: His name appears on the rolls of the 2d Albany County Militia.

CELDER, ABRAHAM: His name appears on the rolls of the 2d Albany County Militia.

CERON, CHRISTOPHER: A joiner. On November 15, 1779, he went bail for Julius Bush.

CESSLER, THOMAS: His name appears on the rolls of the 2d Albany County Militia.

CHANNEL, JOHN: His name appears on the rolls of the 2d Albany County Militia.

CHANNEL, THOMAS: His name appears on the rolls of the 2d Albany County Militia.

CHARLES, HENDRICK: Baptized May 30, 1731. On March 1, 1776, he signed an agreement with Philip Schuyler for service at Lake George and Ticonderoga. His name appears on the rolls of the 2d Albany County Militia.

CHRISTIANNSE, AHASUERAS: Baptized February 26, 1749. His name appears on the rolls of the 2d Albany County Militia and the 2d Albany County Militia, Land Bounty Rights.

CHRISTIANNSE, ISAAC: Born in Schenectady, January 1, 1755, and lived here all his life. In the summer of 1775, he enlisted under Captain John Mynderse, 2d Albany County Militia, and served as a "minute man" until the spring of 1777 when Mynderse's company was disbanded and its members joined to the regular militia under Colonel Abra-

ham Wemple. In January, 1776, he took part in the
expedition to Johnstown, and during the summer was
employed at Ticonderoga and near-by places erecting
storehouses and aiding in the building of boats for the
army. During the summer and fall of 1777 he was stationed at Fort Miller, Fort Ann and Fort Edward. He
took part in the engagement at Snookkill and at Stillwater on September 19. In 1778 he performed garrison
duty at the Upper Fort, Schoharie, under Captain Fink,
and in 1779 was on duty at German Flats guarding
farmers while they were bringing in their crops. In the
fall of 1780 he marched to Ballston in pursuit of the
enemy. A pensioner under the act of June 7, 1832.

CILKER, WILLIAM: His name appears on the rolls of the
2d Albany County Militia.

CLARK, HENRY A.: His name appears on the rolls of the 2d
Albany County Militia.

CLARK, MATTHIS: His name appears on the rolls of the 2d
Albany County Militia.

CLARK, WILLIAM: On April 19, 1777, he was granted a
tavern license by the Committee of Safety, but later fell
under suspicion of having bartered liquor for clothes with
the soldiers. His name appears on the rolls of the 2d
Albany County Militia.

CLEMENT, ARENT: Baptized April 8, 1722. His name
appears on the rolls of the 2d Albany County Militia.

CLEMENT, ELDERT: His name appears on the rolls of the
2d Albany County Militia.

CLEMENT, JOHANNES: Baptized September 24, 1732. On
March 1, 1776, he signed an agreement with Philip Schuyler
for service at Lake George and Ticonderoga. His name
appears on the rolls of the 2d Albany County Militia.

CLEMENT, PETER: Baptized February 22, 1761. His name
appears on the rolls of the 2d Albany County Militia.

CLENCH, RALPH: Born in 1760; died January 19, 1828. A native of Schenectady, where he lived until the commencement of the war. He joined the British forces as a cadet in the 42d Regiment and for his conduct in the action which terminated in the surrender of General Burgoyne was commissioned and transferred to the 8th or King's Regiment. Shortly after, he was given a lieutenancy in Butler's Rangers and in this corps he served until its reduction in 1783.

CLENCH, ROBERT: Died during the latter part of 1781. He kept an inn on the south corner of State and Water Streets, which was spoken of as "a good house of entertainment." This house, which was one of those spared in 1690, was destroyed in the fire of 1819. On February 12, 1776, he was reported to the Committee of Safety for making some unbecoming expressions, which upon investigation were found not serious enough to warrant punishment. In May, 1777, he was recommended to the field officers as "a dangerous person." On May 22 he voluntarily took oath that he would take up arms in defense of the country in case of any invasion. On July 23, 1778, he was cited to appear before the Commissioners of Conspiracies to render satisfaction regarding his conduct conformable to the Act respecting persons of a neutral or equivocal character. On July 25 he requested time to consider taking the Oath of Allegiance and on August 1, the Oath was administered.

CLUTE, BARTHOLOMEW: Born in Schenectady, December 30, 1764. He lived here all his life. During the year 1778 and on various other occasions he performed garrison duty at Schenectady. In March or April, 1779, he enlisted in a company of artificers under Captain John Clute and served three months at Saratoga and other places in the vicinity. On this occasion he found a large twelve-inch brass mortar which had been buried by the

INDIVIDUAL RECORDS OF SERVICE 147

British at the Surrender of Burgoyne. For this he was allowed a compensation by General Schuyler. During the summer of the same year he volunteered with a detachment of militia and Oneida Indians under Captain J. B. Vrooman. They marched to Schoharie and assisted in capturing a party of runaway Tuscarora Indians. In December, 1780, he enrolled under Captain John Mynderse, 2d Albany County Militia, and served in his company to the end of the war. On many occasions he acted as a scout and Indian spy. He was a member of Captain John Crousehorn's company of artillery. In the fall of 1781 he joined the troops in pursuit of Major Ross and Butler under the immediate command of Captain Thomas Brower Banker, marching as far as Caughnawaga, where he mounted guard for some time and then returned to Schenectady. A pensioner under the Act of June 7, 1832.

CLUTE, DANIEL TOLL: Born November 29, 1754; died July 25, 1815. Buried in Vale Cemetery. He was enrolled under Captain Jesse Van Slyck, 2d Albany County Militia, and in 1781 was a member of Captain John Crousehorn's company of artillery. His name appears on the rolls of the 2d Albany County Militia, Land Bounty Rights.

CLUTE, FREDERICK: His name appears on the rolls of the 2d Albany County Militia.

CLUTE, ISAAC: Born March 15, 1756. During the fall of 1777, he served near Fort Stanwix in a company of batteaumen under Captain Jacobus Peek. In 1778, as a private under Captain John Mynderse, 2d Albany County Militia, he performed garrison duty at Stone Arabia and also served as a batteauman at various places along the Hudson River under Captain Jacobus Peek. In 1779 he served at Saratoga in a company of artificers under the immediate command of Lieutenant-Colonel Christopher Yates, and in 1780 he marched to Ballston when it was attacked. His name appears on the rolls of the 2d Albany County Militia, Land Bounty Rights.

CLUTE, JACOB: Born January 18, 1736. On April 1, 1777, he was elected overseer of highways at Schenectady. His name appears on the rolls of the 2d Albany County Militia and in 1778 he was enrolled under Captain Jesse Van Slyck.

CLUTE, JACOB P.: Born in Schenectady, March 4, 1759; died January 16, 1848. In 1775 he was enrolled under Captain Jesse Van Slyck, 2d Albany County Militia. He served the whole of the year 1776 on guard duty at Schenectady. In the summer of 1777 he went on draft to Fort Edward, where, and at other posts, he performed six weeks' service. He was in the engagement at Snookkill. In 1778 he performed nine months' service in Captain Christopher Miller's company of artificers employed in constructing boats at Coeymans. During the spring and fall of 1780 he served with the troops against Sir John Johnson, and in October, 1781, with the troops under Colonel Willett against Major Ross and Butler. He was in the battle of Johnstown and went with the detachment that pursued the enemy to the West Canada Creek. On the return to the main army after Butler was killed a squad of thirteen became detached and "would have been lost in the woods if Jacob P. Clute had not been with them and being a perfect woodsman directed them through to the Mohawk River."

CLUTE, JELLIS: His name appears on the rolls of the 2d Albany County Militia and in 1778, he was enrolled under Captain Jesse Van Slyck. His name also appears on the rolls of the 2d Albany County Militia, Land Bounty Rights.

CLUTE, JOHN: On August 12, 1777, he was serving as captain of a company of fatigue men and laborers. On December 9, 1777, he was elected constable at Schenectady and in 1779 was captain of a company in the Quartermaster's Department, having charge of the public blacksmiths serving at Saratoga.

CLUTE, JOHN BAPTIST: His name appears on the rolls of the 2d Albany County Militia. In 1778 he was enrolled under Captain Jesse Van Slyck. He also served under Captain Thomas Brower Banker. In August, 1782, he was on garrison duty at the Upper Fort, Schoharie, and in September of the same year on scout duty at Sacandaga. A pensioner under the Act of June 7, 1832.

CLUTE, JOHN CURTISS: His name appears on the rolls of the 2d Albany County Militia.

CLUTE, JOHN F.: Born in February, 1748; died July 22, 1805. His name appears on the rolls of the 2d Albany County Militia.

CLUTE, PETER: Born April 28, 1765; died July 7, 1835. His name appears on the rolls of the 2d Albany County Militia.

COMBES, JOHN: Baptized September 8, 1751. He served as a private and as a sergeant under Captain John Mynderse, 2d Albany County Militia.

CONAN, DANIEL: On March 4, 1776, he refused to go to Lake George as overseer of carpenters and batteaumen under General Schuyler.

CONDE, ADAM: Born September 25, 1748; died in Glenville, September 22, 1824. In 1770 he lived on the west corner of Church and Front Streets. He was probably enrolled under Captain Jesse Van Slyck. In 1776 he served at Saratoga in a company of fatigue men under Captain Jacob Vrooman. During the summer and fall of 1777 he was with Colonel Wemple's regiment on duty at Snookkill, Bemis Heights and other posts occupied by the American army. Late in the summer of 1778 he performed six weeks' garrison duty at the Lower Fort, Schoharie, and later six weeks' duty at Fort Plain. In the fall of 1779 he performed three months' garrison duty at Stone Arabia, and in October, 1781, he was on duty at Fort Hunter and other posts after Warren's Bush was destroyed.

CONNER, LANCASTER: On July 11, 1776, he was elected a member of the Committee of Safety and on April 1, 1777, was elected fire master at Schenectady. On June 15, 1779, he was again chosen a member of the Committee of Safety. His name appears on the rolls of the 2d Albany County Militia, Land Bounty Rights.

CONNER, SIMON: His name appears on the rolls of the 2d Albany County Militia.

CONOVER, SAMUEL: Born in Albany in 1759. He moved to Schenectady at the age of sixteen and went to live with John Mynderse in order to learn the blacksmith's trade. In May, 1777, he enlisted for four months under Captain John Mynderse, 2d Albany County Militia, and marched to Fort Edward. He was in the engagement at Snookkill. At Stillwater he was wounded in the ankle by the accidental discharge of a musket in the hands of one of his own company and this rendered him lame for the remainder of his life. He was honorably discharged a short time before the battle of Saratoga. In November, 1777, he was drafted, assigned to Captain Price's company and detailed for guard duty at Albany. He remained there until March, 1778. In July, 1780, he volunteered under Colonel Volkert Veeder and marched to Schoharie, serving also during this year one month at Stone Arabia. A pensioner under the Act of June 7, 1832.

CONSAUL, DAVID: Died previous to May 7, 1818. He served under Captains Jesse Van Slyck and John Van Patten, 2d Albany County Militia. In September, 1782, he went on scout duty to Mayfield and Sacandaga.

CONSAUL, MANUEL: His name appears on the rolls of the 2d Albany County Militia.

CORL, HENRY: His name appears on the rolls of the 2d Albany County Militia and the 2d Albany County Militia, Land Bounty Rights.

CORL, JOHN: Born in 1757; died April 24, 1842. Buried in Vale Cemetery. In the spring of 1775 he enlisted under Captain John Mynderse, 2d Albany County Militia. He took part in the expedition to Johnstown in January, 1776, and in March enlisted in Captain John Clute's company of fatigue men and served in it for one year. In the summer of 1777 he served under Captain John Mynderse with the Northern Army. He was at Bemis Heights. In the fall he enlisted and served in Captain James Peek's company of batteaumen employed in transporting provisions and ammunition from Schenectady to Fort Stanwix. In 1778 he performed garrison duty at the Schoharie Forts under Captain Walter Vrooman. In the fall of 1779 he mounted guard at Fort Paris and served with the troops under General Van Rensselaer at Fort Hunter. In 1780 he was engaged at Watervliet for the Continental Congress under Captain Bowman in cutting wood to make charcoal for the use of the blacksmiths and artisans of the army. In 1781 he was with the troops under Colonel Marinus Willett in the pursuit of Major Ross and Walter Butler. A pensioner.

CORL, WILLIAM: Born in 1760; died March 19, 1848. Buried in Vale Cemetery. In the spring of 1776 as a substitute he marched to the Heldebergh under Captain John B. Vrooman, and in the fall of the same year he enrolled in the company of Captain Jesse Van Slyck, 2d Albany County Militia. In January, 1777, he was serving in a company of fatigue men under Captain Jacobus Peek. From July until the beginning of October (when he was taken sick and obliged to return home) he served with the Northern Army at Fort Edward, Stillwater, Fort Miller, Saratoga, Van Schaick's Island and Snookkill. During the years 1778 and 1779 he performed various scout and garrison duties. On January 1, 1780, he again enlisted in the company of batteaumen under Captain Jacobus Peek. In the fall of 1780 he took part in the expedition to Ballston.

CORNU, DANIEL: Baptized December 21, 1740. His lot was on the north side of State Street, extending easterly from the present line of the canal. His name appears on the rolls of the 2d Albany County Militia and he saw service under Captain Thomas Brower Banker.

CORNU, WESSEL: Baptized March 18, 1764. On March 1, 1780, he enlisted in Captain Thomas Brower Banker's company, 2d Albany County Militia, commencing service in the garrison at Schenectady, serving there until about July 18, when his company was ordered to Beaverdam in pursuit of Tories. He served two weeks in each month from April to July in garrison at Schenectady. On August 1 he marched to Schoharie with a part of Captain Banker's and a part of Captain Mynderse's companies and there served one month guarding farmers while they harvested their crops. On September 1 he returned to Schenectady and served one week on garrison duty. He performed like service three weeks in October and two weeks in November. During 1781 he served in "minute service" under Captains Banker and Jesse Van Slyck, mostly at Schenectady, although he was sometimes called for scout duty along the line of the Mohawk River. In September he marched on an alarm some thirty miles to the north of Schenectady in pursuit of the enemy who retreated without an engagement; during this campaign Cornu was absent about one month, most of the time being quartered at Ballston. In October and November he served two weeks of each month in garrison at Schenectady, and in 1782 performed various garrison and scout duties, marching in July with a detail of forty men under Captain Gerrit S. Veeder to Fort Plain and Fort Plank to serve as guard while the crops were being harvested. A pensioner.

COVEL, WILLIAM: His name appears on the rolls of the 2d Albany County Militia.

CRAWFORD, ALEXANDER: He was enrolled under Captain Thomas Wasson, 2d Albany County Militia. On February 25, 1780, he was promoted to the rank of ensign.

CRAWFORD, JOHN: His name appears on the rolls of the 2d Albany County Militia.

CRAWFORD, JOSEPH: He enlisted for nine months at Schenectady April 1, 1781, as a corporal under Captain Lawrence Gross, Colonel Marinus Willett's New York Levies. He was later promoted to the rank of sergeant and served as such until his discharge in December, 1781. His widow's claim for pension was rejected.

CROUSEHORN, JOHN: He lived on the east corner of State and Jay Streets. He was a tanner by trade. In 1781 he was appointed captain of a volunteer company of artillery enlisted in Schenectady and consisting of fifteen men. To this company was particularly intrusted the cannon of Colonel Wemple's regiment.

CUMMINGS, JOHN: Buried August 25, 1801. On June 19, 1775, he enlisted under Captain Cornelius Van Dyck for the defense of Fort Ticonderoga. His name appears on the rolls of the 2d Albany County Militia enrolled under Captain Thomas Brower Banker.

CUYLER, CORNELIUS: A merchant. On May 26, 1775, he was appointed a member of the first Committee of Safety to fill the vacancy caused by the resignation of John Sanders. On August 11 he was appointed to receive the "donation wheat for the poor of Boston," and on November 17 to draw up articles to be signed by the various officers before receiving their commissions. On December 29 he was one of the town's magistrates. On October 9,

1776, he was appointed by the Committee of Safety of the State of New York one of a committee in Albany County "to purchase all the coarse woolen cloth, linsey-woolsey, blankets, woolen hose, mittens, coarse linen, felt hats and shoes fitting for soldiers and to have the linen made up into shirts."

CUYLER, JOHN: Enrolled under Captain Thomas Brower Banker, 2d Albany County Militia. On December 29, 1775, he was one of the town's magistrates. On February 10, 1776, he was elected a member of the Committee of Safety, and served as a member on several subsequent Committees. On April 1, 1777, he was elected assessor, and on June 7 appointed one of a committee to consult with the inhabitants of Tryon County regarding the election of governor. On June 15, 1779, he was chosen a member of the Committee of Safety and on July 9 appointed chairman of the Board to succeed Abraham Oothout resigned.

DAVIS, ABRAHAM: His name appears on the rolls of the 2d Albany County Militia.

DAVIS, JOHN: His name appears on the rolls of the 2d Albany County Militia.

DE GARMO, MATTHEW: Born in Albany. During the Revolution he lived in Schenectady. He was enrolled part of the time under Captain Jellis J. Fonda and part under Captain Jesse Van Slyck, 2d Albany County Militia. Early in the spring of 1777 he enlisted in a company of batteaumen under Captain Teunis Fisher and served until the fall (when the company was discharged), transporting stores from Albany to Lake George and other places. In January, 1778, he enlisted in the Quartermaster's Department at Saratoga under the immediate charge of Colonel Christopher Yates, and in the fall of the same year served on an expedition up the Mohawk River. In the fall of 1779 under Captain Ahasueras Marselis he went to Fort Hunter and other places along the Valley. In August, 1782, he was on garrison duty at the Upper Fort, Schoharie. His name appears on the rolls of the 2d Albany County Militia, Land Bounty Rights. A pensioner.

DEGOLYER, JAMES: His name appears on the rolls of the 2d Albany County Militia.

DEGOLYER, JOSEPH: Born at Kinderhook in the year 1762. He moved to Glenville in the year 1769. In 1778 he entered the service in Captain John Van Patten's company, 2d Albany County Militia, as a substitute for Harmanus Veeder, and performed garrison duty at the Upper Fort, Schoharie. In 1779 he served at Fort Plank, and in October, 1780, with the troops under General Van Rensselaer took part in the battle of Klock's Field. From the middle of July to the end of November, 1781, he was on garrison duty at the Middle Fort, Schoharie. A pensioner.

DE GRAFF, ABRAHAM: Born April 20, 1754; died June 1, 1810. His name appears on the rolls of the 2d Albany County Militia.

DE GRAFF, ANDREAS: His name appears on the rolls of the 2d Albany County Militia.

DE GRAFF, CORNELIUS: Born November 23, 1738; died July 11, 1830. He lived on the south side of State Street. His name appears on the rolls of the 2d Albany County Militia under Captain Thomas Brower Banker and on the rolls of the 2d Albany County Militia, Land Bounty Rights.

DE GRAFF, DANIEL: Born May 26, 1708; died March 12, 1790. On April 24, 1777, he was detailed as a wagoner for service from Albany to Lake George.

DE GRAFF, ISAAC: Born in Schenectady, November 16, 1757; died December 21, 1844. In October, 1776, he entered the service as a deputy commissary of issues, being appointed by Elisha Avery. He was stationed at Johnstown and served until August, 1777, when Avery resigned. He continued to hold office under various appointments until July 1, 1780, when in consequence of a change in the commissary department his term of service closed. A pensioner under the Act of June 7, 1832.

DE GRAFF, JESSE: Born January 13, 1745; died August 30, 1812. In 1777 he was enrolled under Captain Jesse Van Slyck, 2d Albany County Militia. On July 2, 1779, he was appointed one of a committee of four to sell salt to the people of the district. About 1780 he served as a captain of the guard at Schenectady. His name appears on the rolls of the 2d Albany County Militia, Land Bounty Rights.

DE GRAFF, JOHN: Born in Glenville. In 1775 he enrolled under Captain John Van Patten, 2d Albany County Militia. In January, 1776, he went with the forces under General Schuyler to Johnstown, and in October of the same year was on duty at Fort Ann for one month. In the spring of 1777 he was drafted in a company mustered at Schenectady under Captain Jellis J. Fonda and performed three months' service at West Point. In September, 1777, he marched to Bemis Heights, returning home after Burgoyne's surrender. In May, 1779, he marched with a detachment to Sacandaga to erect a blockhouse, and later performed garrison duty at the Schoharie Forts. From May to December, 1780, he was constantly on duty. His company was stationed in Glenville and at a place called Tinker's Hill erected a picket fort. His company was employed at this time in pursuing Indians and Tories and to prevent incursions of the enemy. In October of this same year De Graff marched on an alarm to Palatine being out two weeks. A pensioner.

INDIVIDUAL RECORDS OF SERVICE 157

DE GRAFF, JOHN N.: His name appears on the rolls of the 2d Albany County Militia.

DE GRAFF, NICHOLAS: His name appears on the rolls of the 2d Albany County Militia, Land Bounty Rights.

DE GRAFF, SIMON: Born April 6, 1753. On March 1, 1776, he signed an agreement with Philip Schuyler for service at Lake George and Ticonderoga. His name appears on the rolls of the 2d Albany County Militia.

DE GRAFF, WILLIAM: Buried September 22, 1803. His name appears on the rolls of the 2d Albany County Militia.

DE LA GRANGE, MYNDERT: On August 12, 1777, he was taken into custody as a "disaffected person."

DELLAMONT, ABRAHAM: Baptized July 19, 1729; died December 23, 1792. He lived at the Norman's Kill. His name appears on the rolls of the 2d Albany County Militia.

DELLAMONT, HENDRICK: Born October 24, 1745; died August 20, 1820. Buried in Vale Cemetery. In 1781 he owned the lot on Union Street where the old Court House now stands. He served as a private and as a sergeant in the 2d Albany County Militia.

DENNY, JOHN: On June 20, 1775, having just returned from Canada he was cross-questioned by the Committee of Safety regarding conditions there. On February 8, 1776, he appeared before the Committee to give information against one John Freel of Johnstown. On February 29 he accepted a recruiting warrant from General Schuyler with the rank of ensign. On November 21, 1776, he was promoted to the rank of second lieutenant, 1st New York Line, and in this capacity he served until October 7, 1778, when he resigned from the service.

DE SPITZER, AARON: Buried in Vale Cemetery. In June, 1780, as a corporal under Captain Jesse Van Slyck, 2d Albany County Militia, he went in command of a detail to

Beaverdam and Harpersfield. He served also in the Levies under Colonel Morris Graham.

DE SPITZER, GERRIT: Born June 28, 1758; died June 2, 1801. Buried in Vale Cemetery. On September 24, 1776, he enlisted in Captain John A. Bradt's company of State Rangers. In 1778 he was serving as a sergeant under Captain Jesse Van Slyck, 2d Albany County Militia. In May he commanded a detail to Sacandaga and in April, 1779, a detail to Ballston and Glens Falls. In November he commanded at the Upper Fort, Schoharie, and went in charge of a detail for scout duty to the Norman's Kill and Beaverdam. In April, 1780, he went on scout duty to Glens Falls and Lake George, and in June, 1781, was in command of a detail sent to Sacandaga to watch the movements of the Sacandaga Indians. In September he went to Beaverdam and Harpersfield on scout duty, and in July, 1782, commanded a party sent by the Schenectady Committee to Harpersfield to reconnoiter and spy on the enemy. In September he was in command of a scout at Sacandaga and Mayfield.

DILLENO, HENDRIC: His name appears on the rolls of the 2d Albany County Militia.

DORN, ABRAHAM: His name appears on the rolls of the 2d Albany County Militia.

DORN, JOHN: His name appears on the rolls of the 2d Albany County Militia and the 2d Albany County Militia, Land Bounty Rights. The name of John Dorn appears also on the rolls of the 3d Company, 1st New York Line. He enlisted on March 11, 1777, and was mustered to the end of the war.

DOTY, REV. JOHN: In 1773 he became rector of St. George's Church. He considered himself bound by the Oath of Allegiance to adhere to the British Government. In May, 1777, he was recommended to the field officers as "a dangerous person." He was brought before the Committee of Safety and accused of plotting against the State. He denied the charge of plotting but declared that he was loyal to England. He was committed to the Albany jail but was soon discharged. He was, subsequent to his return to Schenectady, taken from his bed by two armed men and with some others hurried to Albany where an oath (of neutrality, as he believed) was proposed to him. This oath he refused to take and notwithstanding his refusal he was permitted to return to Schenectady where he remained until the defeat of General Burgoyne, when he procured permission to retire to Canada. General Gates offered him a living of £200 per annum if he would remain, but this he refused. He was later appointed chaplain of Sir John Johnson's 1st Battalion. He retired on half pay and died in England. His property in Schenectady, which was confiscated, was three hundred and fifty-three acres of land, valued at £239; a chamber organ, which he placed in the Church for security, and a "tolerable" library.

Douw, Abraham: His name appears on the rolls of the 2d Albany County Militia.

Duncan, John: Born in 1722; died May 5, 1791. He came to Schenectady in 1755, and was a merchant of considerable means, having his warehouse on the northwest corner of Washington Avenue and Union Street. Soon after his establishment he took into partnership James Phyn, a London merchant. The firm of Duncan & Phyn became widely known, and both men very wealthy. The business was later carried on by the Ellices, on the retirement of Mr. Duncan. Mr. Duncan had a city residence on the southeast corner of Union and Ferry Streets, and a country seat comprising some eight hundred acres known as the Hermitage situated in Niskayuna, of which the present estate of Mr. Welton Stanford comprises a part. He lived in Schenectady after the war and died here. On March 11, 1776, General Washington informed the Committee of Safety that he had been informed that Duncan had three hundred stand of arms. On May 21 the Board was informed that a number of enemies to the cause of liberty were gathered at his house. The Board, however, did not feel justified in taking any action, as the Hermitage was outside the Schenectady district. On December 19 he was ordered confined to the limits of his farm until further notice and required to give a bond of £500 for his good behavior and the carrying out of the order. On March 28, 1777, he was paroled by the Committee of Safety. In May he was recommended to the field officers as "a dangerous person," and on May 3 arrested in order to be taken to Albany, but was released after giving his oath that he would take up arms in defense of the country in case of any invasion. On October 16 the inhabitants petitioned General Gates for his removal as commissary for the purchase of supplies for the hospital, and on November 7 he resigned. On July 23, 1778, he was cited to appear before the Commissioners of Conspiracies to render satisfaction regarding his conduct conformable to the Act respecting persons of a neutral or equivocal character. He was unable to attend because of illness, but on August 1 appeared and requested time to consider taking the Oath of Allegiance. On August 8 he again appeared and stated that while he "conceived himself not to be comprehended within the meaning of the Act nevertheless to show his farther zeal and attachment to the State and the cause of America, he was willing and ready to take the Oath voluntarily." This he accordingly did. On August 16, 1780, he was reported as having received letters from the enemy. His name appears on the rolls of the 2d Albany County Militia and the 2d Albany County Militia, Land Bounty Rights.

DUNCAN, RICHARD: Died in February, 1819. He was living with his father in Schenectady when the war broke out.

In June, 1776, under an assumed name he accompanied
to Johnstown General McLean, an officer of the British
service who had come to the house in disguise, endeavoring to make his way to Canada. In May, 1777, he was
recommended to the field officers as a "dangerous person." He was appointed a captain in the British army
and joined the troops at Saratoga, bringing with him not
a few volunteers. He remained with the troops until a
little while before the Convention, when with General
Burgoyne's permission he left to join his corps at Ticonderoga accompanied by a number of other soldiers. The
band was pursued and fired upon by the American troops
but no one was taken prisoner. He was in immediate
command of a company of regular troops under Sir John
Johnson in his attack upon the Mohawk River settlements
in 1780, and is said to have commanded "with great gal-
lantry and success on the retreats, when attacked by a
spirited regiment of the army of General Robert Van Rensselaer." He remained in the army until the reduction of
his regiment in 1783. Captain Duncan "was never taxed
with cruelty or severity by the settlers" and after his
father's death in 1791, he resided for many years at the
Hermitage, "an accomplished Christian gentleman, of
extremely urbane manners and very much respected."

DUNLAP, JAMES: He served as a private in Captain Jacob
Reed's company, 2d or New York Regiment of artillery.
He lost his eyesight, was transferred to the Corps of
Invalids and discharged April 10, 1783.

EARLEY, EDWARD: On August 20, 1776, he was serving as a
member of Captain John A. Bradt's company of State
Rangers. On April 19, 1777, he was granted a tavern
license by the Committee of Safety. He was probably an
enlisted soldier, for on September 11 he was detailed as a
guard to accompany a prisoner to Albany.

ELLICE, ALEXANDER: A merchant from London in business in Schenectady as early as 1768. Known to have been an open enemy to the American cause. In May, 1775, he was said to have "harangued the people in the street and endeavored to discourage them from forming a committee of safety." In the fall he moved to England.

ELLICE, JAMES: A merchant from London in business in Schenectady as early as 1768. He remained here during and after the war. On April 13, 1776, he was given a certificate by the Committee of Safety to the effect that he had signed the General Association and that to their knowledge he had done nothing against the American cause. On May 25 he was given a pass to go to German Flats on business. In May, 1777, he was recommended to the field officers as a "dangerous person," and on the twenty-second voluntarily took oath that he would take up arms in defense of the country in case of any invasion. On May 1, 1778, he was brought before the Commissioners of Conspiracies for "speaking words that in the opinion of the Board might have a dangerous tendency and prove detrimental to the liberties of America." On July 14 he was summoned "to render satisfaction regarding his conduct as a neutral and equivocal character." On July 16 he refused to take the Oath of Allegiance and was requested "to hold himself in readiness to go off in eight days." On July 20 the matter was reported to the Secretary of State, and on August 1 he declared his readiness to take the Oath. He was not permitted to do so, however, as the law did not allow the Oath to be administered to one who had once refused to take it. He was ordered to be ready on August 14 for transportation to the enemy's lines, and on that day was taken into close confinement in accordance with orders from Governor Clinton. On May 19, 1779, the Oath of Allegiance was administered to him as authorized by the amended Act.

INDIVIDUAL RECORDS OF SERVICE

ELLICE, ROBERT: A merchant from London in business in Schenectady as early as 1768. On April 13, 1776, General Schuyler was informed by the Committee of Safety that he had not signed the General Association and that he was looked upon as an enemy to the American cause of liberty. On April 22 he was refused a certificate for the purpose of obtaining a passport as being an enemy. On April 24 he signed an affidavit to the effect that he had not signed the General Association and openly declared himself as a friend of the American cause for the reason that he had a great deal of property up country and that he felt such action would be detrimental to the settling of his affairs. Upon this declaration he was given the certificate of character requested.

EMPIE, JOHN: Born October 3, 1731. His name appears on the rolls of the 2d Albany County Militia.

FAIRLY, CALEB: Baptized December 7, 1735. His name appears on the rolls of the 2d Albany County Militia and the 2d Albany County Militia, Land Bounty Rights.

FAIRLY, JOHN: Baptized May 28, 1732. In 1778 he was a member of Captain Jesse Van Slyck's company, 2d Albany County Militia.

FELTHOUSEN, CHRISTOFFEL: Died in 1799. On March 1, 1776, he signed an agreement with Philip Schuyler for service at Lake George and Ticonderoga. His name appears on the rolls of the 2d Albany County Militia, Land Bounty Rights.

FELTHOUSEN, JOHN: Born in Schenectady, January 12, 1764. In 1779, when fifteen years old, he substituted for his father Christoffel and others. In the spring of 1780 he enlisted under Captain James McGee, Colonel Morris Graham's Levies, and served four months, during which time he marched to West Point, Dobbs Ferry and other posts. At Dobbs Ferry he took part in an encounter with a British brig. After this period of service he enrolled under Captain J. B. Vrooman, 2d Albany County Militia, and served to the end of the war. He went to Beaverdam twice, to Fort Hunter, Fort Paris and Johnstown, performing garrison duty at the latter places for a period of about one month each. When not out on expeditions he mounted guard at Schenectady. A pensioner under the Act of June 7, 1832.

FETHERLY, JOHN: On August 12, 1777, he was arrested and sent to Albany as implicated in a Tory plot.

FLANSBURGH, WILLIAM F.: Born in Schenectady and resided here at the beginning of the war. At the time of his enlistment in the regular troops he was only twelve or thirteen years of age. He was in the battle of White Plains and Monmouth. In the spring of 1780 he enrolled under Captain Walter Vrooman in the New York Levies, and in the fall of the same year was detailed with a company of about sixty men to destroy boats of the enemy lying on Onondaga Lake. While returning they were all taken prisoners and Flansburgh after many vicissitudes was taken to London. He was later brought back to Canada, whence he made his escape and reached Schenectady soon after the war was over. A pensioner.

FLETCHER, ————: On May 22, 1775, it was reported to the Committee of Safety "by good authority that one Mr. Fletcher a schoolmaster in the Town had said that Col. Guy Johnson would come down the River with 500 Indians and cut us all off, and further that it would be right, and if he had it in his power he would do the same for we were all rebels." Fletcher failed to appear when summoned before the Board.

FOLGER, BENJAMIN: His name appears on the rolls of the 2d Albany County Militia.

FOLGER, THOMAS: Born in England, April 26, 1750. In 1774 he came to Currybush, now Princetown, and in the spring of 1775 volunteered and was assigned to the company of Captain Thomas Wasson, 2d Albany County Militia. In the fall of 1776 he served at Fort Edward. In 1777 he was at Fort George when destroyed by the American troops, and took part in Schuyler's retreat. He was discharged the day after General Gates arrived at Bemis Heights, his service having expired. He returned home and had been there but two days when he was again ordered out. He performed garrison duty on various occasions and several times went in pursuit of Joseph Bettis. In the fall of 1780 he was at the Middle Fort, Schoharie, when Timothy Murphy fired on the flag of truce as it approached the fort with a demand for surrender, and in the fall of 1781 he marched with the troops in pursuit of Major Ross and Butler, on which occasion, accompanying the party of Oneidas who followed Walter Butler, he was present at his death. A pensioner.

FONDA, ABRAHAM: Born July 17, 1715; died February 13, 1805. He lived in the house No. 27 Front Street built by himself in 1752. On May 7, 1776, he was elected a member of the third Committee of Safety, and on January 15, 1777, was appointed chairman. He served also on the Committees taking office June 2, 1777, and January 5, 1778. On August 8, 1778, he was serving as a justice of the peace.

FONDA, JACOB G.: Born in the Schenectady Township, August, 1761; died in West Glenville, December 8, 1859. He was living in Albany in the spring of 1778, when he enlisted under Captain Gerrit Groesbeck, 1st Albany County Militia. He performed various garrison and scout duties and was in the battle of Klock's Field with the troops under General Van Rensselaer. His claim for pension was rejected.

FONDA, JELLIS A.: Born October 25, 1759; died at Chittenango, August 27, 1834. Buried in Vale Cemetery. In 1777 he was serving as an ensign in Captain Jesse Van

Slyck's company, 2d Albany County Militia. He performed service at Fort Ann, Fort George and Fort Edward, and was in the battle of Bemis Heights. In 1778 he was enrolled in Captain John Mynderse's company and attached to General Frederick Visscher's brigade. He was promoted to the rank of lieutenant. During the year 1780 he served as a lieutenant and adjutant in Colonel Morris Graham's Levies at West Point and Harper's Ferry. At West Point he acted as brigade major for a few weeks in the absence of Major Lansing. He "was one of the 1200 men whom General Arnold (previous to his treachery) sent away to Fort Edward to weaken the garrison at West Point." During the years 1781 and 1782 he was attached to the Levies under Colonel Willet with the same rank as before. He saw service at Fort Plain, German Flats, Fort Stanwix and at the battles of Torlock and Johnstown. On November 1, 1782, he was promoted to the rank of captain. In February, 1783, he went with the expedition to Fort Oswego under Colonel Marinus Willett. A pensioner.

FONDA, JELLIS J.: Born January 13, 1751; died in 1839. Buried in the family cemetery in Glenville. On May 27, 1775, he was appointed captain of a company of minute men, which came to be known as "The Greens" because of the color of their uniforms. On July 10, 1775, he refused an offer of a recruiting warrant from the Provincial Congress. On October 20, 1775, a commission as captain was issued in his name by the Provincial Congress. He was reappointed June 20, 1778, the commission being signed by Governor Clinton. In January, 1776, and again in June he went to Johnstown. In the fall of the same year, he marched with his company to Stillwater where they were in camp for some time. From Stillwater they marched to Fort Ann, thence down Wood Creek to Skenesborough as guards for boats. He served with particular distinction in the campaign against Burgoyne and at the battle of Bemis Heights. He served in many expeditions and on various garrison duties during the succeeding years of the war, being especially zealous in the discharge of his offices. While on guard duty at Schenectady he was spoken of as "attending roll call and giving orders every morning at daybreak, sometimes 2 hours before day." He was actively engaged in the battle of Johnstown (October, 1781) and in the pursuit of the enemy, and on this occasion he "so highly distinguished himself that Colonel Willett addressed him a letter of thanks for his services and praising him for his intrepidity." A pensioner under the Act of June 7, 1832.

FORSETH, GEORGE: A clerk in the employment of James Ellice. On April 13, 1776, General Schuyler was informed by the Committee of Safety that he had not signed the General Association and that they looked upon him as an enemy to the American cause of liberty. In May, 1777, he was recommended to the field officers as "a dangerous person." On May 22 he voluntarily took oath that he would take up arms in defense of the country in case of any invasion.

FORT, JOHN: Born June 14, 1725; died in 1821. He served as a sergeant under Captain Thomas Brower Banker, 2d Albany County Militia.

FORT, JOHN D.: Baptized April 1, 1750. He served as a private and as a sergeant under Captain Thomas Brower Banker, 2d Albany County Militia.

FRANK, DAVID: He served as a private under Captain Jacob Schermerhorn and as a private and sergeant under Captain Thomas Brower Banker, 2d Albany County Militia.

FREEMAN, RICHARD: In 1776 he enlisted in a company of Tryon County Rangers and served nine months. In May, 1777, he enlisted under Captain Giles Wolcott, Colonel Seth Warner's regiment, and served until July 15, 1779, when he was taken prisoner by the enemy "on the 14 Mile Island" in Lake George after an engagement "in which the greater part of the troops were killed and scalped." He made his escape in October, 1780, and on his return found his regiment disbanded. His name appears on the rolls of the 2d Albany County Militia, Land Bounty Rights. He lived in Schenectady until 1819. A pensioner under the Act of March 18, 1818.

FRENCH, DAVID: In 1781, he was a member of Captain John Crousehorn's company of artillery. His name appears on the rolls of the 2d Albany County Militia.

FREYS, HENDRICK: His name appears on the rolls of the 2d Albany County Militia, Land Bounty Rights.

FURMAN, JOHN: His name appears on the rolls of the 2d Albany County Militia.

GARDINIER, JAMES: His name appears on the rolls of the 2d Albany County Militia, Land Bounty Rights.

GARDNER, WILLIAM: His name appears on the rolls of the 2d Albany County Militia.

GLEN, HENRY: Baptized July 13, 1739; died January 6, 1814. He was for some years a trader in company with his brother, John, and Jacobus Teller. On May 6, 1775, he was chosen a member of the first Committee of Safety. He served as a representative from Albany County in the first, second and third Provincial Congresses. On July 23, 1775, he was appointed one of a committee to go to Johnstown to inquire into the causes of the disturbances in that section. On February 10, 1776, he was appointed captain of one of the newly organized militia companies but did not serve actively as such. During the war he acted as deputy quartermaster, having charge of all supplies at Schenectady. During the spring of 1781, he pledged his personal credit to build sixteen batteaux for the service. He was appointed one of the three commissioners of Indian affairs in accordance with the Act of March 25, 1783.

GLEN, ISAAC: His name appears on the rolls of the 2d Albany County Militia. In the fall of 1777 he was at Stillwater, but returned home before the battle of Bemis Heights. On July 28, 1778, he was chosen first lieutenant in a company of Exempts formed in Schenectady under Captain Jacob Schermerhorn.

GLEN, JACOB: On April 21, 1779, it was reported to the Commissioners of Conspiracies that he had drunk "success to the British Army and wished they might conquer America with many other Expression's inimical to the American Cause."

GLEN, JOHN: Baptized July 2, 1735; died September 23, 1828. He was a trader in company with his brother, Henry, and Jacobus Teller. He built and occupied the house on Washington Avenue now numbered 58. He was a highly esteemed personal friend of General Washington. In 1775 he bought the tract of land on the Hudson which afterwards became known as Glens Falls. On July 25, 1778, he was cited to appear before the Commissioners of Conspiracies to give satisfaction touching his conduct during the war agreeable to the act respecting persons of neutral and equivocal character, and on August 1 took the Oath prescribed by the Act. His name appears on the rolls of the 2d Albany County Militia.

GLEN, JOHN SANDERS: Baptized January 25, 1733. His name appears on the rolls of the 2d Albany County Militia.

GOFF, ISAAC: On June 19, 1775, he enlisted under Captain Cornelius Van Dyck for the defense of Ticonderoga. He served in the Canadian campaign under Captain Barent Ten Eyck, 2d New York Line, and was at the taking of St. John's, Chamblee, Montreal and at the siege of Quebec. He returned with the regiment to Saratoga and was discharged under Captain Andrew Finck about December 20, 1776.

GORDON, CHARLES: He was living in Schenectady in 1779. His name appears on the rolls of the 2d Albany County Militia.

GORDON, JOSEPH: In 1783 his home was on Church Street next north of the Dutch Church lot. His name appears on the rolls of the 2d Albany County Militia, enrolled under Captain John Mynderse. On March 1, 1776, he signed an agreement with Philip Schuyler for service at Lake George and Ticonderoga.

GORDON, ROBERT: His name appears on the rolls of the 2d Albany County Militia.

GORDON, WILLIAM: His name appears on the rolls of the 2d Albany County Militia, enrolled under Captain John Mynderse. On March 1, 1776, he signed an agreement with Philip Schuyler for service at Lake George and Ticonderoga.

GRAVENBERG, JOHN: His name appears on the rolls of the 2d Albany County Militia. In 1778 he was enrolled under Captain Jesse Van Slyck.

GREGG, ANDREW: His name appears on the rolls of the 2d Albany County Militia.

GREGG, JAMES: His name appears on the rolls of the 2d Albany County Militia.

GREGG, JOHN: On August 6, 1777, the Committee of Safety was informed that he had drunk the health of King George the Third at Bradt's Tavern. On being summoned before the Board he "made the most humble concessions" and "out of compassion to his family he was discharged."

GROOT, ABRAHAM C.: Died in 1818. His name appears on the rolls of the 2d Albany County Militia.

GROOT, AMOS: His name appears on the rolls of the 2d Albany County Militia.

GROOT, ANDREW: His name appears on the rolls of the 2d Albany County Militia.

GROOT, CORNELIUS: His name appears on the rolls of the 2d Albany County Militia.

GROOT, ELIAS: On October 10, 1776, he enlisted in Captain John A. Bradt's company of State Rangers. His name appears on the rolls of the 12th Albany County Militia, Land Bounty Rights.

GROOT, PHILIP: His name appears on the rolls of the 2d Albany County Militia.

GROOT, SIMON: Born in 1749. His name appears on the rolls of the 2d Albany County Militia, enrolled under Captain Jellis J. Fonda. In September, 1777, he was at Stillwater but not in the battle, being out on scout duty.

GROOT, SIMON A.: Baptized October 31, 1756; died March 4, 1838. In the spring of 1775 he was enrolled as a private in the company of Captain Thomas Brower Banker, 2d Albany County Militia. This same year he served six months as an artificer at Lake George under Jacob Vrooman. In January, 1776, he took part in the expedition to Johnstown. He was at Ticonderoga when the fort was evacuated and at Bemis Heights under General Arnold. He took part in Sullivan's expedition and was at the West Canada Creek when Walter Butler was killed, on which occasion he took a prisoner. He performed various garrison duties and went on various details for the apprehension of Tories. He was for a long time captain of the city guard at Schenectady. A pensioner under the Act of June 7, 1832.

GROOT, SIMON C.: Baptized November 17, 1745; died in West Glenville, February 10, 1832. His name appears on

the rolls of the 2d Albany County Militia, as serving under
Captain Thomas Brower Banker.

GUTHRIE, ABRAHAM: He served as a private in the 1st New
York Line.

HACKNEY, GEORGE: In 1778 he served at the Middle Fort,
Schoharie, under Captain W. B. Vrooman, and in the
summer of 1779 at Sacandaga erecting fortifications under
Captain Thomas Brower Banker. In the fall of the same
year he was on duty at Fort Paris. In October, 1781, he
was wounded in the head by a tomahawk at Johnstown
and confined for some time in the hospital. His widow
received a pension.

HAGEDORN, HARMANUS: His name appears on the rolls of
the 2d Albany County Militia.

HALL, JOHN: On October 11, 1776, he enlisted in Captain
John A. Bradt's company of State Rangers. He was
discharged on January 21, 1777, having returned his
bounty. His name appears on the rolls of the 2d Albany
County Militia.

HALL, JOHN W.: On March 1, 1776, he signed an agreement
with Philip Schuyler for service at Lake George and
Ticonderoga. His name appears on the rolls of the 2d
Albany County Militia.

HALL, NICHOLAS: Baptized July 27, 1748; died April 17,
1828. His name appears on the rolls of the 2d Albany
County Militia as serving under Captain Jesse Van Slyck.

HALL, WILLIAM: A weaver. On October 18, 1776, he enlisted in Captain John A. Bradt's company of State
Rangers. His name appears on the rolls of the 2d Albany
County Militia.

HANNA, ALEXANDER: He served as a corporal under Captain Thomas Wasson, 2d Albany County Militia.

HARE, PETER: His name appears on the rolls of the 2d Albany County Militia.

HARNEL (HARNER), SAMUEL: His name appears on the rolls of the 2d Albany County Militia.

HARSEY, WILLIAM: His name appears on the rolls of the 2d Albany County Militia.

HEDGET, ABRAHAM: His name appears on the rolls of the 2d Albany County Militia.

HELMER, HENYOST: His name appears on the rolls of the 2d Albany County Militia.

HENDRICK, PETER: His name appears on the rolls of the 2d Albany County Militia.

HENRY, JOHN: Born in Schenectady, February 24, 1764. In February, 1780, he enlisted under Captain John Mynderse, 2d Albany County Militia. Previous to this enrollment he performed guard duty at Schenectady. He served on several expeditions notably to Ballston in the fall of 1780, and to Warren's Bush after it was burned. His claim for pension was rejected.

HETHERINGTON, JOSEPH: His name appears on the rolls of the 2d Albany County Militia.

HILTON, BENJAMIN: On May 29, 1775, he was appointed a lieutenant in a company for the defense of Ticonderoga, but on June 23 gave in his resignation and refused to serve. On January 14, 1776, a letter signed by Hilton addressed to Sheriff White and containing "some expressions very unfriendly to the American cause" was delivered to the Committee of Safety. On January 15, when brought before the Board, Hilton declared that he was the author of the letter, and that he knew he was doing wrong but never thought it would be discovered. In compliance with a resolution of the Committee he promised to cause the letter and his declaration to be published three weeks successively in "Hugh Gaines newspapers."

HOOGTELING, JACOBUS: On July 12, 1777, he was arrested by order of the Committee of Safety and sent to the Albany jail for endeavoring to persuade two men to desert to the British. There was a Jacobus Hoogteling who, judging from the minutes of the Commissioners of Conspiracies, bore a somewhat unsavory reputation and caused this Board considerable annoyance.

HOOPLE, GEORGE OR JERRY: His name appears on the rolls of the 2d Albany County Militia. In 1781 he was a member of Captain John Crousehorn's company of artillery, and in July, 1782, was on scout duty at Harpersfield.

HORSFORD, JOHN: Baptized November 4, 1758. His name appears on the rolls of the 2d Albany County Militia.

HORSFORD, REUBEN: From Farmington, Connecticut. A hatter. His name appears on the rolls of the 2d Albany County Militia, Land Bounty Rights.

HOUSE, JOHN GEORGE: His name appears on the rolls of the 2d Albany County Militia.

HOUSE, PETER: His name appears on the rolls of the 2d Albany County Militia.

HUGHAN, JOHN: On July 10, 1775, he made application to the Committee of Safety to raise a company, stating that he already had twenty men engaged. Permission was refused because many of the men enlisted had not signed the Association. His name appears on the rolls of the 2d Albany County Militia.

HYDENBURGH, SYBRANT: His name appears on the rolls of the 2d Albany County Militia.

JACQUISH, JOHN: On October 31, 1776, he enlisted in Captain John A. Bradt's company of State Rangers.

JAMES, WILLIAM: On April 19, 1777, he was granted a tavern license by the Committee of Safety. His name appears

on the rolls of the 2d New York Line and the 2d Albany
County Militia, Land Bounty Rights.

KEES, JOHN: His name appears on the rolls of the 2d
Albany County Militia.

KENNEDY, ALEXANDER: His name appears on the rolls of
the 2d Albany County Militia.

KENNEDY, JOHN: His name appears on the rolls of the 2d
Albany County Militia and the 2d Albany County Militia,
Land Bounty Rights.

KENNEDY, SAMUEL: Born at Currybush (Princetown) in
1760. In May, 1776, he enlisted in Captain John Winn's
company of Tryon County Rangers. He served in this
company until about February 1, 1777. In June of this
year he volunteered in an independent company under
a Captain Canute [sic] and served until the end of August,
after which he volunteered under Captain Thomas Wasson, 2d Albany County Militia, and served with the
Northern Army until after the surrender of Burgoyne.
In the spring of 1778 he enlisted as a batteauman and
served for nine months between Albany and New York.
Subsequent to 1778 he served with the militia on various
expeditions. A pensioner.

KINGSLEY, JOSEPH: On February 8, 1776, he stated to
the Committee of Safety under examination that "he
differed with them in sentiments in regard to the present
dispute between Great Britain and the Colonies." He
was ordered committed to the Albany jail to await trial
at the next general meeting of the Committee. He returned to Schenectady on his release and on April 27 was
summoned and ordered to pay twenty shillings, the
amount expended in connection with his imprisonment,
for a sled and two minute men to carry him to Albany. On
his refusal to pay he was given the choice of so doing or of
again being confined in the Albany jail. On May 1 the
chairman reported the account paid.

KINSELA, JOSEPH: Born at Lisburn, Ireland, in 1749; died April 15, 1816. His name appears on the rolls of the 2d Albany County Militia, Land Bounty Rights.

KITTLE, ADAM: On December 28, 1776, he enlisted in Captain John A. Bradt's company of State Rangers. In 1778, he was enrolled in the 2d Albany County Militia under Captain Jesse Van Slyck. He died a little before October 7, 1781, and was said to have been killed in the war.

KITTLE, DANIEL: Baptized September 23, 1733. He was enrolled in Captain Jesse Van Slyck's company, 2d Albany County Militia. In 1777 he served with the Northern Army at Stillwater and Bemis Heights, and in 1778 with a company of batteaumen under Captain Cornelius Barhydt. In 1779 he performed garrison duty at Fort Plain and Fort Plank. He served as batteauman and on garrison duty on various occasions to the end of the war. His widow received a pension.

KITTLE, DAVID: His name appears on the rolls of the 2d Albany County Militia.

KITTLE, EZRA: His name appears on the rolls of the 2d Albany County Militia.

KITTLE, JOHN: His name appears on the rolls of the 2d Albany County Militia.

LAMBERT, JOHN: Born in 1753; died July 26, 1809. A schoolmaster. He lived on the east side of Church Street, about midway between Union and State Streets. On June 19, 1775, he enlisted under Captain Cornelius Van Dyck for the defense of Ticonderoga. He subsequently served as a private under Captain John Mynderse and as a private and sergeant under Captain Jellis J. Fonda, 2d Albany County Militia.

LANSING, ABRAHAM G.: His name appears on the rolls of the 2d Albany County Militia.

INDIVIDUAL RECORDS OF SERVICE 177

LANSING, ALEXANDER C.: Baptized September 8, 1751. On March 1, 1776, he signed an agreement with Philip Schuyler for service at Lake George and Ticonderoga.

LANSING, CORNELIUS: His name appears on the rolls of the 2d Albany County Militia.

LANSING, GERRIT G.: Baptized February 8, 1756. On November 7, 1775, he was elected a member of the second Committee of Safety. On March 4, 1776, he was appointed overseer of batteaumen at Lake George, and on March 5 was objected to by certain persons as being too young to serve, although the objection was not sustained by the Committee. On July 9, 1777, he gave the use of a wagon for the service. He served as a private under Captain Jellis J. Fonda, and as quartermaster in the 2d Albany County Militia.

LANSING, JOHN G.: On May 24, 1775, he was appointed with John Post keeper of three hundred and thirty-eight pounds of gunpowder purchased from Daniel Campbell. On June 23, 1775, he was appointed ensign in Captain Cornelius Van Dyck's company for the defense of Ticonderoga to fill the vacancy caused by the promotion of Cornelius Van Slyck. On July 10, 1775, he was recommended to the Provincial Congress to fill the position of first lieutenant in the recruiting service. On February 28, 1776, he was serving with the New York regiments in Canada with the rank of second lieutenant. On October 7, 1776, he was serving in Colonel John Nicholson's regiment with the rank of first lieutenant. In 1779 he was adjutant in the 3d Tryon County Militia under Colonel Frederick Visscher, serving in September or October of that year at Fort Plank and Stone Arabia.

LANSING, JOHN S.: Baptized March 17, 1745. On September 5, 1776, he enlisted in Captain John A. Bradt's company of State Rangers.

LARAWAY, ISAAC: Born in 1756; died June 3, 1828. He
served as a private in the 5th New York Line and in the
3d Albany County Militia. He received a pension of $96
per annum and after his death his widow was allowed $30
per annum.

LATTA, WILLIAM: On October 30, 1776, he enlisted in Captain John A. Bradt's company of State Rangers, being
discharged on January 23, 1777, as unfit for duty. His
name appears on the rolls of the 3d Albany County Militia.

LEWIS, HENRY: In 1778, he enlisted under Captain James
Rosekrans, 5th New York Line. He served nine months
after which he was discharged for "inability." A pensioner under the Act of March 18, 1818.

LEWIS, JOHN: His name appears on the rolls of the 2d
Albany County Militia.

LEWIS, WILLIAM: Baptized November 5, 1720. His name
appears on the rolls of the 2d Albany County Militia as
serving under Captain John Van Patten.

LIDDLE, ANDREW: A native of Ireland. He was living in
Schenectady when the war broke out. A blacksmith by
trade and evidently prosperous as he is said to have had
a home well furnished and apprentices to aid him in his
work. In July, 1777, he joined General Burgoyne's army
at Saratoga and served until its capitulation. While
attempting to join the British forces in Canada he was
taken prisoner and confined in the Albany jail. On May
2, 1778, he was released on his entering into "Recognizance for his good behaviour and Monthly appearance"
before any of the Commissioners of Conspiracies at Schenectady. All his property was confiscated "some plundered, some sold at vendue."

LIGHTHALL, ABRAHAM (ABRAHAM J. OR W.): Baptized
September 12, 1753. In 1776 he served in a company of
artificers under Captain Jacob Vrooman, and in 1777

two months in the Quartermaster's Department during the campaign against Burgoyne. In 1778 he was drafted for service in the Levies from Captain Jellis J. Fonda's company, 2d Albany County Militia, and served at the Schoharie Forts. In 1779 he was on duty at Fort Plank and Stone Arabia. His widow received a pension.

LIGHTHALL, GEORGE: His name appears on the rolls of the 2d Albany County Militia.

LIGHTHALL, JAMES N.: Born in 1758; died April 22, 1829. On June 14, 1775, he enlisted under Captain Cornelius Van Dyck and took part in the Canadian expedition. In November, when his term expired, he re-enlisted at Montreal under Captain Barent Ten Eyck. He went to Quebec and remained with the army in its retreat in May, 1776. On January 6, 1777, he enlisted in Captain John A. Bradt's company of State Rangers. He served but a short time and then enlisted for the war under Captain Aaron Austin, 3d New York Line. Upon the consolidation of the regiments he was attached to the company under Captain Cornelius T. Jansen, 1st New York Line, and in this company he served until his discharge on June 14, 1783. His discharge was signed by General Washington. A pensioner under the Act of March 18, 1818.

LIGHTHALL, JOHN: Died in Glenville, August 4, 1835. In the spring of 1776 he enlisted at Schenectady for seven months under Captain Gerrit S. Veeder, re-enlisting in January, 1777, at Saratoga for the war under Captain John Copp, 1st New York Line. He remained in this company until July 14, 1779, when Copp resigned and was then transferred to the company of Captain Charles Parsons in the same regiment. He was discharged on June 8, 1783, and "honored with the badge of merit for seven years faithful service." A pensioner under the Act of March 18, 1818.

LIGHTHALL, LANCASTER: Born May 10, 1761. On January 22, 1777, he enlisted in Captain John A. Bradt's company of State Rangers. His name appears on the rolls of the 5th Company, 3d New York Line. On April 7, 1777, he enlisted for the war and served to the end, being promoted in July, 1779, to the rank of corporal.

LIGHTHALL, NICHOLAS: Born at German Flats, August 17, 1750; died January 27, 1838. Buried in Vale Cemetery. In the spring of 1776 he enlisted at Albany for nine months under Captain John Hunn. He served in the Quartermaster's Department, transporting ammunition and provisions to Ticonderoga and other posts. At the expiration of his term he removed to German Flats and enlisted under Captain Frederick Frank, 4th Tryon County Militia. In August, 1777, he fought at the battle of Oriskany. He was on active duty at Fort Herkimer until November, 1780, when he removed to Schenectady and enrolled in Captain John Van Patten's company, 2d Albany County Militia. In October, 1781, he performed three weeks' guard duty at Teunis Swart's Fort and served with the militia in the pursuit of Major Ross and Walter Butler. A pensioner under the Act of June 7, 1832.

LIGHTHALL, WILLIAM: Died October 5, 1822. On June 12, 1776, he enlisted in a company of New York State Rangers under Captain John A. Bradt. On March 7, 1776, he re-enlisted and was attached to Captain Giles Wolcott's company, Colonel Seth Warner's regiment. He remained in this company as sergeant until November 14, 1778, when he was promoted to the rank of ensign and commissioned. Under General Stark he "was highly distinguished for his bravery in the battle of Bennington." (Sanders.) In 1779 he was promoted to the rank of lieutenant. He remained in active service until October, 1780, when at Fort George, N. Y., he was captured and taken

to Canada. Here he remained a prisoner of war until
November, 1782, when he was paroled and permitted to
return home until exchanged. He remained on parole
until the army was disbanded in 1783. A pensioner under
the Act of March 18, 1818.

LITTLE, DAVID: His name appears on the rolls of the 2d
Albany County Militia.

LITTLE, JOHN: On June 20, 1778, he was appointed first
lieutenant in Captain Thomas Wasson's company, 2d
Albany County Militia.

LITTLE, THOMAS: His name appears on the rolls of the 2d
Albany County Militia as serving under Captain Thomas
Wasson.

LITTLEJOHN, DUNCAN: His name appears on the rolls of the
2d Albany County Militia.

LYNE, MATTHEW: On August 16, 1776, he enlisted in Captain John A. Bradt's company of State Rangers. From
December 16, 1776, to January 15, 1777, he was at Fort
Constitution.

LYPORT, DAVID: His name appears on the rolls of the 2d
Albany County Militia, Land Bounty Rights.

LYPORT, JACOB: Born in Glenville in 1759. He was enrolled
in Captain Abraham Van Eps's company, 2d Albany
County Militia, during the whole of the war. In 1776 he
went on an expedition to Clifton Park and Ballston in
pursuit of Joseph Bettis. From May to September, 1777
(when he returned home on account of sickness), he served
with the Northern Army. From August to the latter part
of November, 1779, he was on duty at the Upper Fort,
Schoharie. Regarding this service one Van Patten affirms
that "Lyport was a faithful soldier and did duty barefooted late in the fall." In the fall of 1780 he performed
two months' service at Fort Paris until discharged in
December. A pensioner under the Act of June 7, 1832.

McBeen, John: His name appears on the rolls of the 2d Albany County Militia.

McCallum, James: His name appears on the rolls of the 2d Albany County Militia.

McCarty, John: His name appears on the rolls of the 2d Albany County Militia.

McCarty, William: His name appears on the rolls of the 2d Albany County Militia.

McCue, James: From March 1, 1777, to January 1, 1778, he served in a company of batteaumen under Captain Myndert R. Wemple at Fort Dayton, Fort Stanwix and on the Mohawk River. In 1778, he served about a fortnight under Captain John Van Patten when Cobleskill was attacked, and in 1780 was on duty when the Mohawk settlements were destroyed. His widow received a pension.

McDonald, James: Born in 1737; died in 1818. He is buried in a private cemetery on the old McDonald farm (now owned by George McClain) in Princetown. In 1781 he was a member of Captain John Crousehorn's company of artillery.

McDougal, Duncan: His name appears on the rolls of the 2d Albany County Militia.

McDougal, John: He enlisted under Captain Robert McKean, 1st New York Line, and was later transferred to a company under a Captain Van Rensselaer. He was in the retreat from Ticonderoga, at the siege of Fort Stanwix, with the main army at Valley Forge, at White Plains and in the battle of Monmouth. From 1779 until his discharge in 1780 he served as a corporal. A pensioner under the Act of March 18, 1818.

McFarlan, Andrew: Born in 1733; died July 17, 1805. Buried in Vale Cemetery. A merchant in Schenectady as early as 1767. He resided on the west corner of Church and Water Streets. On April 22, 1776, he was granted a certificate of character in order to obtain a passport. On June 2, 1777, he was a member of the Committee of Safety, and on September 5 was elected chairman of the Board, being replaced on November 1, as it was stated that he was going abroad. On January 5, 1778, he was again elected chairman of the Committee of Safety. On July 2, 1779, he was appointed one of a committee of four to sell salt to the people of the district. His name appears on the rolls of the 2d Albany County Militia.

McFARLIN, JOHN: His name appears on the rolls of the 2d Albany County Militia.

McGINNIS, ROBERT: His name appears on the rolls of the 2d Albany County Militia.

McINTOSH, JOHN: He served as a sergeant in the New York Militia. A pensioner under the Act of June 7, 1832.

McINTYRE, WILLIAM: In 1774, he was a trader located at the corner of State and Ferry Streets. His name appears on the rolls of the 2d Albany County Militia as serving under Captain Thomas Brower Banker.

McKELLOP, ARCHIBALD: A farmer. On August 11, 1778, while a prisoner in the City Hall at Albany he was ordered removed to the fort by the Commissioners of Conspiracies because of sickness. On September 7 he was released on bail, the charges against him being but trivial. On January 5, 1781, it was reported to the Board by the Commissioners at Schenectady that he had refused to do military duty and that he was adjudged a dangerous person. On January 12 he appeared before the Board and denied the charges against him, whereupon he was released, having given bond for his good behavior during the remainder of the war.

McKINNEY, ANDREW: Born in Ireland in 1750; died November 12, 1825. Buried in the churchyard of the Cobblestone

Church in Rotterdam. He served as a private in the Pennsylvania Line. A pensioner under the Act of March 18, 1818.

McMARTIN, WILLIAM: His name appears on the rolls of the 2d Albany County Militia.

McMICHAEL, ALEXANDER: Born in 1758; died in 1818. Buried on the old Valk farm in the town of Princetown. In May, 1779, he was on duty at Schoharie as a sergeant under Captain John Mynderse, 2d Albany County Militia. In 1781 he was a member of Captain John Crousehorn's company of artillery.

McMICHAEL, DANIEL: Born near Albany, December 15, 1758. In the spring of 1775 he entered service from the township of Schenectady under Captain Abraham Oothout, 2d Albany County Militia. Shortly afterwards he was selected by Major Wemple as his servant and remained in that capacity for a period of two years. In the fall of 1777, previous to Burgoyne's surrender, he served two weeks at Fort Edward, and in the spring of 1778 at Fort Plank. He later enrolled under Captain Jesse Van Slyck, was appointed orderly sergeant and so served to the end of the war. In the fall of 1779 he served at Fort Hunter and Fort Plain, and in 1780 served as a volunteer in a company of Rangers in pursuit of Sir John Johnson after the destruction of the Mohawk settlements. He volunteered under Captain Jellis J. Fonda when Ballston was burned, and on his return to Schenectady was ordered to Fort Herkimer. In October, 1781, he marched with the troops under Colonel Willett in pursuit of Major Ross and Butler. He served in many expeditions and once had charge of the ammunition and one of the redoubts at Fort Plank. In the fall of 1782 he went with scouts under Abraham Van Eps in pursuit of Joseph Bettis. A pensioner.

McMICHAEL, JAMES: On March 1, 1776, he signed an agreement with Philip Schuyler for service at Lake George and Ticonderoga. His name appears on the rolls of the 2d Albany County Militia as enrolled under Captain John Mynderse.

McMICHAEL, ROBERT: He is mentioned on the State Treasurer's pay book as having served as a lieutenant.

McNUTT, SAMUEL: His name appears on the rolls of the 2d Albany County Militia.

McQUEEN, JAMES: His name appears on the rolls of the 2d Albany County Militia.

MABB, JOHN: He enlisted early in the war under Lieutenant-Colonel Christopher C. Yates. In 1779 he served under Captain Thomas Hicks, 12th Albany County Militia, and in 1780 under Captain Lawrence Gross, Colonel Marinus Willett's Levies, to which regiment he was also attached during the summer of 1781. His widow received a pension.

MABB, ROBERT: His name appears on the rolls of the 2d Albany County Militia.

MAIN, WILLIAM: His name appears on the rolls of the 2d Albany County Militia as serving under Captain John Mynderse.

MANNING, EDWARD: His name appears on the rolls of the 2d Albany County Militia.

MANNING, JOHN: Of Princetown. His name appears on the rolls of the 2d Albany County Militia.

MARKLE, DIRK: His name appears on the rolls of the 2d Albany County Militia.

MARKLE, MATTHEW: His name appears on the rolls of the 2d Albany County Militia as serving under Captain John Van Patten.

MARKLE, WILLIAM: His name appears on the rolls of the 2d Albany County Militia as serving under Captain John Van Patten.

MARSELIS, AHASUERAS: Baptized April 12, 1740. On February 10, 1776, he was elected captain of one of the newly organized militia companies although he probably did not serve actively as such. On March 4 he was appointed overseer of batteaumen for service at Lake George and Ticonderoga. In the fall of 1779 he commanded a detachment (probably of fatigue men) to Fort Hunter and other places along the Mohawk. In 1781 he was a member of Captain John Crousehorn's company of artillery.

MARSELIS, ALEXANDER: Born September 20, 1747. His name appears on the rolls of the 2d Albany County Militia as serving under Captain John Mynderse.

MARSELIS, ARENT: Baptized November 26, 1732. On March 30, 1776, he complained to the Committee of Safety that the poll kept on February 10 by Abraham Wemple at the Widow Vrooman's for the choosing of officers was irregular. His name appears on the rolls of the 2d Albany County Militia.

MARSELIS, GYSBERT: His name appears on the rolls of the 2d Albany County Militia and the 2d Albany County Militia, Land Bounty Rights.

MARSELIS, HENRY A.: Born May 25, 1753; died August 12, 1821. On May 13, 1776, General Schuyler was requested by the Committee of Safety to send him back from Lake George because he had not signed the General Association. From April 21 to 28, 1778, he was in command of four whites and four Indians on an expedition to Harpersfield for scout duty. In October he performed the same duty at Cobleskill. In April, 1780, he went on scout duty to Glens Falls and Lake George, and in June was in command of a detail of thirty-six whites and seven

Indians on an expedition to Beaverdam and Harpersfield. In July and August he served under Captain Jesse Van Slyck in pursuit of Sir John Johnson. In July, 1781, he is spoken of as a lieutenant on garrison duty at Fort Hunter. In June, 1782, he was again on garrison duty at Fort Hunter.

MARSELIS, JOHN BAPTIST: On February 10, 1776, he was elected first lieutenant in Captain Thomas Brower Banker's company, 2d Albany County Militia. He served in this capacity until August, when he was transferred as first lieutenant to a company of State Rangers under Captain John A. Bradt.

MARSELIS, JOHN J.: He enlisted at Schenectady for three years under Captain David Van Ness, 1st New York Line. He remained on duty at Schenectady until detailed to accompany a drove of cattle to Fort Stanwix. He was in the fort during the attack by St. Leger and remained there until his time of enlistment had expired. At the solicitation of his captain and other officers he was induced to re-enlist for the war and was given a commission as ensign in his company. He remained in the service until the end of the war.

MARSELIS, JOHN N.: Born January 27, 1760; died December 15, 1833. Buried in Vale Cemetery. He lived on Ferry Street opposite St. George's Church. On March 1, 1776, he signed an agreement with Philip Schuyler for service at Lake George and Ticonderoga. In 1777 he was enrolled in Captain Jesse Van Slyck's company, 2d Albany County Militia. He served to the end of the war. He was with the Northern Army in the campaign against Burgoyne; at various times at the Upper Fort, Schoharie, Fort Herkimer, Fort Plank, Fort Plain and Fort Clyde; and in 1778 at Saratoga in a company under Lieutenant-Colonel Christopher Yates. In October, 1780, he marched to Ballston in pursuit of the enemy after the raid, and in

1781 to Canajoharie when Major Ross descended on the Mohawk settlements. A pensioner under the Act of June 7, 1832.

MARSELIS, RICHARD: His name appears on the rolls of the 2d Albany County Militia, Land Bounty Rights.

MARTIN, CHARLES: Buried January 30, 1818. A merchant. On April 22, 1776, he was granted a certificate from the Commitee of Safety that he might obtain a passport from General Schuyler. It was stated at that time that "he appeared a true friend to the American cause, although he had not signed the General Association." His name appears on the rolls of the 2d Albany County Militia as enrolled under Captain John Mynderse.

MARTIN, JOHN: On August 2, 1777, he was taken prisoner by a band of Seneca Indians and carried to the Seneca country. He escaped but was later recaptured by a party of Rangers in the British service and taken to Quebec by way of Niagara and Montreal. Here he remained a prisoner from December 17, 1777, until May 27 of the following year, when he embarked on board the ship Maria for Halifax, whence he was sent by a flag ship to Boston.

MARTIN, ROBERT: Baptized December 2, 1758. On May 31, 1775, the Committee of Safety arranged that part of the men of Captain Cornelius Van Dyck's company be quartered at his house while the company was being recruited and drilled.

MEAD, WILLIAM: Died February 1, 1829. He served as a surgeon in the 1st New York Line from November 21, 1776, to October 13, 1779, when he was obliged to resign from the service because he had expended a greater part of his property and his pay had depreciated to such an extent that he was unable longer to adequately provide for his family. He was at the battle of Monmouth. He moved to Schenectady soon after his resignation from the service. A pensioner under the Act of March 18, 1818.

INDIVIDUAL RECORDS OF SERVICE 189

MEAL, CAREL: His name appears on the rolls of the 2d Albany County Militia.

MEBIE, ALBERT: Baptized May 14, 1738; died previous to 1799. On November, 7, 1775, he was elected a member of the second Committee of Safety. He served also on the third Committee and on the Boards taking office June 2, 1777, and January 5, 1778. On April 1, 1777, he was elected fence viewer, and on August 11 was serving as captain of the town guard. On June 24, 1779, he was again elected a member of the Committee of Safety. His name appears on the rolls of the 2d Albany County Militia.

MEBIE, ARENT: Baptized in 1729. His name appears on the rolls of the 2d Albany County Militia as serving under Captain John Van Patten.

MEBIE, CORNELIUS: Born March 18, 1741; died May 10, 1789. On October 20, 1775, he was commissioned first lieutenant in Captain John Van Patten's company, 2d Albany County Militia. His name does not appear on the roster of regimental officers, June 20, 1778 (Archives, State of New York), although John Van Eps (Pension Office Records W 27862) states that Mebie was serving as a lieutenant under Captain Van Patten in the fall of 1779.

MEBIE, JOHN: His name appears on the rolls of the 2d Albany County Militia.

MEBIE, JUITER: His name appears on the rolls of the 2d Albany County Militia.

MEBIE, PATRICK: His name appears on the rolls of the 2d Albany County Militia.

MEBIE, PETER: Baptized November 14, 1742; died before 1782. In 1780 he was living at the junction of the Schoharie Creek and the Mohawk River, but removed his family to Rotterdam to avoid the incursions of the Indians. He served with the troops under Colonel Marinus Willett against Major Ross and Walter Butler in 1781. His name appears on the rolls of the 2d Albany County Militia.

MERCER, ALEXANDER: Born in 1732; died January 18, 1798. His name appears on the rolls of the 2d Albany County Militia as serving under Captain Jesse Van Slyck.

MERCKER, WILLIAM: His name appears on the rolls of the 2d Albany County Militia.

MILS, CHRIS: His name appears on the rolls of the 2d Albany County Militia.

MITCHELL, HUGH: Born in 1741; died February 21, 1784. On May 6, 1775, he was chosen a member of the first Committee of Safety and on the ninth was elected clerk of the Board. On May 10 he was appointed a deputy for the election of delegates to the first Provincial Congress, and on June 27 appointed to attend the council with the Indians at German Flats. On November 7 he was elected clerk of the second Committee of Safety. He served also on the Committees taking office June 2, 1777, and January 5, 1778. On December 18, 1775, he was ordered to hold in trust £73 N. Y. C. raised for the relief of the poor of Boston until it could be transferred to Boston, and on May 25, 1776, he was appointed to receive the amount due for sleds, etc., employed in the expedition to Johnstown and to pay it out where due. On May 27 he was appointed caretaker of the papers of the Committee. On December 19, 1777, he was appointed to purchase a quantity of salt in certain states not to exceed six hundred bushels, to be paid for in flour or money. On April 4, 1778, he was appointed one of the Commissioners of Conspiracies and as such served until March 8, 1781. His name appears on the rolls of the 2d Albany County Militia.

MOORE, JOHN: Born in 1751; died April 7, 1821. He kept an inn at the corner of Liberty and Ferry Streets. In June, 1777, he enlisted at Schenectady in Captain Leonard

Bleeker's company, 3d New York Line. He was afterwards transferred to the 1st New York, under Colonel Goose Van Schaick. He was in Fort Stanwix when it was besieged by St. Leger and was at the capture of Lord Cornwallis at Yorktown. He served until June, 1783, when he was honorably discharged by General Washington. A pensioner.

MOORE, WILLIAM: In the spring of 1775 he was appointed an ensign in Captain Thomas Wasson's company, 2d Albany County Militia. On August 5, 1777, he informed the Committee against one John Gregg who had drunk the health of King George the Third at Bradt's Tavern. On February 25, 1780, he was commissioned second lieutenant in Captain Wasson's company, and on April 27, 1781, was serving as a lieutenant in the Levies under Colonel Marinus Willett.

MORREL, THOMAS: A merchant. On August 10, 1777, it was reported to the Committee of Safety that he was harboring a band of Tories. His name appears on the rolls of the 2d Albany County Militia as enrolled under Captain Thomas Brower Banker.

MOYSTON, ROBERT: Born April 24, 1745; died August 3, 1798. His name appears on the rolls of the 2d Albany County Militia, and the 2d Albany County Militia, Land Bounty Rights.

MULLER, JACOB JR.: His name appears on the rolls of the 2d Albany County Militia.

MUNRO, JOHN: He was a merchant in Schenectady for some time after 1760, but previous to the Revolution moved to Albany. On May 24, 1776, the Committee of Safety at Schenectady was ordered by Colonel Dayton to apprehend and treat him as a common enemy to the liberty of America. On the next day he was summoned before the Board and sent to Albany under guard for confinement in the Albany

192 HISTORY OF SCHENECTADY

jail. This is the Major Munro who led the attack on the settlement of Ballston in October, 1780.

MUNROE, ALEXANDER: Born in 1743; died April 21, 1823. On August 31, 1776, he enlisted in Captain John A. Bradt's company of State Rangers. On March 12, 1777, he enlisted for three years and was assigned to the 8th Company, 3d New York Line. A pensioner under the Act of March 18, 1818.

MURRAY, ALEXANDER: He served in the Levies under Colonel Marinus Willett. A pensioner under the Act of June 7, 1832.

MURRAY, JOHN: Baptized April 5, 1752. His name appears on the rolls of the 2d Albany County Militia as serving under Captain Thomas Wasson and on the rolls of the 2d Albany County Militia, Land Bounty Rights.

MURRAY, WILLIAM: In 1775 he enlisted under Captain Cornelius Van Dyck. He served under General Montgomery at St. John's, Chamblee and Montreal. In the spring of 1777 he enlisted for the war under Captain Robert McKean. He served until June 8, 1783, when he was discharged. He was in the battle of Monmouth and was at Yorktown at the surrender of Lord Cornwallis. A pensioner.

MYNDERSE, HARMEN: Baptized July 2, 1749. His name appears on the rolls of the 2d Albany County Militia.

MYNDERSE, JOHN: Born October 18, 1741; died October 29, 1815. On May 27, 1775, he was elected first lieutenant in Captain Cornelius Van Dyck's company. On October 20 he was commissioned captain of militia by the Provincial Congress, and assigned to the command of a company of minute men (an intermediate corps between the regular troops and the militia). This company came to be known as "The Blues" because of the color of the uniforms, and its motto, painted on the colors, was "Liberty or Death." On January 14, 1776, he went to Albany with sixty minute men under his command, and from there went with the troops on the expedition to Johnstown. From September, 1777, he served with the Northern Army until the surrender of General Burgoyne. In 1778 he was attached with his company to the brigade of Colonel Frederick Visscher. On June 20, 1778, he was recommissioned captain, and in August was stationed with his company at Fort Paris. In May, 1779, he was at Schoharie, and in the fall commanded an expedition to Beaverdam. In the fall of 1780 he marched with the troops under General Van Rensselaer against Sir John Johnson. In March, 1782, he commanded the guard at Fort Volunteer, Schenectady.

MYNDERSE, JOHN R.: Baptized December 25, 1743; died September 6, 1819. His name appears on the rolls of the 2d Albany County Militia.

MYNDERSE, LAWRENCE: Born October 12, 1751; died August 7, 1789. Buried in Vale Cemetery. On October 20, 1775, he was commissioned ensign in Captain John Mynderse's company, 2d Albany County Militia. On June 20, 1778, he was commissioned first lieutenant, but declined to serve.

MYNDERSE, REINIER: Born October 6, 1710; died August 6, 1788. A merchant. In 1781 he lived on the west corner of State Street and Mill Lane. On May 6, 1775, he was elected a member of the first Committee of Safety, and on August 9 was appointed chairman of the Board to fill the vacancy caused by the resignation of Christopher Yates. On November 7 he was elected chairman of the second Committee of Safety and served until December 29, when he was replaced by Dirk Van Ingen. On June 2, 1777, he was again elected chairman of the Board and served as such until September 5, when he was replaced probably because of his duties in attending the Senate and Assembly at Kingston. From 1777 to 1781 he served as a state senator under the first constitution. On November 1, 1777, he was again appointed chairman of the Committee of Safety and served also as a member of the Board taking office January 5, 1778. On July 1, 1780, he was appointed one of the Commissioners of Conspiracies.

NEALLY, MATTHEW: He served as a private and fifer under Captain Thomas Wasson, 2d Albany County Militia.

NEARD, CHRISTOPHER: His name appears on the rolls of the 2d Albany County Militia.

NEIGER, JOHN: His name appears on the rolls of the 2d Albany County Militia.

NESBIT, JOSEPH: On October 3, 1776, he enlisted for the war and was assigned to the 8th Company, 1st New York Line. In October, 1777, he was serving as a corporal and in June, 1778, as a private. He received land bounty rights.

NESTLE, GEORGE: He served as a private under Captain Simeon Newell, Colonel Marinus Willett's New York Levies. He was shot through the body (engagement and date not known), but not killed.

NIXON, JOSHUA: Baptized November 22, 1761. His name appears on the rolls of the 2d Albany County Militia.

OGDEN, JOHN: Buried August 23, 1801. His name appears on the rolls of the 2d Albany County Militia.

OHLEN, HENRY GEORGE: Born in London, September 16, 1758; died October 1, 1837. Buried in Vale Cemetery. He enlisted January 14, 1777, and was assigned to the 6th Company, 3d New York Line. He was promoted to the rank of sergeant on April 21, 1779. A pensioner under the Act of May 15, 1828.

OOTHOUT, ABRAHAM: Born May 27, 1744; died in July, 1822. On May 6, 1775, he was elected a member of the first Committee of Safety. He served also on the second

Committee and the Committees taking office January 15, 1777, June 2, 1777 and January 5, 1778. He was a deputy from Albany County to the first Provincial Congress. He served throughout the war as a captain in the 2d Albany County Militia, being appointed soon after January 26, 1776. On June 27, 1775, he was appointed to attend the council with the Indians at German Flats, and on February 24, 1776, he was appointed with Christopher Yates to collect donations from the inhabitants to pay for sleds to transport the troops from Albany to Lake George. In the fall he was in command of a detail to Fort Ann, Fort Edward and Skenesborough. On April 24, 1777, he was detailed as a wagoner for duty from Albany to Lake George. On May 21 he was a member of a court martial at Albany. He served with the troops against General Burgoyne at Saratoga, Stillwater and Bemis Heights. On December 20, 1777, he was appointed with Abraham Fonda to purchase two hundred pounds of flour to barter for salt. On June 20, 1778, he was regularly commissioned captain, and in the summer commanded a detachment to Stone Arabia. On June 24, 1779, he was again appointed a member of the Committee of Safety, and on June 2 was appointed chairman of the Board, which office he resigned on July 8, because of the pressure of public business. On July 1, 1780, he was appointed one of the Commissioners of Conspiracies. In August he marched with the troops to Fort Plain after the destruction of Canajoharie, and in the fall of 1781 was stationed at Fort Hunter. After the battle of Johnstown he marched in pursuit of the enemy. Towards the end of the war he was promoted to the rank of colonel in the 2d Albany County Militia to succeed Colonel Wemple, resigned.

OUDERKIRK, ARENT: Baptized July 9, 1737. His name appears on the rolls of the 2d Albany County Militia.

OUDERKIRK, JOHN: In February, 1776, he enlisted at Schenectady for one year in a company of fatigue and batteaumen under Captain John Clute, but was discharged after ten months' duty. In 1777 he again enlisted under Captain Clute at Schenectady and served nine or ten months. In 1779 he enlisted at Schenectady as a boatman under Captain Peter Adair. Adair was later discharged from the service at Fishkill and Ouderkirk there enlisted under Captain John Denny as a fatigue man, boatman and laborer. He served in this capacity and also as a baker and washer for a period of ten or eleven months. A pensioner under the Act of June 7, 1832.

PASSAGE, GEORGE: Born in Philadelphia May 12, 1761. He lived at the Norman's Kill. In the spring of 1778, he enlisted in Captain Abraham Oothout's company, 2d Albany County Militia, and shortly after was ordered to Beaverdam. While the company was on parade and Colonel Wemple was reading the orders, Passage received a kick from the horse of one of the field officers which broke two of his ribs and rendered him unfit for military duty until the following spring. In the fall of 1779 he was drafted into Captain Walter Vrooman's company of Levies and performed four weeks' garrison duty at Schoharie. In the fall of 1780 he marched with the troops to Ballston when it was attacked. In the year 1781 he served one month at Fort Hunter. He often served on guard duty at Schenectady. His claim for pension was rejected on the ground of insufficient service.

PASSAGE, GEORGE, JR.: Born in 1763; died in 1840. Buried in the cemetery of the Reformed Church at Giffords. His name appears on the rolls of the 2d Albany County Militia.

PATTERSON, OLIVER: Of Princetown. His name appears on the rolls of the 2d Albany County Militia.

PATTERSON, THOMAS: During the year 1778, he served as a batteauman and carpenter under Captain Cornelius Barhydt both on the Mohawk and Hudson Rivers. In

1779 treasury certificates were issued to Patterson covering three periods; the first and second, August and October for service under Captain Thomas Wasson, and the third dated November 30 for service under Captain Jellis Fonda. His widow received a pension.

PEEK, ARENT: Baptized December 25, 1743. His name appears on the rolls of the 2d Albany County Militia as serving under Captain John Van Patten.

PEEK, CHRISTOPHER: On March 1, 1776, he accepted a commission as ensign from the Provincial Congress through the Committee of Safety at Schenectady. He, however, later tendered his resignation to the Committee because of his father's displeasure at his having accepted it. This resignation was accepted on March 11, 1777. He later served as a lieutenant and quartermaster in the 2d Albany County Militia, and in 1778 received a commission as quartermaster and served as such until 1782, when he was appointed ensign in the New York Levies under Colonel Marinus Willett. This position he held until the end of the war.

PEEK, CORNELIUS: Born December 1, 1729; died August 22, 1802. Buried in Vale Cemetery. On May 8, 1776, complaint was made to the Committee of Safety that he was working as a carpenter at Lake George without having signed the General Association. His name appears on the rolls of the 2d Albany County Militia. In 1778 he was enrolled under Captain Jesse Van Slyck.

PEEK, CORNELIUS, JR.: Born August 21, 1763. In 1778 he was enrolled under Captain Jesse Van Slyck, 2d Albany County Militia. In August, 1782, he was on garrison duty at the Upper Fort, Schoharie, and in September on scout duty at Sacandaga.

PEEK, DANIEL: Baptized June 30, 1745. His name appears on the rolls of the 2d Albany County Militia as serving under Captain John Van Patten.

PEEK, HARMANUS: Baptized January 14, 1759. His name appears on the rolls of the 2d Albany County Militia, Land Bounty Rights.

PEEK, HENRY H.: Born in Schenectady, April 18, 1764. In the spring of 1776 he went with a detachment to the Heldebergh. In the fall of 1779 he volunteered under Captain John Mynderse, 2d Albany County Militia, for service at Beaverdam and on his return to Schenectady mounted guard under John J. Vrooman. In the spring of 1780 he regularly enrolled in the company of Captain John Mynderse, and in the fall of the same year marched with the troops under General Van Rensselaer. He served at this time one month at Fort Plain and from there marched to Fort Plank, where he assisted in burying the dead after the battle. In October, 1781, he marched with the troops to Johnstown and was with the detachment that pursued Walter Butler to the West Canada Creek. A pensioner under the Act of June 7, 1832.

PEEK, JACOBUS C.: Baptized November 10, 1752. His name appears on the rolls of the 2d Albany County Militia, Land Bounty Rights.

PEEK, JACOBUS VEDDER: Baptized January 29, 1764. His name appears on the rolls of the 2d Albany County Militia.

PEEK, JAMES: He served as a sergeant under Captain Jesse Van Slyck, 2d Albany County Militia.

PEEK, JAMES H. (OR JACOBUS): Born in Schenectady, August 16, 1758; died September 23, 1835. Buried in Vale Cemetery. In the fall of 1775 he was enrolled as a second lieutenant in the company of Captain John Mynderse, 2d Albany County Militia. In January, 1776, he took part in the expedition to Johnstown, and in the spring of the same year went to Sacandaga under General Clinton to erect fortifications. In July, 1777, he marched with his company to Fort Edward. He served during Schuyler's retreat, engaging in most of the skirmishes

during the campaign and in the battles of Snookkill and
Bemis Heights. On June 20, 1778, a commission as second
lieutenant was assigned to him by Governor Clinton.
During the years 1778 and 1779 he performed various
garrison and scout duties, and on August 16, 1780, re-
ceived a commission as lieutenant in the State Levies,
being assigned to the company of Captain Benjamin
Dubois, Colonel Lewis Dubois's regiment. He served three
months and two weeks in the Levies, doing duty at Fort
Herkimer (where he was in command for five weeks),
Albany, West Point, Tappan and other posts. After this
service he again entered the company of Captain John
Mynderse. He often served as captain of the guard at
Schenectady. A pensioner under the Act of June 7, 1832.

PEEK, JESSE: Born January 28, 1752; died June 3, 1810.
Buried in Vale Cemetery. On March 1, 1776, he signed
an agreement with Philip Schuyler for service at Lake
George and Ticonderoga. His name appears on the rolls
of the 2d Albany County Militia as serving under Captain
Jellis J. Fonda and on the rolls of the 2d Albany County
Militia, Land Bounty Rights.

PEEK, JOHN: On October 5, 1775, he was recommended to
the Provincial Congress by the Committee of Safety for
the office of quartermaster among the field officers to be
assigned to the newly organized Schenectady companies,
and on October 20 a commission was issued in his name.
On December 9 he tendered his resignation to the Board.
On March 1, 1776, he signed an agreement with Philip
Schuyler for service at Lake George and Ticonderoga.
On May 7 he was elected a member of the third Committee
of Safety. His name appears on the rolls of the 2d Albany
County Militia.

PEEK, JOSEPH: Born in Schenectady, November 25, 1755;
died May 25, 1842. Buried in Vale Cemetery. In the
spring of 1775 he enlisted under Captain John Mynderse,

2d Albany County Militia. Soon after he went to Ticonderoga in another company where he was employed in erecting works of defense and in the construction of boats. In January, 1776, he took part in the expedition to Johnstown, and later in the spring enlisted in a company of artificers under Captain Teunis Bradt and served the whole season building boats for service on Lake Champlain. In April, 1777, he was drafted into Captain Jesse Van Slyck's company and subsequently made orderly sergeant. He marched to Jessup's Patent in pursuit of Tories, and in the summer of the same year to Fort Edward, performing service there, at Stillwater, Bemis Heights and other posts until the surrender of Burgoyne. In the spring of 1778 he again enlisted under Captain Teunis Bradt and performed seven months' service at Coeymans. In the winter of the same year he performed guard duty at Schenectady. During the winter of 1779 he was appointed a captain on the Continental Establishment and served to the end of the war in the Quartermaster's Department, having charge of the forwarding of supplies to the frontier posts. A pensioner under the Act of June 7, 1832.

PEEK, LEWIS D.: Born in Rotterdam, January 6, 1764. In 1779 he was enrolled as a private under Captain John Van Patten, 2d Albany County Militia. He was later made a corporal and served as such to the end of the war. His service seems to have been mostly patrol, guard and garrison duty, the latter at Schenectady. In 1780 he marched with the troops to Jessup's Patent to intercept Sir John Johnson after the Mohawk settlements were destroyed, and in October, 1781, he went with the troops to the West Canada Creek in pursuit of Walter Butler. A pensioner under the Act of June 7, 1832.

PENDLETON, SOLOMON: On October 20, 1775, he was commissioned second lieutenant in Captain John Mynderse's company, 2d Albany County Militia. On February 14, 1776, he was recommended for the office of first lieutenant in a company to be formed under Captain John A. Bradt. He received his commission on March 1, and on April 12 applied to the Committee for leave to resign, giving as his reason that the men were mutinous and dissatisfied because Gerrit S. Veeder had been appointed their captain without awaiting the return of Bradt. On April 13 he delivered his commission to the Board, but was later induced to ask for its return. His request was granted but with an admonition regarding his future behavior. On October 6, 1777, while enrolled as first lieutenant in Captain Henry Godwin's company, Colonel Lewis Dubois's regiment, he was taken prisoner at Fort Montgomery. In 1778, during his imprisonment, he became mentally deranged. He was exchanged on February 8, 1781, but did not return to the army.

PETERS, HARMON: Born in Schenectady and lived here during the war. In 1832 he was a resident of Charlton. On December 22, 1777, he enrolled under Captain John Mynderse, 2d Albany County Militia. From January 10 to April 10, 1778, he performed guard duty in his regular turn at Schenectady. In the spring of 1779 he went on scout duty to Beaverdam, and in April of the same year he went to Fort Plain, where he served two months. In March, 1780, he volunteered under Captain Jesse Van Slyck, and served one month at Stone Arabia. In March, 1782, he volunteered under Walter Swits for guard duty at Fort Volunteer, Schenectady, and in the fall of the same year went on scout duty to Jessup's Patent with a detail of Oneida Indians in search of deserters from the American service.

PETERS, WILLIAM: On March 4, 1776, he was appointed overseer of batteaumen for service at Lake George and Ticonderoga. His appointment was objected to by certain persons because they considered him too young to serve. The objection was not sustained by the Committee of Safety. In 1778 he commanded a company of state troops engaged as batteaumen in transporting stores from Schenectady to Fort Stanwix. On June 29, 1781, he was appointed ensign in the 8th Company, 2d New York Line.

PETERSON, CHARLES: His name appears on the rolls of the 2d Albany County Militia.

PETERSON, HARMANUS: His name appears on the rolls of the 2d Albany County Militia, as serving under Captain Thomas Wasson.

PHILIPS, THOMAS: His name appears on the rolls of the 2d Albany County Militia.

PHYN, JAMES: Born March 12, 1742; died November 2, 1821. Buried in Vale Cemetery. A native of County Kent, England. He was in business in Schenectady as early as 1768. On April 24, 1776, it was stated by the Committee of Safety that he had resided for some time past in England. He was at that time in partnership with Alexander Ellice, who had also retired to England during the previous fall. The accounts of the firm were being collected by Robert Ellice.

POST, ELIAS: Baptized in New York, January 7, 1708. His name appears on the rolls of the 2d Albany County Militia, Land Bounty Rights.

POST, JOHN: Born January 1, 1749. On May 24, 1775, he was appointed with John G. Lansing keeper of three hundred and thirty-eight pounds of gunpowder purchased from Daniel Campbell. On January 13, 1776, he was appointed quartermaster of the 2d Albany County Militia, and on March 5 Henry Glen was instructed to apply to Congress for his commission. Some time in the fall of 1776 he was appointed commissary of issues for the New York Line, and in this position continued to the end of the war, serving at Herkimer, German Flats, Yorktown, Princeton, Monmouth and in General Sullivan's expedition against the Indians. His widow received a pension.

PUTMAN, ARENT J.: Born June 13, 1745; died August 1, 1830. Buried in the cemetery of the Cobblestone Church, Rotterdam. His name appears on the rolls of the 2d Albany County Militia. In 1778 he was enrolled under Captain Jesse Van Slyck.

PUTMAN, ARENT L.: Baptized July 10, 1751. His name appears on the rolls of the 2d Albany County Militia as serving under Captain Thomas Brower Banker.

PUTMAN, CORNELIUS: Baptized April 20, 1755. His name appears on the rolls of the 2d Albany County Militia.

PUTMAN, JOHN: His name appears on the rolls of the 2d Albany County Militia.

PUTMAN, TEUNIS: Baptized March 31, 1716. His name appears on the rolls of the 2d Albany County Militia, Land Bounty Rights.

PUTNAM, ARENT: He is said to have served two years in the militia and also as a butcher in the Commissary Department at Schenectady under Henry Glen. His daughter's claim for pension was rejected.

QUACKENBUSH, GERARDUS: Baptized March 11, 1721. On October 14, 1776, he was a member of Captain John A. Bradt's company of State Rangers. His name appears on the rolls of the 2d Albany County Militia.

QUACKENBUSH, JOHN: Born in Schenectady, August 19, 1750; died July 28, 1839. He lived at the junction of Lafayette and Liberty Streets. In the spring of 1775 he was enrolled under Captain Thomas Brower Banker, 2d Albany County Militia. About November 1, 1775, he was appointed a lieutenant in this company and as such served to the end of the war. His lieutenant's commission was not renewed by the Council of Appointment, but after the war he received that of a captain. He was spoken of as "always evincing the utmost alacrity, zeal and fidelity in the cause of his country." Most of his service in 1776 was that of guarding boats laden with stores from Fort Ann to Skenesborough. He marched on various alarms and was often on guard duty, especially at Schenectady, where he frequently had command of the guard. A pensioner under the Act of June 7, 1832.

RAMSEY, GEORGE: On September 25, 1775, it was reported to the Committee of Safety that he had spoken very disrespectfully of some of the members of the Board and that he was strongly suspected of being concerned in putting tar and feathers on several of their doors. On January 31, 1776, he appeared before the Committee to answer charges that he had made some reflections against the friends of the American cause in general and against one William Murray in particular, having called him "a traitor and a rebel." Ramsey admitted the truth of the accusations but said that he "only did it to put Murray in a passion as he knew he was of a quick temper." On February 12 it was decided by the Committee that he was a "high offender" against the American cause and he was ordered sent to the Albany jail to await trial. On his release Ramsey returned to Schenectady and on April 27 was summoned and ordered to pay the amount expended in connection with his imprisonment (sixteen shillings) for a sled and one minute man to carry him to Albany. This amount he promised to pay.

REIS, JOHN: His name appears on the rolls of the 2d Albany County Militia.

RIGHTER, MICHAEL: On November 22, 1777, he was reported as an enemy to the American cause. On December 1 he was arrested by order of the Committee of Safety and committed to the Albany jail.

ROBISON, JOHN: A merchant. Buried in the cemetery of the Presbyterian Church at Rynex Corners. His name appears on the rolls of the 2d Albany County Militia, Land Bounty Rights.

ROSA, ELIAS: Born in Ulster County, March 4, 1753. He was living in Schenectady in July, 1775, when he enlisted under Captain Jellis J. Fonda, 2d Albany County Militia. He served during the whole war as orderly sergeant in this company. In the summer of 1775 he was engaged in building boats and erecting fortifications at Ticonderoga. In the early fall he enlisted with the troops for Canadian service, marching to St. John's, and serving at the reduction of Chamblee, after which he returned to Fort Edward and remained there until the close of the year. In January, 1776, he took part in the expedition to Johnstown. From the latter part of May to the end of October, 1777, he was with the Northern Army, serving at Fort Edward and Fort Ann and in the battles of Fort Miller and Snookkill. In 1779 he performed garrison duty at Fort Plank and Stone Arabia, and in the fall of 1780 was on duty when Caughnawaga was destroyed. In October, 1781, he was at Fort Herkimer.

ROSA, ISAAC: On May 25, 1776, he promised a contribution for the poor of Boston. His name appears on the rolls of the 2d Albany County Militia.

ROSE, JOHN: In 1775 he enlisted for six months under Captain Cornelius Van Dyck. He was at the siege of St. John's. He volunteered under Ethan Allen and was taken prisoner on the Island of Montreal. He jumped overboard from the Gaspee, swam ashore and again joined the army under Montgomery. He was in the siege and at the storming of Quebec, where he was wounded in the arm. He subsequently enlisted under Captain Joseph McCracken, 1st New York Line, and remained with this company until the advance of Burgoyne, when he enlisted at Saratoga for the war under Captain John Copp, 1st New York Line. He served during the campaign against Burgoyne, and in 1778 took part in the battle of Monmouth, where he was wounded in the throat. In 1779 he marched with the expedition under General Sullivan against the Indians. In 1780 or 1781 he was transferred to Captain Aaron Austin's company, 3d New York Line. He was in the battle of Yorktown and there had his leg broken by a bombshell. He remained in the army until it was disbanded and received an honorable discharge at Snake Hill, Orange County, N. Y., in 1783. He received a sergeant's commission in 1778, and several times acted as a recruiting sergeant.

ROSEBOOM, JOHN: Born in Albany, October 23, 1739; died in Canajoharie, April 4, 1805. He moved from Schenectady some time previous to 1790. He is buried in the Prospect Hill cemetery, Canajoharie. A merchant. He lived on the northeast corner of Ferry and Union Streets. On May 6, 1775, he was elected a member of the first Committee of Safety. On May 24 he was appointed one of a committee to go to Guy Park to deliver an answer to a speech made by the Mohawk Indians, and on June 23 he was appointed to accompany the Rev. Samuel Kirkland and five Oneida Indians to Albany. In August, 1776, he was appointed first lieutenant in Captain Abraham Oothout's company, 2d Albany County Militia, but was not so commissioned until June 20, 1778. He served in the capacity of lieutenant until the end of the war. On January 15, 1777, he was a member of the Committee of Safety and on July 2, 1779, he was appointed one of a committee of four to sell salt to the people of the district. On July 26 he was again elected a member of the Committee of Safety. In 1780 he was on garrison duty at the Upper Fort, Schoharie.

RYKMAN, CORNELIUS: His name appears on the rolls of the 2d Albany County Militia as serving under Captain Jesse

Van Slyck. In 1781 he was a member of Captain John Crousehorn's company of artillery.

RYKMAN, JOHN: His name appears on the rolls of the 2d Albany County Militia, Land Bounty Rights.

RYLEY, JACOBUS: His name appears on the rolls of the 2d Albany County Militia.

RYLEY, JAMES VAN SLYCK: Born October 3, 1761; died January 8, 1848. In 1778 and 1779 he served under Lieutenant James H. Peek at Stone Arabia and elsewhere.

RYLEY, JOHN: Born April 3, 1757; died April 24, 1842. He served as a private under Captain John Clute in the Quartermaster's Department.

RYLEY, PHILIP: Born in New York, April 29, 1719, O. S. He served as a private and sergeant under Captain John Mynderse, 2d Albany County Militia.

RYLEY, WILLIAM: Born November 16, 1760; died March 19, 1848. He served under Captain Jacob Vrooman in the Quartermaster's Department.

RYNEX, ANDREW: He served as a sergeant under Captain Thomas Wasson, 2d Albany County Militia, and in the same capacity in the Levies under Colonel John Harper. On October 23, 1780, he was taken prisoner by the forces under Sir John Johnson and Joseph Brant and by them taken to Canada. He was exchanged the next year and was back in Schenectady on July 23, 1781. On December 26, 1780, at a meeting of St. George's Lodge of which he was a member it was resolved "that fifty shilling, hard money, out of the funds of the lodge be delivered for the use of Brother Andrew Rynex's family, he being taken captive."

RYNEX, JOHN: He served as a private and drummer under Captain Thomas Wasson, 2d Albany County Militia. His name appears also on the rolls of the 2d Albany County Militia, Land Bounty Rights.

RYNEX, RICHARD: His name appears on the rolls of the 2d Albany County Militia.

SACIA, DAVID: He was enrolled under Captain Abraham Oothout, 2d Albany County Militia. At various times he served as "an express rider" and on one occasion was taken prisoner by the Indians and carried to their camp. He made his escape on the following night and returned to the service. He was often on duty drawing wood to and from various posts. Once while returning from Lake George the Indians drove him from his regular crossing, and he had to swim the river with his horses and wagon. He was at the Upper Fort, Schoharie, when Timothy Murphy fired on the flag of truce sent forward by Sir John Johnson, in the engagement at Cobleskill and in pursuit of the enemy after the raid on Ballston. He performed various garrison and guard duties, being stationed from August to October, 1781, at Claas Viele's Rifts. His widow received a pension.

ST. JOHN, THADDEUS: On May 25, 1776, he promised a contribution for the poor of Boston. His name appears on the rolls of the 2d Albany County Militia and the 2d New York Line.

SANDERS, JOHN: Born in Albany, August 10, 1714; died September 13, 1782. He removed to Scotia immediately after his marriage to Deborah Glen on December 6, 1739. He lived in the Glen-Sanders house which Deborah inherited on the death of her father in 1762. In 1765, by the purchase of the other outstanding interests, John Sanders and his wife became owners of the entire Glen estate. On May 6, 1775, he was elected a member of the first Committee of Safety but immediately refused to serve. On July 30, 1777, he was ordered arrested and to appear before the State Committee for refusing to receive Continental currency in payment of a debt. His name appears on the rolls of the 2d Albany County Militia. In

INDIVIDUAL RECORDS OF SERVICE

the fall of 1780 he was in command of the guard at Schenectady.

SAWYER, JAMES: His name appears on the rolls of the 2d Albany County Militia.

SCHERMERHORN, AARON: From August to October, 1781, an Aaron Schermerhorn was on duty at Claas Viele's Fort under Sergeant William Teller of Captain Abraham Oothout's company, 2d Albany County Militia.

SCHERMERHORN, ABRAHAM: Baptized October 21, 1721; died in 1811. He lived near Haverly's in Glenville and died there. During the war he suffered much from the Indians and Tories, and was compelled to flee repeatedly from his home to Schenectady for safety. On one occasion a party led by Walter Butler came to Schermerhorn's house and after plundering it carried away two boys, one a German and the other a negro. The former of the boys was scalped but later recovered. Schermerhorn's name appears on the rolls of the 2d Albany County Militia, Land Bounty Rights.

SCHERMERHORN, ANDREW (ANDREAS): Born July 11, 1762; died in Rotterdam about 1815. His name appears on the rolls of the 2d Albany County Militia.

SCHERMERHORN, BARNHARDUS FREEMAN: Born October 14, 1739; died July 14, 1799. On June 20, 1778, he was commissioned ensign in Captain Thomas Brower Banker's company, 2d Albany County Militia. In September or October, 1779, he was on duty at Fort Plank and Stone Arabia.

SCHERMERHORN, BARTHOLOMEW: Baptized in Schenectady, August 24, 1757. He lived in Rotterdam and died July 16, 1845. In the fall of 1775 he was enrolled under Captain Abraham Oothout, 2d Albany County Militia. In the spring of 1776 he went to Fort Dayton, and in the fall of the same year with the regiment to Fort Edward, thence under Captain Jesse Van Slyck to Fort Ann and Skenesborough as a guard for boats plying between these posts.

He then returned to Fort Edward. In the spring of 1777, under Captain Jesse Van Slyck, he went with the troops of Colonel Warner to Jessup's Patent in pursuit of Tories. He was with the main army at Bemis Heights. In the spring of 1778 he marched to Schoharie and Cobleskill, where he assisted in burying the dead slain by the enemy. In February, 1779, he served in a company of fatigue men under Captain Joseph Peek. On July 23, 1780, he was sent a prisoner to Albany, accused of being apprehended on his way to the enemy or of supplying them with provisions; he was, however, on August 10 released on bail. In October, under Major Swits, he marched to Ballston when it was attacked. He performed considerable garrison and guard duty, especially at Fort Plain, Fort Clyde and at Claas Viele's Rifts. A pensioner under the Act of June 7, 1832.

SCHERMERHORN, GERRIT: Born in the Schenectady Township, October 22, 1763; died in Rotterdam, March 24, 1848. In the fall of 1779 he enrolled under Captain Abraham Oothout, 2d Albany County Militia, and served at Fort Hunter, Fort Plank, Stone Arabia and at the Middle Fort, Schoharie. In the spring of 1780 he marched to Caughnawaga when it was destroyed, and in October to Ballston after the raid. During that year he also performed six months' guard duty at Claas Viele's Rifts. In October, 1781, he went with the troops under Colonel Willett in pursuit of Major Ross and Butler. A pensioner under the Act of June 7, 1832.

SCHERMERHORN, HENRY J.: His name appears on the rolls of the 2d Albany County Militia.

SCHERMERHORN, JACOB: Born November 21, 1729; died April 18, 1814. He lived about six miles south of Schenectady, near the Norman's Kill, and is buried in Homer or East Homer, N. Y. On October 5, 1775, he was recommended to the Provincial Congress by the Committee of

Safety for the office of lieutenant-colonel in the 2d Albany
County Militia. On October 20 a commission was issued
in his name. In November he was elected a captain of
militia but declined to serve, and on January 23, 1776, he
also refused to accept the commission of lieutenant-colonel.
On July 28, 1778, he was appointed captain of a company
of Exempts formed in Schenectady, and as such served
during the years 1779 and 1780. On June 29, 1780, he is
mentioned in the records of the Commissioners of Conspiracies as "Major."

SCHERMERHORN, JACOB: His name appears on the rolls of
the 2d Albany County Militia. This might be Jacob, son
of Arent, baptized December 20, 1752; or Jacob, son of
William, baptized December 1, 1745.

SCHERMERHORN, JACOB J.: Baptized January 20, 1751. His
name appears on the rolls of the 2d Albany County Militia.

SCHERMERHORN, JACOBUS: Baptized January 31, 1720; died
July 28, 1782. His name appears on the rolls of the 2d
Albany County Militia, Land Bounty Rights.

SCHERMERHORN, JOHN J.: Born in Schenectady, January
23, 1764. In August, 1777, being too young to enroll in
the militia, he volunteered and served under Major Swits
on a scout to the Heldebergh. In 1778 he performed guard
duty at Claas Viele's Rifts, and in 1779, as a substitute
for his father, Jacob Schermerhorn, performed garrison
duty at Stone Arabia. In 1780 he performed garrison duty
on various occasions at the Schoharie Forts, Fort Plank
and Fort Herkimer, and took part in several scouting
expeditions. He was at Ballston when the town was
attacked.

SCHERMERHORN, LAWRENCE: Born in Schenectady, February 9, 1749; died in Rotterdam, March 26, 1837. In
1775 he was enrolled under Captain Jellis J. Fonda, 2d
Albany County Militia. In January, 1776, he took part

in the expedition to Johnstown and in the spring of the
same year served at Sacandaga erecting fortifications. In
1777 he served in the campaign against Burgoyne at Fort
Edward, Stillwater and other posts. From May to June,
1778, he was on duty when Cobleskill was destroyed, and
in the fall of the same year he enlisted in Captain Martin
Mynderse's company of artificers and served in it two
years. Just previous to this enlistment he served on draft
with a detail bringing military stores from Ticonderoga
to Albany. In the fall of 1781 he went with the troops
under Colonel Willett in pursuit of Major Ross and Butler. A pensioner under the Act of June 7, 1832.

SCHERMERHORN, MAUS: Born March 9, 1753; died January
26, 1830. Buried in Vale Cemetery. His name appears on
the rolls of the 2d Albany County Militia, Land Bounty
Rights. He received a land bounty in 1829.

SCHERMERHORN, NICHOLAS W.: Baptized in Schenectady,
September 21, 1760. He served as a sergeant under Captain Jesse Van Slyck, 2d Albany County Militia.

SCHERMERHORN, RICHARD: Born March 7, 1755. A laborer.
He was enrolled under Captain Jellis J. Fonda, 2d Albany
County Militia. About January 1, 1780, he enlisted as
a batteauman under Captain Joseph Peek in the Quartermaster's Department and served for one year. On July
23 he was ordered confined at Albany by the Commissioners of Conspiracies at Schenectady for being connected
with a party that intended to join the enemy. On August
9, having answered "in a candid and open manner" the
questions put to him under examination by the Board at
Albany, he was released on bail. His widow received a
pension.

SCHERMERHORN, RYER: His name appears on the rolls of
the 2d Albany County Militia as enrolled under Captain
John Van Patten. Through his marriage with the widow
of Gerrit Veeder the property around "Veeder's Mills"

later became known as the Schermerhorn "Mill farm." During the Revolution Ryer Schermerhorn built the stone house opposite the mill to be used as a fort in case of necessity. There was also a log house near the mill that was used as a place of refuge.

SCHERMERHORN, SIMON: Born January 3, 1723; died May 6, 1808. Buried in Vale Cemetery. He resided at the "Mills," located at the east end of State Street. His name appears on the rolls of the 2d Albany County Militia.

SCHERMERHORN, WILLIAM: Baptized November 10, 1722. On May 10, 1776, the Committee of Safety at Schenectady informed General Schuyler that he had gone to Lake George without the permission of the Board and that he had repeatedly refused to sign the General Association. On January 15, 1777, he was a member of the Committee of Safety. His name appears on the rolls of the 2d Albany County Militia, Land Bounty Rights.

SCHUYLER, REUBEN: He came to Schenectady in 1779 and lived here until 1781. He was enrolled under Captain Jellis J. Fonda, 2d Albany County Militia, and performed duty during the years of 1779 and 1780, "on all occasions when called into service either for repelling inroads on the frontier or mounting guard to defend the compact part of the Town of Schenectady."

SHANNON, ALEXANDER: His name appears on the rolls of the 2d Albany County Militia.

SHANNON, GEORGE: Baptized March 17, 1751; died January 8, 1829. A farmer. On March 13, 1776, he enlisted under Captain Gerrit S. Veeder, in Colonel Cornelius D. Wynkoop's regiment, and served until February, 1777, when he was discharged. On July 23, 1780, he was sent to Albany under arrest as being connected with a plot to join the enemy or of supplying them with provisions. He was on August 11 released on bail. A pensioner under the Act of March 18, 1818.

SHANNON, JOHN: Died in April, 1821. In the fall of 1775 he was enrolled under Captain Abraham Oothout, 2d Albany County Militia. In the fall of 1776 he went to Jessup's Patent with the troops under Colonel Warner, and in the summer of the same year he marched to Fort Edward. He served with the Northern Army during Schuyler's retreat and was at the battle of Bemis Heights. From May to June, 1778, he was on duty when Cobleskill was attacked; during the latter part of the summer he was at the Middle Fort, Schoharie, and in November at Switzerberg near Caughnawaga. In the fall of 1779 he was on duty at Fort Paris and Fort Plain, serving during this year both as a corporal and as a sergeant. In 1781 he again served as a corporal. His widow received a pension.

SHANNON, ROBERT: His name appears on the rolls of the 2d Albany County Militia. On July 10, 1780, a Robert Shannon enlisted for the war and was assigned to the 8th Company, 4th New York Line. He deserted on October 23, was taken on November 20 and mustered to January, 1782.

SHANNON, THOMAS: Baptized December 20, 1752. His name appears on the rolls of the 2d Albany County Militia. On October 28, 1776, a Thomas Shannon enlisted for the war and was assigned to the 4th Company, 1st New York Line.

SHANNON, WILLIAM: His name appears on the rolls of the 2d Albany County Militia.

SHEARER (alias SHERWOOD), JAMES: Died December 31, 1818. He served as a private in the New York Line. A pensioner under the Act of March 18, 1818.

SHELLING, ALEXANDER: His name appears on the rolls of the 2d Albany County Militia.

SHELLY, SAMUEL: He was enrolled under Captain Thomas Brower Banker, 2d Albany County Militia. In January, 1776, he took part in the expedition to Johnstown, on which occasion he and three others constituted the party entrusted with the flag of truce. On March 1, 1776, he signed an agreement with Philip Schuyler for service at Lake George and Ticonderoga, and on September 23, enlisted for one year in Captain John A. Bradt's company of State Rangers. He held the rank of sergeant. On December 4 he was discharged as unfit for duty, but later he returned and served for nearly a year, when he was again taken sick and placed in the hospital at Albany. After three weeks he was removed to Schenectady. In consequence of his continued illness he was not required to join the army, "but he felt such anxiety for the success of the American cause that he procured one Donelly as a substitute and said Donelly served to near the end of the war when he died." In spite of his ailments Shelly again entered the service, for in the summer of 1777 he was on duty six weeks with the Northern Army, and in 1778 at Fort Plain and the Lower Fort, Schoharie. In 1779 he was at Fort Paris, and in 1780, under Abraham Van Eps, he marched to Ballston. He later moved to Saybrook, Connecticut. His widow received a pension.

SHIELDS, DANIEL: A resident of Schenectady before and after the Revolution. In 1780 he enlisted under Lieutenant Philip Conine, 3d New York Line, and was later transferred to the company of Captain George Sytez, 1st New York Line. In this company he served to the end of the war. He was at Yorktown. He received five hundred acres of land as a bounty. A pensioner.

SIMONDS, REUBEN: Born in 1736; died May 5, 1810. On April 19, 1777, he was granted a tavern license by the Committee of Safety. His inn was on the west side of Church Street and came to be a popular place for the holding of public meetings. His name appears on the rolls of the 2d Albany County Militia and the 2d Albany County Militia, Land Bounty Rights.

SMILIE, JOHN: His name appears on the rolls of the 2d Albany County Militia.

SMITH, ADAM: Baptized January 28, 1750. His name appears on the rolls of the 2d Albany County Militia.

SMITH, JOHN: His name appears on the rolls of the 2d Albany County Militia.

SMITH, ROBERT: He was enrolled under Captain Jellis J. Fonda, 2d Albany County Militia. In the summer of 1780 he was attached to Colonel Malcolm Graham's regiment, having been drafted from the Schenectady militia. He marched to West Point and while there every fifteenth man was selected to join the Regular Army. He was among those selected. He is said to have served at least six months in the Levies under Colonel Marinus Willett. His widow's claim for a pension was rejected.

SNELL, MAJOR: Born April 26, 1720; died September 24, 1818. He came from Yorkshire, England. A merchant. On September 11, 1776, he was ordered confined to the Albany jail by the Schenectady Committee of Safety. On the eighteenth he refused to sign the Association or to swear allegiance and was therefore ordered recommitted. In May, 1777, he was recommended to the field officers as "a dangerous person," and on the twenty-second voluntarily took an oath that he would take up arms in defense of the country in case of any invasion.

SNOW, EPHRAIM: He was appointed an ensign under Captain Gerrit S. Veeder, Colonel Cornelius D. Wynkoop's regiment. On April 12, 1776, he delivered his commission to the Committee of Safety, giving as his reason for resigning that the men were mutinous and dissatisfied with the appointment of Veeder as captain. He was later induced to ask for the return of his commission and his request was granted by the Board, but with a word of caution regarding his future behavior. On November 21, 1776,

INDIVIDUAL RECORDS OF SERVICE 217

he was serving as a second lieutenant in the 1st New York Line. He was promoted to the rank of first lieutenant on March 26, 1779, and served in this capacity until June, 1783.

SPECK, ABRAHAM: His name appears on the rolls of the 2d Albany County Militia.

SPECK, TOBIAS: His name appears on the rolls of the 2d Albany County Militia.

STALEY, GEORGE: Born at Truxberry, N. J., July 6, 1753; died June 7, 1832. In the spring of 1775 he lived in Princetown and was enrolled under Captain Thomas Wasson, 2d Albany County Militia. He was not called upon until 1776, after which time he served to the end of the war. In 1776 after the defeat of the American forces on Lake Champlain he served with a detachment of Colonel Wemple's regiment under General Ten Broeck in guarding ammunition conveyed from Albany to Skenesborough. In the summer of 1777 he served with the Northern Army from the evacuation of Ticonderoga to the surrender of Burgoyne, with the exception of about three weeks, when he hired a substitute. He was in the encounter at Snookkill, but not in the battle of Bemis Heights, being on sentry duty and among the troops not called upon. In 1778 he served under Colonel Wemple in bringing ammunition and cannon from Ticonderoga to Albany. He performed duties at various times at Schoharie, Cobleskill, Fort Paris, Fort Plain, Fort Plank, Ballston, and in the expeditions to Cherry Valley, Warren's Bush and Caughnawaga. A pensioner under the Act of June 7, 1832.

STALEY, JACOB: His name appears on the rolls of the 2d Albany County Militia.

STALEY, MATTHIAS: Born in New Jersey in 1737. In 1776 he enlisted at Schenectady, where he then lived, under

Myndert Wemple and during the year served six months. During the year 1777 he served three months under Captain Thomas Wasson, 2d Albany County Militia, being present at the surrender of General Burgoyne. In 1778 he enlisted for six months in the batteau service on the North River. In 1779 he served at Stone Arabia on draft. His name appears on the rolls of the 2d Albany County Militia, Land Bounty Rights. He lived in Schenectady and Duanesburgh after the Revolution and in 1804 moved to Blenheim, Schoharie County. A pensioner.

STANLEY, JOHN: His name appears on the rolls of the 2d Albany County Militia.

STEELEY, HENRY: His name appears on the rolls of the 2d Albany County Militia.

STEERS, JOHN: Baptized October 15, 1732; died February 12, 1811. His name appears on the rolls of the 2d Albany County Militia and the 2d Albany County Militia, Land Bounty Rights. In 1778 he was enrolled under Captain Jesse Van Slyck.

STEERS, PETER: Baptized January 7, 1739. In 1778 he was enrolled under Captain Jesse Van Slyck, 2d Albany County Militia.

STEVENS, JOHN: Baptized March 31, 1745. On March 1, 1776, he signed an agreement with Philip Schuyler for service at Lake George and Ticonderoga. On April 1, 1777, he was elected fire master at Schenectady, and on September 11 was sent to give information to the Albany Committee regarding the condition of the army at Saratoga. His name appears on the rolls of the 2d Albany County Militia.

STEVENS, NICHOLAS: Born November 14, 1734; died September 19, 1788. On April 12, 1776, it was reported to the Schenectady Committee that he had gone up the North River to trade without a certificate from the Board. On the same day General Schuyler was informed regarding him, as it was suspected that he had or might obtain a pass through a misrepresentation. On August 8, 1778, he was summoned before the Commissioners of Conspiracies to render satisfaction touching his conduct during the war, in accordance with the Act regarding neutral and equivocal characters. He was tendered the Oath of Allegiance and granted time to consider its acceptance. On August 15 he refused to take the Oath and was cited to appear on September 5, ready for removal to the enemy's lines. On August 28 he was authorized to go to Canada, on his promise of thereafter maintaining a strict neutrality. On September 3 his name was transmitted to General Clinton that he might, if he thought proper, detain him for the purpose of an exchange. On September 8 he was ordered removed.

STEVENS, WILLIAM: Baptized September 10, 1732. On February 10, 1776, he was elected a second lieutenant in one of the newly organized Schenectady militia companies. On April 1, 1777, he was elected overseer of highways. His name appears on the rolls of the 2d Albany County Militia, Land Bounty Rights.

STEWART, DANIEL: His name appears on the rolls of the 2d Albany County Militia.

STEWART, DAVID: His name appears on the rolls of the 2d Albany County Militia.

STUART, GEORGE: His name appears on the rolls of the 2d Albany County Militia and the 2d Albany County Militia, Land Bounty Rights.

STUART, JAMES: His name appears on the rolls of the 2d Albany County Militia, Land Bounty Rights.

STUART, JOHN: In October, 1778, he was serving as a sergeant in the 2d Albany County Militia in command of a detail to Cobleskill. In 1781 he was a member of Captain

. John Crousehorn's company of artillery, and in July, 1782, was on scout duty at Harpersfield.

STUART, JOHN: "At the commencement of the unhappy contest betwixt Great Britain and her colonies, I acquainted the Society [for the Propagation of the Gospel] of the firm reliance I had on the fidelity and loyalty of my congregation, which has justified my opinion; for the faithful Mohawks, rather than swerve from their allegiance, chose rather to abandon their dwellings and property; and accordingly went in a body to General Burgoyne, and afterwards were obliged to take shelter in Canada. While they remained at Fort Hunter I continued to officiate as usual, performing the public service entire, even after the Declaration of Independence, notwithstanding by so doing I incurred the penalty of high treason by the new laws. As soon as my protectors were fled I was made a prisoner, and ordered to depart the province with my family, within the space of four days or be put into close confinement, and this only upon suspicion that I was a loyal subject of the King of Great Britain. Upon this I was admitted to 'paroles' and confined to the limits of the town of Schenectady [June, 1778], in which situation I have remained for upwards of three years. My house has been frequently broken open by mobs, my property plundered, and, indeed, every kind of indignity offered to my person by the lowest of the populace. At length my farm, and the produce of it, was formally taken from me in May last, as forfeited to the State; and, as the last resource, I proposed to open a Latin school for the support of my family. But this priviledge was denied, on pretence that, as a prisoner of war, I was not entitled to exercise any lucrative occupation in the State. I then applied [March 30, 1781] for permission to remove to Canada, which, after much difficulty and expence, I obtained upon the following conditions:—to give bail in the sum of £400, to send a rebel colonel in my room, or else return to Albany, and surrender myself a prisoner whenever required. In consequence I set out on my journey from Schenectady on the 19th of September last, with my wife and three small children; and, after suffering much fatigue and difficulty, we arrived safe at St. John's in Canada. . . . I cannot omit to mention that my church was plundered by the rebels, and the pulpit-cloth taken away from the pulpit; it was afterwards employed as a tavern, and a barrel of rum placed in the reading-desk. The succeeding year it was used for a stable, and now serves as a fort.'' Letter of John Stuart, n.d.

SULLIVAN, CHARLES: His name appears on the rolls of the 2d Albany County Militia. His widow's application for pension gives no facts regarding his service and her claim was rejected.

SULLIVAN, JACOB: Died before February 25, 1780. On June 20, 1778, he was commissioned ensign in Captain Thomas Wasson's company, 2d Albany County Militia.

SWART, JACOBUS: Baptized October 19, 1740. His name appears on the rolls of the 2d Albany County Militia.

SWART, JAMES: His name appears on the rolls of the 2d Albany County Militia.

SWART, NICHOLAS: Died March 1, 1825. He lived in Glenville, five miles above Schenectady, near the Fourth Flat. He served as a sergeant under Captain John Van Patten, 2d Albany County Militia.

SWART, TEUNIS: Lived in Glenville near the Fourth Flat about five miles from Schenectady on the north side of the river. His house which stood on the river bank, was of brick, and during the Revolution it was stockaded and used as a fort, having as an armament a small field piece. The house was removed prior to 1873. Swart served as a lieutenant in the company of Captain John Van Patten, 2d Albany County Militia, his commission being dated

June 20, 1778. He also served eight months as a lieutenant in the Levies. He was spoken of as having been a brave, active, vigilant and much beloved officer, ready on all occasions to turn out with his men. He served in all the principal expeditions up the Mohawk from 1778 to the end of the war. When the troops under Colonel Willett went in pursuit of Walter Butler he commanded the advance guard and was in the battle when Butler was killed. The claim for pension made by his two sons was rejected on the ground that Swart had died prior to the Act of 1832.

SWEET, CALEB: Born in Schenectady and practiced medicine here after the war. He died in 1823. On November 21, 1776, he was serving as surgeon's mate in the 1st New York Line. From October 13, 1779, until the close of the war he served as a surgeon in the same regiment.

SWITS, ABRAHAM: Born October 31, 1730; died August 17, 1814. On October 5, 1775, he was recommended to the Provincial Congress by the Committee of Safety for the office of first major among the field officers to be assigned to the Schenectady militia. On October 20 a commission was issued in his name. On July 9, 1777, he was under orders to march with the militia to Fort Edward, but on August 10 was ordered detained in town with his troops by the Committee because of a Tory plot. On August 11, assisted by a detachment of Continental troops, he arrested seventeen Tories. From April 7 to 14, 1778, he commanded a detachment of one hundred and twenty-five whites and a few Indians to Beaverdam to apprehend Tories. On June 20 he was reappointed major. In the fall of 1780 he served at Fort Hunter, and in October marched to Ballston after the raid. In November, he performed garrison duty at Fort Paris, and in August, 1781, a like service at the Upper Fort, Schoharie.

SWITS, HENDRICK: Baptized in October, 1762; died September 18, 1825. His name appears on the rolls of the 2d Albany County Militia as serving under Captain John Mynderse.

SWITS, ISAAC: Born in 1721; died in 1790. His name appears on the rolls of the 2d Albany County Militia and the 2d Albany County Militia, Land Bounty Rights.

SWITS, JACOB: His name appears on the rolls of the 2d Albany County Militia.

SWITS, JACOB A.: Born November 3, 1762; died November 21, 1835. He served as a private under Captain John Mynderse and as a corporal under Captain Jellis J. Fonda, 2d Albany County Militia.

SWITS, WALTER: Born in 1754; died October 31, 1823. Buried in Vale Cemetery. On May 1, 1776, he made application to the Committee of Safety to be dismissed from Captain Gerrit S. Veeder's company on a plea that he had not been fairly enlisted. On the testimony of Lieutenant Bates that the enlistment was regular the Committee, however, refused to interfere. On May 6 he complained to the Committee that the officers of the company had refused to "take a sufficient man in his place." In June, 1776, he was serving as a lieutenant in Captain John A. Bradt's company of State Rangers. About February 15, 1777, he was enlisted as a lieutenant in Captain Giles Wolcott's company, Colonel Seth Warner's regiment. He remained in this company until September, 1780, when he resigned and returned to Schenectady. In March, 1782, he commanded a company of forty-six men raised to keep guard at Forts Volunteer and Squash, Schenectady. His widow received a pension.

SWORDS, THOMAS: His name appears on the rolls of the 2d Albany County Militia as serving under Captain Thomas Brower Banker.

TAWS, DAVID: Born in Scotland, December, 1748. He was living at Princetown when, on July 1, 1776, he enlisted for six months in the company of Captain Henry Marselis, 1st New York Line. He served until December, performing duty at Skenesborough, Fort George and Fort Ann. In 1777 he was enrolled under Captain John Mynderse, 2d Albany County Militia, and later served under Captain Thomas Wasson. In the fall he was at Fort Miller and Fort Ann. In 1780 he was on duty when the Mohawk settlements were destroyed. He served to the end of the war. A pensioner under the Act of June 7, 1832.

TAYLOR, SOLOMON: His name appears on the rolls of the 2d Albany County Militia as serving under Captain John Mynderse.

TAYLOR, WALTER: In 1777 he was on duty with Colonel Wemple's regiment at Bemis Heights, and in the summer of 1778 he performed six weeks' garrison duty at the Middle Fort, Schoharie. In the fall of the same year he performed six weeks' garrison duty at the Lower Fort. On April 27, 1782, he enlisted in the Levies, "for Cornelius Van Santvoord and class," under the Act of March 23, 1782. His widow received a pension.

TELLER, JACOBUS: Baptized March 17, 1738; killed by the Indians at Detroit, September 27, 1784. In 1764 he was an Indian trader in company with John and Henry Glen. From his father he inherited part of the Teller lot on the east corner of Washington Avenue and Union Street. On May 26, 1775, he was appointed a member of the first Committee of Safety in place of Tobias Ten Eyck, who had refused to serve. He served on the second Committee of Safety and on the Boards taking office June 2, 1777, and January 5, 1778. On January 14, 1776, he was appointed, with Harmanus Wendel, to confer with the magistrates with a view of having the watch doubled as on account of the number of strangers in town the Board feared "some roil might happen." On June 2, 1777, he was elected assessor, and on June 7 appointed one of a committee to confer with the inhabitants regarding the election of governor. On June 24, 1779, he was again elected a member of the Committee of Safety. His name appears on the rolls of the 2d Albany County Militia.

TELLER, JOHN, JR.: Born May 18, 1765; died March 29, 1790. His name appears on the rolls of the 2d Albany County Militia.

TELLER, WILLIAM: Baptized June 14, 1740. He served as a sergeant in Captain Abraham Oothout's company, 2d Albany County Militia. From August to October, 1781, he was in command at Claas Viele's Fort.

TEN EYCK, HENRY: Born July 27, 1755. He served as a captain in a Connecticut regiment. He took part in many battles and was distinguished for gallant service. On July 15, 1779, he fought in the advance column at the storming of Stony Point under General Wayne and was wounded in the arm by a bayonet thrust. "He became very deaf [Judge Sanders quotes this from the veteran's own lips], owing to the fact that while crawling through a cannon port-hole in the assault the piece was simultaneously fired over his body." A pensioner.

TEN EYCK, JACOB T.: Baptized February 15, 1761. A merchant. His name appears on the rolls of the 2d Albany County Militia and the 2d Albany County Militia, Land Bounty Rights.

TEN EYCK, MYNDERT: Born February 9, 1753; died October 4, 1805. A merchant. On July 11, 1776, he was elected a member of the Committee of Safety. On January 15, 1777, he was again elected a member of the Board. On May 8 he was appointed to purchase and deliver certain boards to the barkmaster at Fishkill. His name appears on the rolls of the 2d Albany County Militia.

TEN EYCK, TOBIAS: Born August 15, 1717; died February 9, 1785. He moved to Schenectady about 1750. A merchant. He lived on the northeast corner of Governor's Lane and Front Street. On May 6, 1775, he was chosen a member of the first Committee of Safety but refused to serve. His name appears on the rolls of the 2d Albany County Militia, Land Bounty Rights.

TERWILLIGER, ISAAC: His name appears on the rolls of the 2d Albany County Militia.

TERWILLIGER, JACOBUS: His name appears on the rolls of the 2d Albany County Militia.

TERWILLIGER, SOLOMON: Baptized March 26, 1749. On February 28, 1776, he refused to accept a recruiting warrant with rank of ensign from the Provincial Congress. His name appears on the rolls of the 2d Albany County Militia as serving under Captain John Van Patten.

THOMPSON, JOHN: Born in Schenectady, June 21, 1755. On March 15, 1776, he enlisted in the Quartermaster's Department. He served nine months at Albany, Coeymans, Dobbs Ferry, Tarrytown, Dover and other places, performing guard as well as fatigue duty. He served also at Troy in preparing posts for stockades and at Saratoga erecting fortifications. A pensioner.

THOMSON, PETER: His name appears on the rolls of the 2d Albany County Militia.

THORN, SAMUEL: His name appears on the rolls of the 2d Albany County Militia.

THORNTON, JAMES: In 1775 he was enrolled under Captain Thomas Wasson, 2d Albany County Militia. In January, 1776, he took part in the expedition to Johnstown. In 1777 he performed three weeks' service at Fort George and Fort Edward, after which he was ordered to Oriskany. Dorcas Wright, his daughter, stated that her father was in David McMaster's company, 3d Tryon County Militia, and was at the battle of Oriskany. She remembered her father taking a chest containing the papers relating to the farm and some other things of value and concealing them in the woods for safety, but that notwithstanding this they were destroyed, causing him to suffer considerable loss of property. She remembered also that frequently her mother and the children spent the night concealed in the woods for fear of being molested. In the summer of 1780 he was on duty at the Middle Fort, Schoharie, and marched in pursuit of the enemy after the destruction of the Schoharie settlements, later serving at Fort Plain. In October, 1781, he was at the battle of Johnstown. His widow received a pension.

THORNTON, JOHN: Born in Schenectady in 1753; died here, March 22, 1819. On June 20, 1778, he was commissioned second lieutenant in Captain Thomas Wasson's company, 2d Albany County Militia. He performed service during the summer at Stone Arabia. On February 25, 1780, he was promoted to the rank of first lieutenant in Captain Wasson's company, and in the fall marched as far as Palatine when Sir John Johnson raided the settlements. On April 27, 1781, he was appointed a lieutenant in the nine-months Levies under Colonel Marinus Willett, and was attached to the company of Captain Stephen White. He served the full term in this company and in 1782 he was appointed a lieutenant in Captain Guy Young's company of Levies under Colonel Willett. He served in this company until the summer of that year, when he was transferred to the company of Captain Peter B. Tearse. In October, 1783, he was detached from this company and assigned to the command of Fort Stanwix. He continued in command there until May 10, 1784, when he was relieved and later discharged from the service. His widow received a pension.

THORNTON, THOMAS: He is mentioned as having served as a private and as a lieutenant in Captain Thomas Wasson's company, 2d Albany County Militia.

TOLL, CHARLES: His name appears on the rolls of the 2d Albany County Militia.

TOLL, DANIEL: Baptized October 27, 1751. On October 20, 1775, he was commissioned ensign in Captain John Van Patten's company, 2d Albany County Militia. He was reappointed June 20, 1778. In January, 1776, he took part in the expedition to Johnstown, and in May, 1778, was at Cobleskill. His name appears also as ensign in the 2d Albany County Militia, Land Bounty Rights.

TOLL, JOHN: Buried September 12, 1804. His name appears on the rolls of the 2d Albany County Militia.

TRUAX, ABRAHAM I.: He is mentioned as having served as an ensign in Captain Thomas Wasson's Company, 2d Albany County Militia.

TRUAX, ABRAHAM J.: Born April 4, 1737. On March 1, 1776, he signed an agreement with Philip Schuyler for service at Lake George and Ticonderoga. He served as an ensign in Captain John Mynderse's company, 2d Albany County Militia. On April 1, 1777, he was elected poundmaster at Schenectady, and on April 24 commanded a squad of forty-five men detailed for duty between Albany and Lake George. It is stated that he served as a lieutenant at the battle of Bemis Heights. On June 20, 1778, he was regularly commissioned ensign, and in the fall of 1780 marched on an alarm to Fort Hunter.

TRUAX, ABRAHAM P.: Baptized April 28, 1753; died March 13, 1822. Buried in Vale Cemetery. His name appears on the rolls of the 2d Albany County Militia.

TRUAX, ANDRIES: Baptized April 29, 1739. His name appears on the rolls of the 2d Albany County Militia, Land Bounty Rights.

INDIVIDUAL RECORDS OF SERVICE

TRUAX, CALEB: Born November 19, 1747; died in 1808. Buried on the old Van Auken farm in the town of Guilderland. The grave is on the south bank of the Bozen-Kill and about five hundred feet east of the house. His name appears on the rolls of the 2d Albany County Militia.

TRUAX, ISAAC: On April 1, 1777, he was elected a collector, and on May 8, was engaged by the Committee of Safety to "tend the watch for the ensuing year, he having performed this service the past year."

TRUAX, ISAAC I.: Born in Schenectady, July 16, 1756; died December 21, 1854. In March, 1777, he enlisted under Lieutenant-Colonel Christopher Yates and performed duty at Fort Ann and Skenesborough until January, 1778, when he was honorably discharged. In October, 1781, he was drafted under Captain Walter Vrooman and served at the battle of Johnstown. Later in the same year, while serving in the same company he took part in an engagement with the enemy under Sir John Johnson and Joseph Brant. With sixty-three others he was taken prisoner and carried to Canada, where he was confined at Buck's Island. He remained a prisoner during the rest of the war and then returned to Schenectady. A pensioner under the Act of June 7, 1832.

TRUAX, JACOB J.: Born April 4, 1737. On May 8, 1777, he was sent to Albany a prisoner by the Committee of Safety because it was reported that he had said that "he was no Tory but that he was a King's man, that he had been taken prisoner once before by the Committee of Schenectady and that he had a tomahawk ready if they came to take him again." He probably settled in Albany soon after this time.

TRUAX, JOHN: Born August 29, 1749. From March, 1777, to October, 1780, he served in Captain Giles Wolcott's company, Colonel Seth Warner's regiment. He was in the retreat from Ticonderoga, the battle of Bennington and at Fort George, where his regiment was "almost entirely cut up and destroyed." Truax was paroled by his officer at Saratoga and permitted to return to Schenectady. During the years 1780 and 1781 he served under Colonel Willett in the Levies. A pensioner.

TRUAX, JOHN P.: Baptized July 27, 1755; died August 12, 1817. His name appears on the rolls of the 2d Albany County Militia as serving under Captain John Mynderse.

TRUAX, PETER: Born August 27, 1725; died August 27, 1797. Buried in Vale Cemetery. His name appears on the rolls of the 2d Albany County Militia, Land Bounty Rights.

TRUMBULL, JOHN: His name appears on the rolls of the 2d Albany County Militia.

TUTTLE, EZRA: His name appears on the rolls of the 2d Albany County Militia.

TUTTLE, SOLOMON: His name appears on the rolls of the 2d Albany County Militia. The name of Solomon Tuttle appears on the rolls of the 4th Company, 2d New York Line. He enlisted on May 5, 1778, for nine months and was discharged on February 9, 1779.

TYMS, MICHAEL: Baptized September 18, 1763; died August 28, 1804. Buried in Vale Cemetery. His name appears on the rolls of the 2d Albany County Militia.

VAN ANTWERP, ARENT J.: On June 20, 1778, he was appointed ensign in Captain Abraham Van Eps's company, 2d Albany County Militia, but declined to serve.

VAN ANTWERP, GERRIT: Born October 15, 1753; died May 10, 1809. His name appears on the rolls of the 2d Albany County Militia as serving under Captain Jellis J. Fonda.

VAN ANTWERP, JOHN: His name appears on the rolls of the 2d Albany County Militia. On February 8, 1776, as a guard he accompanied a prisoner to the Albany jail.

VAN ANTWERP, PETER: Baptized December 15, 1745. He lived at Princetown. His name appears on the rolls of the 2d Albany County Militia.

VAN ANTWERP, PETER A.: Born December 4, 1755. His name appears on the rolls of the 2d Albany County Militia.

VAN ANTWERP, SIMON J.: Born at Schaghticoke, Albany County, February 2, 1751; died September 11, 1834. He was living in Schenectady when in September, 1775, he enlisted as orderly sergeant under Captain Tacarus Van der Bogart in a company of artificers. He served three months at Ticonderoga. From March 6 to November 20, 1776, he served in Captain Ahasueras Marselis's company of artificers, with the same rank as before, employed in erecting barracks, storehouses and works of defense at Fort Ann and Lake George. He served thereafter until the end of the war, for the most part as orderly sergeant in the company of Captain Thomas Brower Banker, 2d Albany County Militia. In 1777 he served throughout the campaign against Burgoyne. He was at Lake George at the time of the surrender of Ticonderoga. He retreated to Fort Edward, then to Stillwater, where his company was stationed on September 14, when Burgoyne crossed the river. He took part in the battle of September 19, and in the battle of Bemis Heights. In 1778 he was stationed at the Schoharie Forts and at Sacandaga erecting blockhouses. In 1780 he marched with the troops under Colonel Willett in pursuit of Sir John Johnson and took part in the expedition to Ballston. A pension was allowed him but it was later suspended.

VAN BENTHEUYSEN, MARTIN: On September 5, 1776, he enlisted in Captain John A. Bradt's company of State Rangers. On March 13, 1777, he enlisted for the war and was assigned to the 8th Company, 1st New York Line. He was discharged on November 13, 1778. His name appears on the rolls of the 2d Albany County Militia, Land Bounty Rights.

VAN BENTHUYSEN, PETER: His name appears on the rolls of the 2d Albany County Militia.

VAN DER BOGART, JOSEPH: Born November 21, 1756. He was enrolled under Captain Jellis J. Fonda, 2d Albany County Militia. In 1777 he served in the campaign against Burgoyne. From December 24, 1779, to December 24, 1780, he served as a sergeant under Captain Joseph Peek in the Quartermaster's Department. In October, 1781, he went with a detachment of militia to Fort Herkimer, where they joined the troops under Colonel Willett and marched to Jerseyfield. His widow received a pension.

VAN DER BOGART, NICHOLAS: On December 5, 1776, he enlisted for the war and was assigned to the 8th Company, 1st New York Line. On May 1, 1779, he was promoted to the rank of corporal. He served seven years and three months and received six hundred acres of land as a bounty.

VAN DER BOGART, TACARUS: Baptized March 23, 1717; died in 1799. He lived on the north side of Front Street opposite Church Street. In September, 1775, he commanded a company of artificers at Ticonderoga. On March 1, 1776, he signed an agreement with Philip Schuyler for service at Lake George and Ticonderoga.

VAN DERHEYDEN, DANIEL: Born February 22, 1760. His name appears on the rolls of the 2d Albany County Militia.

VAN DERHEYDEN, DAVID: Baptized in Albany, February 26, 1758; died July 9, 1840. Buried in Vale Cemetery. A cooper by trade. He moved with his family to Schenectady about 1780. His village lot was on the north corner of Union and College Streets. In the spring of 1776, while living in Albany, he enlisted for six months under Captain Henry Marselis, 1st New York Line. He served at Skenesborough, Fort George and Fort Ann. In March, 1777, he enlisted and served for nine months in Captain

Teunis Fisher's company of state troops under Lieutenant-Colonel Christopher C. Yates. He was on duty at Fort Ticonderoga on its evacuation and served during General Schuyler's retreat and until the surrender of General Burgoyne. In 1778 he served for nine months in the state troops under Captain William Peters, employed in the transportation of military stores and in regular duty on the Mohawk River from Schenectady to Fort Stanwix. In 1779 he served four months in a company of artificers at Saratoga and later marched with the troops of General Clinton's division against the Indians. He helped build the dam across the outlet of Otsego Lake necessary to transfer the boats to the Susquehanna River. He remained at Tioga Point and there helped to take care of the sick soldiers who were left behind as the army proceeded into the Indian country. On his removal to Schenectady he was enrolled under Captain Thomas Brower Banker, 2d Albany County Militia, and with his company marched to Ballston in pursuit of the enemy after the raid. In 1781 he enlisted and served four months in the Levies under Colonel Willett. A pensioner under the Act of June 7, 1832.

VAN DER VOLGEN, CORNELIUS: Born July 25, 1731; died January 18, 1786. Buried in Vale Cemetery. On May 7, 1776, he was elected a member of the third Committee of Safety. His name appears on the rolls of the 2d Albany County Militia.

VAN DER VOLGEN, NICHOLAS: Born in August, 1722; died May 21, 1797. Buried in Vale Cemetery. A merchant living on State Street. On July 2, 1779, he was appointed one of a committee of four to sell salt to the people of the district.

VAN DER VOLGEN, PETER: Born June 10, 1733. He lived in Princetown. His name appears on the rolls of the 2d Albany County Militia.

VAN DER WERKEN, MARTIN: On December 5, 1776, he enlisted in Captain John A. Bradt's company of State Rangers. On March 20, 1777, he enlisted for three years in the 8th Company, 3d New York Line. He was discharged on March 20, 1780.

VAN DRIESEN, HENRY: A member of the third and fourth Committees of Safety.

VAN DRIESEN, JOHN: Baptized March 11, 1744. On February 10, 1776, he was appointed by the Committee of Safety adjutant of the 2d Albany County Militia, and on March 5 Henry Glen was instructed to apply to Congress for his commission. He was reappointed on June 20, 1778. In the fall of 1780 he was serving at Fort Hunter.

VAN DRIESEN, PETER: Born in Schenectady, May 4, 1763. He was residing at Palatine when he entered the service. In April, 1777, he volunteered for one year under Captain Christian House, 2d Tryon County Militia. He served seven months and then, because of his father's illness, procured a substitute who served three months in his stead, after which time he returned and completed his term of service. At the expiration of his term he re-enlisted and served to the end of the war, with the exception of three months when Dennis Holembolt acted as a substitute for him. A pensioner.

VAN DYCK, CORNELIUS: Born October 8, 1740; died June 9, 1792. Buried in Vale Cemetery. On May 27, 1775, he was appointed captain of militia by the Committee of Safety. On May 29 he was given orders for recruiting a company for the defense of Fort Ticonderoga, and on June 29 was commissioned captain by the Provincial Congress and assigned to the 2d New York Line. He served with distinction under General Montgomery and during the remainder of the Canadian campaign as a military aide-de-camp. On May 7, 1776, he was elected a member of the third Committee of Safety. On November

21 he was commissioned a lieutenant-colonel and assigned to the 1st New York Line. During this year he was at one time acting as commandant at Fort George. On August 21, 1777, he was a member of a council of war held at German Flats under the presidency of Major Arnold. He was at the battle of Monmouth (June 28, 1778), and on December 23 was in command of Fort Schuyler. He was in command of Fort Schuyler on October 25 of the following year and on April 17, 1780. He served to the end of the war, and on September 30, 1783, was appointed colonel of the 1st New York Line.

VAN DYCK, CORNELIUS H.: Baptized February 27, 1763; died August 31, 1832. In 1777 he was enrolled under Captain Abraham Oothout, 2d Albany County Militia. During the fall and winter he performed three months' service at Saratoga, and is believed to have served throughout the campaign against Burgoyne. During the year 1778 he was twice on duty at Schoharie, and in the fall served one month at Stone Arabia. He performed considerable service from 1779 to 1781 under various officers. A pensioner under the Act of June 7, 1832.

VAN DYCK, CORNELIUS N.: His name appears on the rolls of the 2d Albany County Militia.

VAN DYCK, HENRY: Baptized August 29, 1731. His name appears on the rolls of the 2d Albany County Militia and the 2d Albany County Militia, Land Bounty Rights.

VAN DYCK, HENRY H.: His name appears on the rolls of the 2d Albany County Militia.

VAN DYCK, HENRY I.: His name appears on the rolls of the 2d Albany County Militia.

VAN EPS, ABRAHAM: Born October 15, 1738. He had a farm at the Aalplaats. On February 10, 1776, he was elected ensign of one of the newly organized Schenectady militia companies. During the summer of 1777 he served in the campaign against Burgoyne as captain of militia. He probably also served previous to this time as a captain, although the first recorded commission is that granted by the Council of Appointment June 20, 1778. He was in command of various details for the apprehension of Tories and for guard duty, his "beat" being the Aalplaats, a particularly exposed district. In the fall of 1780 he marched to Caughnawaga when the Mohawk settlements were destroyed.

VAN EPS, ALEXANDER: Born in Schenectady, February 28, 1762. He lived in Charlton. In February, 1778, he went out on scout duty twice in search of Joseph Bettis. In March, 1779, he enlisted under Lieutenant-Colonel Christopher C. Yates and for nine months performed fatigue duty at Schuyler's Mills, building boats, erecting barracks, etc. He was honorably discharged in December. In 1780 he was drafted into Captain John Mynderse's company, 2d Albany County Militia, for service at Schoharie, and in 1781 twice drafted into Captain Abraham Van Eps's company, the first time for service at Stone Arabia and the second for service at Tribes Hill. A pensioner under the Act of June 7, 1832.

VAN EPS, GERRIT: Born in Schenectady, January 30, 1764; died in Glenville, May 19, 1844. In 1780 he was drafted, assigned to the company under Captain Abraham Van Eps, 2d Albany County Militia, and detailed for garrison duty at Stone Arabia. In 1781 he was again drafted into the same company and served at Fort Plank for a period of about three months. On one occasion he served on a scouting expedition to Clifton Park and Ballston in pursuit of the famous Tory, Joseph Bettis. He was frequently out on emergency duty.

VAN EPS, JAMES: In March, 1777, he enlisted for nine months in Captain Abraham Van Eps's company, 2d Albany County Militia. He served at Stillwater. He "was also in Captain Daniel Toll's company and went from his residence, about five miles from Schenectady to Caughnawaga and served one month when Caughnawaga was burnt." His widow's application for pension was rejected.

VAN EPS, JOHN: Born in Glenville, December 27, 1764; died August 29, 1847. Buried in West Glenville. Family tradition says that he took part in the battle of Oriskany and was one of those who helped carry General Herkimer under the tree after he was wounded. In the fall of 1779 he entered service as a substitute for his father and was enrolled under Captain John Van Patten, 2d Albany County Militia. His first expedition was to Fort Paris soon after he enlisted. In August, 1780, he was on duty when Brant laid waste the country around Canajoharie, and in October of the same year he marched with the troops under General Van Rensselaer in pursuit of Sir John Johnson after the destruction of the Mohawk settlements. In October, 1781, he went with the troops under Colonel Willett in pursuit of Major Ross and Butler. He fought at the battle of Johnstown and went with the Indians who pursued Walter Butler to the West Canada Creek. He took part in numerous expeditions and performed garrison duties on various occasions at many of the forts throughout the Valley.

VAN EPS, JOHN BAPTIST: Baptized April 29, 1739; buried July 13, 1805. Buried in Vale Cemetery. He lived in Glenville. On January 14, 1776, the Committee of Safety was informed that last summer he had supplied Sir John Johnson with a quantity of powder. On May 13 he complained to the Board regarding the wrongful enlistment of an apprentice boy who was under him. On April 19, 1777, he was granted a tavern license by the Committee, and on July 9 he furnished a wagon for use in the service. His name appears on the rolls of the 2d Albany County Militia.

VAN EPS, JOHN J.: Born in Schenectady, October 24, 1751. In 1775, he was enrolled in Captain John Mynderse's company, 2d Albany County Militia, and served in it until 1777, when he was attached to the company under Captain Abraham Oothout. In 1775 he performed six months' service at Lake George in a company of artificers under Captain Jacob Vrooman, and in this company served eight months at Skenesborough in 1776 and eight months at Coeymans in 1778. In 1776 he took part in the expedition to Johnstown. In 1777 he was ordered to Fort Edward and served with the Northern Army until after the surrender of Burgoyne. He was one of the detachment that brought Burgoyne a prisoner to Albany. During the summer of 1778 he performed garrison and field duty at Fort Plank and Fort Plain when Brant laid waste the Canajoharie district. In 1779 he was on garrison duty at the Middle Fort, Schoharie, and in the fall of 1780 was under arms at the time of the Ballston raid. He performed various garrison duties especially at Schenectady.

VAN ESS, GERRIT: On April 19, 1777, he was granted a tavern license by the Committee of Safety. His name appears on the rolls of the 2d Albany County Militia.

VAN ETTEN, BENJAMIN: Born in 1757; died April 22, 1823. On March 17, 1776, he enlisted for nine months under Captain Gerrit S. Veeder, Colonel Cornelius D. Wynkoop's regiment. He served until February 15, 1777, when he was discharged. He was afterwards drafted and was present at the surrender of General Burgoyne. A pensioner under the Act of March 18, 1818.

VAN GUYSLING, CORNELIUS: Baptized November 13, 1726. His name appears on the rolls of the 2d Albany County Militia.

VAN GUYSLING, ELIAS: Died September 5, 1802. On April 1, 1777, he was elected overseer of highways. His name appears on the rolls of the 2d Albany County Militia, Land Bounty Rights.

VAN GUYSLING, JACOB: Born January 18, 1736; died November 19, 1803. His name appears on the rolls of the 2d Albany County Militia and the 2d Albany County Militia, Land Bounty Rights.

VAN GUYSLING, PETER: Born in 1744; died November 20, 1824. He lived on the north side of Front Street, his house being removed at the laying out of Governor's Lane, part of the lot on which it stood being used for the street. His name appears on the rolls of the 2d Albany County Militia and the 2d Albany County Militia, Land Bounty Rights.

VAN INGEN, DIRK: Born September 19, 1738; died February 27, 1814. Buried in Vale Cemetery. He lived on Church Street in the second house north of the Dutch Church. On November 7, 1775, he was elected a member of the second Committee of Safety, being appointed chairman on December 29. He was clerk of the Committee, taking office June 2, 1777, and served on several subsequent Committees. From May 9, 1777, to January 18, 1780 (when he was reduced as a supernumerary), he served in the general hospitals of the Northern Department, eight months as junior and the remainder of the time as senior surgeon. From May to June, 1778, he was at the Schoharie Forts, where he took charge of the wounded after the battle of Cobleskill. On June 24, 1779, he was again elected a member of the Committee of Safety and on July 2 was appointed clerk of the Board. During the fall of 1780 he was in charge of the hospital at Schenectady, where he dressed the wounds of Colonel Brown's soldiers who were brought down after the battle of Klock's Field.

VAN INGEN, JOHN: His name appears on the rolls of the 2d Albany County Militia.

VAN INGEN, JOHN VISSCHER: Born November 11, 1764; died August 30, 1839. His name appears on the rolls of the 2d Albany County Militia. In the fall of 1782 he served on scout duty at Jessup's Patent with a detail of Oneida Indians to apprehend Tories and deserters from the American cause.

VAN INGEN, JOSEPH: Baptized October 3, 1762. He was living in Schenectady when he entered service. From November, 1778, to May 1, 1779, he acted as surgeon's mate under his father, Dirk Van Ingen, at Schenectady, with the rank of first lieutenant; from June to November, 1779, he acted as clerk and surgeon's mate under Doctor Stephen McCrea, physician and surgeon-general of the Flying Hospital, Continental Army; from November, 1779, to May, 1780, he acted as clerk and surgeon's mate under his father; from May to June, 1780, as clerk in the Quartermaster's Department of General Clinton's brigade; from June to August 1, 1780, as clerk to the Commissary General; from August 1, 1780, to May 1, 1781, as conductor of ordnance and military stores under appointment from General Clinton, with rank and pay of first lieutenant; from May 1 to September 1, 1781, as first lieutenant in Captain Hale's company, Colonel Willett's Levies. He served in Sullivan's campaign against the Indians and was in the battle of Newtown. He often performed duty as a surgeon at the hospital in Schenectady, and while conductor of ordnance had charge of a United States gunsmith's or armorer's shop located on Ferry Street. Here several gunsmiths were employed for about a year in repairing arms. Van Ingen is remembered at this time as wearing "a kind of mixed coat and a cocked hat with a cockade thereon." He is spoken of as having been "actively and zealously engaged throughout the war." A pensioner.

VAN PATTEN, AARON N.: Baptized July 1, 1744. On October, 1775, he was recommended to the Provincial

INDIVIDUAL RECORDS OF SERVICE 241

Congress by the Committee of Safety to fill the office of adjutant among the field officers to be assigned to the 2d Albany County Militia. On October 20 a commission was issued in his name, but on January 13, 1776, he refused to accept it. On January 15, 1777, he was a member of the Committee of Safety. His name appears on the rolls of the 2d Albany County Militia.

VAN PATTEN, ADAM: Born in Glenville, November 17, 1757. He lived there during the war and afterwards moved to Rotterdam. Early in 1776 he enrolled under Captain John Van Patten, 2d Albany County Militia, serving as a drummer. In the fall of the same year he performed garrison duty at Fort Edward and Fort Ann, and in the summer of 1777 he was at Fort Edward. He served two months during Schuyler's retreat, after which he was taken sick and permitted to return home. In 1778 he performed garrison duty at the Schoharie Forts, and later went on several tours in pursuit of Tories. A pensioner under the Act of June 7, 1832.

VAN PATTEN, ANDREW: Baptized March 5, 1754. On May 27, 1775, he was appointed first lieutenant in Captain Jellis J. Fonda's company, 2d Albany County Militia, and on October 20 he was commissioned by the Provincial Congress, being reappointed on June 20, 1778.

VAN PATTEN, DIRK: Baptized January 3, 1724-5. His name appears on the rolls of the 2d Albany County Militia, Land Bounty Rights.

VAN PATTEN, FREDERICK: Born in Glenville, November 11, 1760. He lived there during and after the war. In November, 1776, he was enrolled as orderly sergeant under Captain John Van Patten, 2d Albany County Militia. In March, 1777, he enlisted for ten months in a company of batteaumen under Captain Myndert R. Wemple. He performed service cutting wood for the garrison at Schenectady and in transporting provisions and ammunition from

Schenectady to Fort Stanwix. In June, 1778, after the destruction of Cobleskill, he assisted in burying the dead and in pursuit of the enemy. In 1780 he served two months on guard duty at Saratoga after the burning of Caughnawaga. In October, 1781, he marched to Johnstown, but was there taken sick and sent home. A pensioner under the Act of June 7, 1832.

VAN PATTEN, FREDERICK D.: Baptized February 15, 1761; died September 3, 1832. Cornelius Z. Van Santvoord stated that while he was serving as an ensign in Captain Abraham Oothout's company, 2d Albany County Militia, Van Patten "told him that he was about sixteen and prayed to be enrolled in said company, which request [was] complied with by advice and consent of his superior officers. When warned he [Van Patten] was always at his post and conducted himself with zeal and fidelity." Van Santvoord further stated that he "was with him at Saratoga, Fort Edward, Fort Plain, Fort Plank, Ballston, Schoharie and Cobleskill, said Frederick ever evincing the utmost readiness to serve his country and to risk his life on perilous occasions for her benefit." His widow received a pension.

VAN PATTEN, FREDERICK S.: His name appears on the rolls of the 2d Albany County Militia.

VAN PATTEN, HENRY: Baptized April 2, 1753. He served as a private and as a sergeant under Captain John Van Patten, 2d Albany County Militia.

VAN PATTEN, JOHN: Born September 29, 1739; died January 10, 1809. Buried in a private cemetery on the old Teunis Swart farm about one and a half miles west from the village of West Charlton. On May 27, 1775, he was elected captain of the 3d Company of Schenectady militia, and on October 20 a commission was issued in his name by the Provincial Congress. In January, 1776, he took part in the expedition to Johnstown. On January 14, he was

ordered to place guards at William De Graff's, Teunis
Swart's and Lewis Peek's "to prevent any unfriendly
persons or letters from passing upwards." On March 1
he signed an agreement with Philip Schuyler for service
at Lake George and Ticonderoga. On April 1, 1777, he
was elected overseer of highways at Schenectady. He
served throughout the campaign against General Burgoyne, was mentioned for bravery by General Gates at
the battle of Saratoga and was assigned to carry the news
of the British surrender to Albany. (Family tradition.)
On June 20, 1778, he was appointed "captain of the company of the Beat wherein he resided" (the Westina).
Captain Van Patten's company performed guard and
patrol duty throughout his "beat" during the whole of
the war, this being an especially exposed position. In
November, 1778, he was in command of a detail on garrison duty at Switzerbergh near Caughnawaga. In the fall
of 1779 he was at Fort Paris, and in October, 1780, in
command of a detachment in pursuit of Sir John Johnson.
Van Patten resigned from the service towards the close
of the war.

VAN PATTEN, NICHOLAS: On August 11, 1777, he was
arrested by a detail of militia and Continental troops with
sixteen Tories found in his house and barn with their
arms and accoutrements. He was sent to the Albany jail.
On August 13 the Albany Committee refused his release.

VAN PATTEN, NICHOLAS A.: He served as a corporal and as
a sergeant in the 2d Albany County Militia.

VAN PATTEN, NICHOLAS H.: His name appears on the rolls
of the 2d Albany County Militia.

VAN PATTEN, NICHOLAS R.: His name appears on the rolls
of the 2d Albany County Militia.

VAN PATTEN, NICHOLAS S.: Baptized October 21, 1750; died
in Glenville, July 15, 1829. His name appears on the rolls

of the 2d Albany County Militia as serving under Captain John Van Patten.

VAN PATTEN, PETER: Baptized May 5, 1751. His name appears on the rolls of the 2d Albany County Militia, Land Bounty Rights.

VAN PATTEN, PHILIP: Born February 12, 1743; died September 15, 1812. His name appears on the rolls of the 2d Albany County Militia.

VAN PATTEN, SIMON F.: Baptized January 6, 1751. On October 20, 1775, he was commissioned second lieutenant in Captain John Van Patten's company, 2d Albany County Militia. His name does not appear on the roster of regimental officers June 20, 1778 (Archives, State of New York), although John De Graff states (Pension Office Records R 10947) that in November, 1778, he served under him at a place called Switzerburgh near Caughnawaga, at which time he was acting as a second lieutenant in Captain Van Patten's company. John Van Eps also states (Pension Office Records W 27862) that Van Patten occupied such a position in the fall of 1779.

VAN SANTVOORD, CORNELIUS Z.: Born in Schenectady, May 29, 1757; died March 12, 1845. He lived in Schenectady all his life. In 1776 he was an ensign in Captain Abraham Oothout's company, 2d Albany County Militia. In June, 1776, he went to German Flats with General Schuyler when he went to effect the Indian treaty. The same year he marched to Fort Ann, Fort Edward and Skenesborough. He was with the Northern Army during Schuyler's retreat and at the battle of Bemis Heights. On June 20, 1778, he was commissioned ensign by Governor Clinton. He performed service at Sacandaga under General Clinton, twice at Fort Hunter, at Caughnawaga, Johnstown, Canajoharie, Fort Plain, Fort Plank, the Schoharie Forts, Cobleskill, Ballston and Stone Arabia. The details of these duties are not available but they were undoubtedly performed in connection with the raids made at the various points enumerated. A pensioner under the Act of June 7, 1832.

VAN SANTVOORD, ZEGER: Born October 12, 1733; died April 18, 1813. His name appears on the rolls of the 2d Albany County Militia, Land Bounty Rights.

VAN SCHAICK, GERRIT: On March 1, 1776, he signed an agreement with Philip Schuyler for service at Lake George and Ticonderoga. His name appears on the rolls of the 2d Albany County Militia. In 1778 he was enrolled under Captain Jesse Van Slyck.

VAN SICE, ABRAHAM: Born November 27, 1763. In June, 1779, he enlisted under Captain Thomas Brower Banker, 2d Albany County Militia, for duty at Caughnawaga, and in August of the same year, he went to Fort Plank as a volunteer also under Captain Banker. He served at various times thereafter at Fort Plank, Beaverdam, Ballston, Schoharie, Stone Arabia, Canajoharie and on several scouting expeditions with the Oneidas, being assigned to the detachments at the special request of the Indians. In 1781 he was a member of Captain John Crousehorn's company of artillery.

VAN SICE, CORNELIUS: Born March 29, 1737. On March 1, 1776, he signed an agreement with Philip Schuyler for service at Lake George and Ticonderoga. His name appears on the rolls of the 2d Albany County Militia. In 1778 he was enrolled under Captain Jesse Van Slyck.

VAN SICE, GYSBERT: Baptized October 17, 1762. His name appears on the rolls of the 2d Albany County Militia and the 2d Albany County Militia, Land Bounty Rights. From May 1, 1779, to January 1, 1780, he served in the 3d Company, 4th New York Line.

VAN SICE, ISAAC: His name appears on the rolls of the 2d Albany County Militia.

VAN SICE, JACOBUS: Born August 19, 1733. On March 1, 1776, he signed an agreement with Philip Schuyler for service at Lake George and Ticonderoga. On December 6, 1777, he was reported as having "suffered greatly" in a late fire. His name appears on the rolls of the 2d Albany County Militia.

VAN SICE, JOHN: Born January 16, 1726. His name appears on the rolls of the 2d Albany County Militia.

VAN SICE, JOSEPH: Baptized June 29, 1755. His name appears on the rolls of the 2d Albany County Militia. In 1778 he was enrolled under Captain Jesse Van Slyck.

VAN SLYCK, ADRIAN: Baptized June 23, 1751. He served as a corporal and sergeant under Captain Jellis J. Fonda, 2d Albany County Militia, and as a sergeant under Captain John Mynderse. In 1778 he was enrolled under Captain Jesse Van Slyck.

VAN SLYCK, ANDREW: His name appears on the rolls of the 2d Albany County Militia.

VAN SLYCK, ANTHONY: Baptized April 29, 1733. His name appears on the rolls of the 2d Albany County Militia.

VAN SLYCK, ARENT: His name appears on the rolls of the 2d Albany County Militia.

VAN SLYCK, CORNELIUS A.: Born June 3, 1744; died January 27, 1799. On July 28, 1778, he was appointed second lieutenant in a company of Exempts formed in Schenectady under Captain Jacob Schermerhorn.

VAN SLYCK, CORNELIUS P.: Baptized December 1, 1736. On May 27, 1775, he was elected first lieutenant in Captain John Van Patten's company, 2d Albany County Militia. On May 29 he was appointed ensign in a company in the Continental Service under Captain Cornelius Van Dyck, for duty at Ticonderoga. On June 23 he was promoted to the rank of lieutenant and in this capacity served in the Canadian campaign, his company taking part in the siege of St. John's and forming part of the detachment that reduced Chamblee. On March 1, 1776, he signed an agreement with Philip Schuyler for service at Lake George and Ticonderoga, and on April 24, 1777, was in command of a detail of forty-five men for duty between Albany and Lake George. On May 7 he was elected a member of the third Committee of Safety.

VAN SLYCK, HARMANUS: His name appears on the rolls of the 2d Albany County Militia. On February 8, 1776, he was detailed as a guard over a prisoner under committment to the Albany jail.

VAN SLYCK, HARMANUS A.: Baptized June 3, 1750. His name appears on the rolls of the 2d Albany County Militia, Land Bounty Rights.

VAN SLYCK, JESSE: Born June 29, 1744; died in September, 1815. On February 10, 1776, he was appointed first lieutenant in Captain Ahasueras Marselis's company, 2d Albany County Militia. He probably was appointed captain soon after. In April, 1777, he was in command of a detail which marched to Saratoga, where they joined four hundred of the Vermont militia under Colonel Seth Warner and proceeded to Jessup's Patent, where "one Morrell," sent by the British, was actively engaged in enlisting troops and erecting fortifications. He commanded a company throughout the campaign against General Burgoyne, and in April, 1778, commanded part of his company which joined a detachment of one hundred and twenty-five whites and a few Indians under Major Abraham Swits for service in apprehending Tories at Beaverdam. In June he commanded a scout of fifteen whites and seven Indians to Cobleskill. On June 20 he was regularly commissioned captain, and in July was at Fort Plain on garrison duty. In March, 1780, he commanded a detail of thirty men to Stone Arabia, and in

April went on scout duty to Glens Falls with fifteen whites and five Indians. From July to August he was stationed with a company of eighty men at the Middle Fort, Schoharie, and marched in command of a company against Joseph Brant after the destruction of Canajoharie. In October he was on garrison duty at Fort Plank. He did not go with the troops under General Van Rensselaer against Sir John Johnson but remained at Fort Plain. In July, 1781, he was with a detail of thirty men from Schenectady on garrison duty at Fort Hunter, and in October commanded a company in pursuit of Major Ross and Butler after the burning of Warren's Bush, on which occasion his detachment captured twenty-seven prisoners. In October and November, 1782, he was on garrison duty at Fort Herkimer.

VAN SLYCK, MARTIN: Baptized October 20, 1748. On March 1, 1776, he signed an agreement with Philip Schuyler for service at Lake George and Ticonderoga. His name appears on the rolls of the 2d Albany County Militia and the 2d Albany County Militia, Land Bounty Rights. In 1778 he was enrolled under Captain Jesse Van Slyck.

VAN SLYCK, PETER: His name appears on the rolls of the 2d Albany County Militia.

VAN SLYCK, SAMUEL: Baptized March 17, 1738. His name appears on the rolls of the 2d Albany County Militia, Land Bounty Rights.

VAN VLECK, BENJAMIN: Born in Schenectady, January 10, 1756; living in 1837. A carpenter and wagoner by trade. On March 1, 1776, he enlisted as an artificer under Captain Jacob Vrooman and served at Fort George until December. On March 1, 1777, he again enlisted as an artificer under Jacob Van Deusen of Albany. He was stationed at Fort Miller, Fort Edward, Fort George and Ticonderoga, building boats in each of these places. He left Ticonderoga when the fortress was evacuated by Gen-

eral St. Clair and proceeded to within a few miles of
Albany, returning later to Saratoga. He was present at
the surrender of General Burgoyne. On March 1, 1778,
he again enlisted as an artificer under Captain Jacob Vrooman, and served in building barracks and batteaux at Saratoga and in rebuilding General Schuyler's mills and house.
His claim for pension was rejected.

VAN VORST, ABRAHAM: Baptized April 3, 1743; died about
1833. He lived near Burnt Hills. His name appears on
the rolls of the 2d Albany County Militia, Land Bounty
Rights.

VAN VORST, AHASUERAS: Baptized August 24, 1735. His
name appears on the rolls of the 2d Albany County Militia,
Land Bounty Rights.

VAN VORST, JAMES: He first entered the service under Captain Van Sice, and from the spring of 1777 to the winter
of 1780 he served as baggage master under appointment
from Henry Glen, being stationed at Schenectady, where
he assisted in the transportation of supplies. His widow's
claim for pension was rejected.

VAN VORST, JAMES J.: Born in 1763. In 1778 he was
enrolled in Captain Jesse Van Slyck's company, 2d Albany
County Militia. In the spring of 1779 he enlisted in
Captain Silas Grey's company, 4th New York Line, and
continued in this company until 1781, when he was detailed
under Colonel Henry Glen for service in the Quartermaster's Department for duty as a hostler at the Continental stables in Schenectady. A pensioner under the Act
of May 15, 1828.

VAN VORST, JELLIS: Born October 14, 1747; died August
9, 1823. In 1775 he enlisted under Captain Cornelius Van
Dyck and served eleven months. He was at Quebec. In
August, 1777, he enlisted in Captain Giles Wolcott's
company, Colonel Seth Warner's regiment, and served

until October, 1780, when he was taken prisoner by the enemy at Fort George. He was taken to Canada and remained there until 1782, when he managed to escape and returned to find his regiment disbanded. His name appears on the rolls of the 2d Albany County Militia. He received bounty lands from the State. A pensioner under the Act of March 18, 1818.

VAN VORST, JOHN B.: On August 15, 1778, it was certified by several of the more prominent inhabitants that he had kept a ferry for some time past across the Mohawk River at his house about a mile below the town, that a ferry was necessary there and that said Van Vorst was the proper person to keep it.

VAN VORST, JOHN JACOB: Born in Schenectady, January 19, 1741; died in Glenville, May 23, 1844. In the winter of 1775, with a detachment under Captain Jesse Van Slyck, he joined the troops destined to attack Quebec. He performed three weeks' service, probably with the force that went as far as Skenesborough and returned. In 1776, at Fort Edward, he was drafted from the ranks by the quartermaster general to serve as wagon master. He received no regular appointment as such until September, 1777, when a commission was issued in his name under which he served to the close of the war. In addition to his own personal services "at his own individual cost of £28 in specie in March, 1778, [he] furnished a recruit named John Able to enlist and serve as private in the army during the War." Van Vorst served in the campaign against Burgoyne at Fort Edward, Snookkill and Bemis Heights. The greater part of his service was, however, performed as barrack master at Schenectady, where, under Henry Glen, he superintended the transportation of ammunition, baggage and provisions to the different posts. He "was frequently employed on important and confidential occasions as an Express rider," and is spoken of

INDIVIDUAL RECORDS OF SERVICE 251

as having been "a faithful and highly useful friend to his Country."

VAN VORST, PETER: Baptized February 14, 1739. His name appears on the rolls of the 2d Albany County Militia.

VAN VORST, PHILIP D.: Baptized December 22, 1745; died April 3, 1830. On June 20, 1778, he was commissioned second lieutenant in Captain Abraham Van Eps's company, 2d Albany County Militia. His name appears on the rolls of the 2d Albany County Militia, Land Bounty Rights.

VAN VRANKEN, DERICK: His name appears on the rolls of the 2d Albany County Militia. A pensioner under the Act of June 7, 1832.

VAN VRANKEN, GERRIT: Born in Niskayuna, March 10, 1757. From June to December, 1776, he was enrolled under Captain Nicholas Van de Kar, 12th Albany County Militia. From June to October 4, 1777, he served as a volunteer under Captain Nanning Visscher of the same regiment. He went to Fort Edward, Saratoga, Stillwater and then to Niskayuna, where he remained until after Burgoyne's surrender. In June, 1778, he volunteered for service at Cherry Valley under Captain Collins, and in July went to Fort Plain under Captain John Vanderburgh. During the year 1779 he moved to Schenectady and resided here for one year. He was enrolled under Captain Jellis J. Fonda, 2d Albany County Militia, and in September went as a volunteer to Stone Arabia. His claim for pension was rejected.

VAN VRANKEN, MAUS: Born in Schenectady, May 23, 1756; died July 1, 1833. He resided in Schenectady until 1830. He entered service some time in 1776 under Captain Jellis J. Fonda, 2d Albany County Militia, and served throughout the war whenever called upon. He served about nine months in each of the years 1776 and 1777, mostly with the Northern Army. He was at Stillwater, but not in the battle, being out on scout duty. He served at Skenesborough, Fort Ann, Fort George and was present at Burgoyne's surrender. He volunteered to go to Bennington but was recalled after having started because some of the officers claimed they had no right to take their troops outside the State. In 1778 he served about six months, principally at Fort Hunter, Fort Plain and Caughnawaga. On the call to Fort Hunter, Van Vranken and six others took with them a "six pounder." He volunteered to march to Fort Plain to check the raid of Butler and on this occasion also took the cannon, his detachment firing it as they approached the fort to alarm the enemy. They pursued the enemy for three days. He served about four months each year in each of the four succeeding years. This service was mostly in and about Schenectady, Ballston, Schoharie and Caughnawaga. A pensioner.

VAN VRANKEN, NICHOLAS: His name appears on the rolls of the 2d Albany County Militia.

VAN VRANKEN, NICHOLAS N.: His name appears on the rolls of the 2d Albany County Militia.

VAN VRANKEN, RICHARD: Born in Schenectady, August 15, 1763. In 1779 he volunteered under Captain Thomas Brower Banker, 2d Albany County Militia, and in August was on duty for three weeks on a tour to Herkimer and again in the fall for two weeks to Fort Plank. In the summer of 1780 he was on garrison duty at Fort Plank, and in October of the same year he volunteered to march to Fort Hunter with a party of twenty or thirty others from Schenectady. They did not, however, arrive at the fort until after the battle of Johnstown and while the troops were in pursuit of the enemy. In 1781 he was on various tours to Fort Hunter, Stone Arabia and Fort Plank. On one occasion he served as a sergeant. A pensioner.

INDIVIDUAL RECORDS OF SERVICE 253

VAN VRANKEN, RYCKERT: Buried September 12, 1805. On March 1, 1776, he signed an agreement with Philip Schuyler for service at Lake George and Ticonderoga. His name appears on the rolls of the 2d Albany County Militia. In 1779 he was in command of the guard at Schenectady.

VEDDER, ALBERT A.: His name appears on the rolls of the 2d Albany County Militia.

VEDDER, ALBERT H.: Born in Schenectady; baptized March 17, 1737; died in Amsterdam, June 21, 1800. "A man of note and a recognized patriot. He was captured by the Indians and Tories in a raid through the Valley but during the retreat to Canada escaped and returned home."

VEDDER, ALBERT L.: Born in the Schenectady Township, October 28, 1759. In October, 1775, he was enrolled under Captain Abraham Oothout, 2d Albany County Militia. In the spring of 1776 he enlisted for four months in a company of artificers under Jacob Vrooman and was employed in building boats, storehouses, etc., at Ticonderoga, Lake George, Skenesborough and Saratoga. In the spring of 1777 he again enrolled under Captain Oothout, and in the summer of the same year served under Captain John Mynderse with the Northern Army during Schuyler's retreat and until the surrender of Burgoyne. In the fall of 1778 he served two months on draft at Fort Paris, and in the summer of 1779 was at Fort Plain. When Canajoharie was burned he was ordered to Fort Plank. In the spring of 1780 he was ordered to Fort Hunter when Caughnawaga was destroyed. He performed various guard and garrison duties. A pensioner.

VEDDER, ALEXANDER: Born in Albany, February 20, 1709; died in October, 1780. A member of the Committees of Safety taking office June 2, 1777, and January 5, 1778. The election of members to the Board taking office January 5, 1778, was held at his house, where were also held many of the Committee meetings. His name appears on the rolls of the 2d Albany County Militia.

VEDDER, ARENT A.: His name appears on the rolls of the 2d Albany County Militia.

VEDDER, ARENT S.: Born August 14, 1735. He lived in Niskayuna. On February 10, 1776, he was elected second lieutenant in Captain Thomas Brower Banker's company, 2d Albany County Militia. On March 1, 1776, he signed an agreement with Philip Schuyler for service at Lake George and Ticonderoga. On June 20, 1778, he was regularly commissioned second lieutenant in Captain Banker's company. In September or October, he served at Fort Plank and Stone Arabia, and in 1781 at Fort Hunter, Fort Plank and Stone Arabia.

VEDDER, FRANCIS: Baptized August 27, 1749. A merchant. On March 1, 1776, he signed an agreement with Philip Schuyler for service at Lake George and Ticonderoga. In May, 1778, he commanded a scout to Sacandaga, and on June 20 was commissioned second lieutenant in Captain Jesse Van Slyck's company, 2d Albany County Militia. In November he commanded a detail of thirty-six men for garrison duty at Fort Plain, and in May, 1780, commanded a detail of thirteen men to Viele's Rifts to bring scows from the north to the south side of the river to prevent the enemy from crossing. In June, as an ensign, he commanded a detachment on an alarm to Schoharie in pursuit of Sir John Johnson, Brant and Butler, and on his return performed garrison duty at Schenectady. In August, 1781, he went to Viele's Rifts on scout duty with a squad of ten men, and in May, 1782, he was on patrol duty at Harpersfield.

VEDDER, FREDERICK: Born in Glenville, April 28, 1761. In 1779 he enrolled under Captain Abraham Oothout; 2d Albany County Militia, and in September performed duty at Stone Arabia and in October at Caughnawaga. On May

22, 1780, he was sent to warn out the company to go to Caughnawaga at the time the family of the Visschers was murdered. He was on duty three weeks. In 1780 he served two weeks at Fort Hunter; two weeks at Canajoharie, when the town was destroyed; two weeks at Fort Clyde, and in October eight days at Ballston. From August 1 to November 1, 1781, he was stationed at Claas Viele's Rifts. A pensioner under the Act of June 7, 1832.

VEDDER, HARMANUS: Baptized March 4, 1739. His name appears on the rolls of the 2d Albany County Militia. In 1778 he employed Joseph De Golyer as a substitute.

VEDDER, JOHN: Early in 1776, he went to Caughnawaga as a private under Captain John Van Patten, 2d Albany County Militia. On September 17 he enlisted in Captain John A. Bradt's company of State Rangers, and served in it until the company was disbanded in the spring of 1777, after which he enlisted as a minute man under Captain Jellis J. Fonda. In 1778 he served under Captain Jesse Van Slyck, and in October, 1779, was on duty at Stone Arabia. In 1781 he was a member of Captain John Crousehorn's company of artillery. His widow received a pension.

VEDDER, JOHN: On February 25, 1780, he was commissioned ensign in Captain John Van Eps's company, 2d Albany County Militia.

VEDDER, NICHOLAS ALEXANDER: On July 9, 1777, he was appointed to serve in the commissary department during the absence of the militia at Fort Edward, but on account of complaints (he being enrolled in the militia) he was later ordered to accompany the troops. He served as a private in the 2d Albany County Militia under various captains and as a corporal under Captain Abraham Oothout.

VEDDER, PHILIP: Baptized July 9, 1737; died May 6, 1822. He lived in Rotterdam. In November, 1776, he was serving as a lieutenant under Captain John Van Patten, 2d Albany County Militia. In May, 1778, he was on duty at Cobleskill. On June 20 he was regularly commissioned second lieutenant in Captain Van Patten's company.

VEDDER, SIMON H.: Baptized November 11, 1744. His name appears on the rolls of the 2d Albany County Militia.

VEEDER, BARENT: His name appears on the rolls of the 2d Albany County Militia.

VEEDER, CORNELIUS: His name appears on the rolls of the 2d Albany County Militia.

VEEDER, GERRIT (S. OR N.): Born in 1751. On May 27, 1775, he was appointed a second lieutenant in a company of minute men formed in Schenectady. In July he was appointed first lieutenant in Captain John Mynderse's company, being granted a commission by the Provincial Congress on October 20. In January, 1776, he took part in the expedition to Johnstown. In February he was appointed captain of a company raised in Schenectady for the Canadian service, and on March 1 he was commissioned a captain in the Continental Line under Colonel Cornelius D. Wynkoop. On April 10 he was appointed captain of a company of State Rangers in place of John A. Bradt, and on October 7 was commissioned captain of the 8th Company, 1st New York Line. On December 5 he resigned this commission but served as a captain with the New York troops to the end of the war. In 1777 he served in the campaign against Burgoyne and had command of a detachment at the battle of Bemis Heights. On July 1, 1782, he commanded a detail of forty men to Fort Plain and Fort Plank to act as guards while the crops were being harvested. A pensioner under the Act of June 7, 1832.

VEEDER, HELMAR S.: His name appears on the rolls of the 2d Albany County Militia.

INDIVIDUAL RECORDS OF SERVICE 257

VEEDER, HENDRICK: His name appears on the rolls of the 2d Albany County Militia, Land Bounty Rights.

VEEDER, JOHN B.: Born in the Schenectady Township, November 6, 1760; died in Munroe County in August, 1847. He lived in the Schenectady Township for fourteen years after the Revolution. In 1777 he served a short time on guard duty at Schenectady as a substitute. In June, 1779, he served under Captain Thomas Brower Banker, 2d Albany County Militia, erecting blockhouses at Sacandaga. In the fall of 1779, he was drafted for duty at Fort Plank and Fort Paris, and in the spring of 1780 he went to Caughnawaga under Captain Banker. He was at Fort Plain when the Canajoharie settlements were destroyed and when Colonel Willett asked for volunteers for the pursuit of the enemy, Veeder "was the first man who spoke and expressed his willingness to go and he did go together with a large detachment." In 1781 he was a member of Captain John Crousehorn's company of artillery. He performed various garrison and guard duties and went on several expeditions in pursuit of Tories.

VEEDER, JOHN H.: Born June 2, 1718; died August 4, 1794. On March 1, 1776, he signed an agreement with Philip Schuyler for service at Lake George and Ticonderoga. On April 1, 1777, he was elected overseer of highways at Schenectady. His name appears on the rolls of the 2d Albany County Militia, Land Bounty Rights.

VEEDER, NICHOLAS G.: Born in Glenville, December 25, 1761; died April 7, 1862. Toward the end of the year 1777 he enrolled under Captain Jesse Van Slyck, 2d Albany County Militia. In July, 1778, he went on a scout to Ballston and Galway, and in November, 1779, he was on garrison duty at Fort Paris. In August, 1780, he marched with a detachment against a party of the enemy under Joseph Brant after the destruction of Canajoharie, and in October of the same year went to Ballston when it was attacked. In October, 1781, he marched to Johnstown and on his return guarded some prisoners to Schenectady. He was out on many alarms in pursuit of Tories and performed various guard and garrison duties. This is the Nicholas Veeder who is well remembered by many of the older generation as the last survivor of the Revolution in Schenectady. After the war he lived in a building known as the "Old Fort," situated in the present village of Scotia a few hundred feet north of the Vley Road and about one hundred feet west of Halcyon Street. The building was removed in 1891. A pensioner under the Act of June 7, 1832.

VEEDER, NICHOLAS P.: Born February 9, 1734; died November 11, 1807. His house was on the lot bounded by Front, Green and Ferry Streets. On October 5, 1775, he was recommended to the Provincial Congress by the Committee of Safety to fill the office of second major among the field officers to be assigned to the Schenectady militia. On October 20 a commission was issued in his name, but on January 13, 1776, he refused to accept it. He is spoken of as having served as a captain in the Quartermaster's Department during the year 1776, although the records at Washington make special mention of the fact that there is no evidence to show that he so served. On March 3, 1777, he was a member of the Committee of Safety. His name appears on the rolls of the 2d Albany County Militia.

VEEDER, PETER S.: On May 10, 1776, General Schuyler was informed by the Committee of Safety that he had gone to Lake George without the permission of the Board and that he had repeatedly refused to sign the General Association. His name appears on the rolls of the 2d Albany County Militia. In 1778 he was enrolled under Captain Jesse Van Slyck.

VEEDER, SIMON: Born in Schenectady, May 1, 1748. Early in 1776, while living at Caughnawaga, he was appointed a

sergeant under Captain John Davis, 3d Tryon County
Militia. In July he was drafted for the Line but hired
a substitute. During the fall he was stationed at Johnstown. He was not at the battle of Oriskany but was with
the troops that went to the relief of Fort Stanwix, later
marching to Saratoga and being present at the surrender
of Burgoyne. In October, 1780, acting as quartermaster,
he went with the troops under General Van Rensselaer
in pursuit of Sir John Johnson and fought at the battle
of Klock's Field. During this raid of the enemy Veeder's
barn, mills, tannery and brewery were burned and he
"very narrowly escaped with his life, under a discharge
of more than 100 guns at him." In the spring of 1781
he received the appointment of quartermaster in the 3d
Tryon County Militia and served in this capacity to the
end of the war, commanding a detachment of the troops
that marched against Major Ross in October of that year.
In May, 1782, he was again drafted and again hired a
substitute; he, however, performed military duty during
both this year and 1783.

VEEDER, SIMON B.: Born in Schenectady in 1753; died in
1810. His name appears on the rolls of the 2d Albany
County Militia. "He was at the storming of the blockhouse at Johnstown, where his wife nursed the sick and
wounded."

VEEDER, SIMON H.: His name appears on the rolls of the
2d Albany County Militia.

VEEDER, WILHELMUS: His name appears on the rolls of the
2d Albany County Militia.

VIELE, PHILIP: Born July 7, 1745; died August 7, 1797. In
1776 he was enrolled under Captain John Van Patten,
2d Albany County Militia, serving in January on the
expedition to Johnstown, and in the fall performing garrison duty at Fort Ann. In 1777 he performed two
months' service with the Northern Army as sergeant,

which rank he seems to have held to the end of the war. He was present at the battle of Bemis Heights. During the summer and early fall of 1778 he was on duty at the Lower Fort, Schoharie. In the fall of 1779 he served at Fort Plain and Stone Arabia, and in the fall of 1781 was on guard duty at Claas Viele's Fort. His son's application for pension was rejected.

VISSCHER, JOHN: Before the war a justice of the peace at Schenectady. On October 25, 1776, he was reported to the General Committee at Albany as "a person disaffected to the cause of American liberty." In May, 1777, he was recommended to the field officers as "a dangerous person." On May 22, he voluntarily took the oath that he would take up arms in defense of the country in case of any invasion. On July 14, 1778, he was cited to appear before the Commissioners of Conspiracies to render satisfaction regarding his conduct during the war, conformable to the act respecting persons of neutral or equivocal characters. On July 17 he refused to take the Oath of Allegiance, and on July 18 was ordered to hold himself in readiness to be removed to within the enemy's lines. On August 1 he expressed a willingness to take the Oath but was not permitted to do so, as the Act did not permit of the Oath being administered to one who had once refused to take it. He was ordered to appear on August 14 ready for deportation. On May 24, 1779, the Oath of Allegiance was administered to him in accordance with the amended Act.

VISSCHER, JOHN, JR.: His name appears on the rolls of the 2d Albany County Militia.

VROOMAN, ABRAHAM: Born in 1761; died February 5, 1815. He is buried in the old Vrooman Cemetery on the Bartholomew Vrooman farm, Albany Road. The graves are on a knoll in a small grove of evergreen trees surrounded by a fence. His name appears on the rolls of the 2d

Albany County Militia and the 2d Albany County Militia, Land Bounty Rights.

VROOMAN, ADAM: Born in Schenectady, May 25, 1760. In October, 1776, he enlisted under Captain John Mynderse, 2d Albany County Militia, and served to the end of the war, during the first part as a corporal and for more than two years as a sergeant. In the summer of 1777 he was with the Northern Army during Schuyler's retreat, actively engaged in the battle of Snookkill, in the battle of September 19 and in several other skirmishes. He remained on duty until after the surrender of Burgoyne. In 1778 he performed garrison duty at Caughnawaga, Palatine, Fort Paris and Fort Plank, one month at each place except at Fort Plank, where he remained two months. He mounted guard at the three forts in Schoharie both before and after the destruction of the Schoharie settlements; also at Cobleskill and Brakabeen. In October, 1781, he marched to Johnstown. On numerous occasions he served as a scout and spy, and when not out on expeditions performed guard duty at Schenectady. A pensioner under the Act of June 7, 1832.

VROOMAN, ADAM S.: Baptized March 5, 1754; died August 3, 1808. His name appears on the rolls of the 2d Albany County Militia.

VROOMAN, ARENT: Born June 14, 1758; died February 18, 1814. He served under Captain Thomas Brower Banker, 2d Albany County Militia.

VROOMAN, BARENT: Born December 24, 1725; died November 16, 1784. He was pastor of the First Dutch Church during the Revolution.

VROOMAN, CORNELIUS: Born February 4, 1722; died in 1806. His name appears on the rolls of the 2d Albany County Militia, Land Bounty Rights.

VROOMAN, DAVID: His name appears on the rolls of the 2d Albany County Militia.

VROOMAN, HENDRICK: Born October 23, 1757; died January 30, 1813. He is buried in the old Vrooman Cemetery on the Bartholomew Vrooman farm, Albany Road. The graves are on a knoll in a small grove of evergreen trees surrounded by a fence. His name appears on the rolls of the 2d Albany County Militia.

VROOMAN, ISAAC: Born November 13, 1712; died June 1, 1807. He had a farm at the Brandywine Mills. On May 7, 1776, he was elected a member of the third Committee of Safety. He was also a member of the fourth Committee and on March 3, 1777, was elected a member of the fifth Committee of Safety. On April 1, 1777, he was elected a supervisor. In 1779 he was a member of Assembly under the first State Constitution.

VROOMAN, JACOB A.: Baptized December 30, 1747; died in Glenville, July 21, 1831. On March 1, 1776, he signed an agreement with Philip Schuyler for service at Lake George and Ticonderoga.

VROOMAN, JACOB I.: His name appears on the rolls of the 2d Albany County Militia.

VROOMAN, JACOB J.: Baptized March 30, 1755. He inherited his father's farm three and one half miles south of Schenectady. His name appears on the rolls of the 2d Albany County Militia.

VROOMAN, JACOB S.: Baptized November 13, 1723. A carpenter. In 1775 a company under his command served at Ticonderoga and vicinity, building boats preparatory for the American invasion of Canada. On March 1, 1776, he signed an agreement with Philip Schuyler as an overseer of a company of carpenters for service at Lake George and Ticonderoga. In March, 1778, he commanded a company which marched to Saratoga and remained there throughout the season, building boats and rebuilding General Schuyler's house and mills which had been burned by the British the year previous. His name appears on the rolls of the 2d Albany County Militia, Land Bounty Rights.

VROOMAN, JOHN B.: Baptized January 13, 1745. On October 20, 1775, he was commissioned ensign in the 4th Company, 2d Albany County Militia. On November 22 he received a commission as first lieutenant from the Provincial Congress, and on February 10, 1776, was assigned to Captain Thomas Brower Banker's company. In the spring he was in command of a detail for the apprehension of Tories at the Heldebergh. On April 1, 1777, he was elected overseer of highways at Schenectady. On June 20, 1778, he was reappointed first lieutenant in Captain Banker's company. On June 15, 1779, he was elected a member of the Committee of Safety. In the summer he commanded a detachment of militia and Oneida Indians to Schoharie to capture a party of runaway Tuscarora Indians. In September or October he served at Fort Plank and Stone Arabia, and in the fall of 1780 marched to Ballston in pursuit of the enemy after the raid.

VROOMAN, JOHN J.: Born in the Schenectady Township, April 5, 1763. In the spring of 1779 he enlisted under Captain John Mynderse, 2d Albany County Militia, and in the fall of that year was on duty at Fort Paris. He also acted as captain of the guard at Schenectady. From January 1 to December 24, 1780, he served in a company of batteau and fatigue men under Captain Joseph Peek. At various times he served under Colonels Dayton, Van Dyck and Gansevoort. A pensioner.

VROOMAN, JOHN T.: His name appears on the rolls of the 2d Albany County Militia.

VROOMAN, LAWRENCE: Born in Schenectady, July 26, 1757. In 1775 he enlisted under Captain Jellis J. Fonda, 2d Albany County Militia, and served as a private until

1778 when he was promoted to the rank of ensign. He did not, however, receive a regular commission until February 25, 1780. In the fall of 1776 he marched to Stillwater, thence to Fort Ann, remaining some time on duty at each place. From Fort Ann he proceeded down the Wood Creek to Skenesborough as a guard for provision boats. From September 27, 1777, until a few days before Burgoyne's surrender, when he was taken sick and obliged to return home, he served with the Northern Army. In the fall of the same year he was appointed a deputy commissary of the Northern Department to purchase hospital supplies, and served in this capacity until April, 1778. During the year 1778 he performed garrison duty at Fort Paris, and was at one of the Schoharie Forts when Cobleskill was destroyed. He was at Fort Plain and Fort Plank when the Indians and Tories raided that section, and when the alarm gun was fired at Fort Plain he was one of the men who went in front of the cannon for the relief. In October, 1781, he was on duty at Canajoharie when Walter Butler was killed. He was spoken of as "a valiant officer." He died before his claim for pension was granted and his son's application was rejected.

VROOMAN, NICHOLAS: On August 12, 1777, he was arrested and sent to Albany as implicated in a Tory plot.

VROOMAN, SIMON J.: Born in Schenectady, August 3, 1760; died November 10, 1841. He removed from Schenectady in 1787. In March, 1777, he entered the service in the the Quartermaster's Department under Lieutenant-Colonel Christopher Yates, being stationed at Fort Ann. He was in active service during Schuyler's retreat, in the battle of Bemis Heights and with the troops under General Arnold to the relief of Fort Stanwix. In March or April, 1778, he performed three months' service at Schuyler's Farms, building boats, and in August of the same year he enrolled in the company of Captain John Mynderse. He was stationed three months at Fort Paris. In June, 1779, under

Lieutenant-Colonel Christopher Yates he went to Tioga Point with the boats conveying baggage and ammunition for General Clinton's division. He was afterwards stationed six weeks with Captain John Mynderse's company at Fort Herkimer. In August, 1780, he was commissioned a subaltern by the Council of Appointment and assigned to the company of Captain John Burnett, Colonel Lewis Dubois's Levies. He performed guard duty at Fishkill, Dobbs Ferry and later at Fort Plain, and on the approach of Sir John Johnson was sent as an express to Schenectady, returning to the fort on the third day. He was in the engagement at Stone Arabia when Colonel Brown was killed, and in the second action after the arrival of General Van Rensselaer. He went in pursuit of the enemy as far as Fort Herkimer, remaining there six weeks until relieved by the Regulars, when he returned to Schenectady. In April, 1781, he was commissioned a subaltern and assigned to the company of Captain John Gross, Colonel Willett's Levies. He was stationed at Fort Plain, and in July took part in the engagement known as the battle of Torlock, in which Captain Robert McKean was killed. He went in pursuit of the enemy after the destruction of Warren's Bush, was in the battle of Johnstown and joined in the pursuit of the enemy after the battle. His widow stated that at the close of the war Vrooman held a commission as lieutenant. A pensioner.

VROOMAN, WALTER: On June 20, 1778, he was commissioned first lieutenant in Captain Jesse Van Slyck's company, 2d Albany County Militia. In September he was on garrison duty at the Middle Fort, Schoharie. In 1779 he was serving as a lieutenant in the Levies. From August to November he commanded a company at Schoharie mustered at Schenectady and attached to Colonel Butler's regiment. On October 23, 1780, while serving as a lieutenant in Colonel Harper's Levies, he was taken prisoner by forces under Sir John Johnson and Joseph Brant and removed to Canada, where he was held until the end of the war.

WAGGERMAN, GEORGE: On January 22, 1777, he enlisted in Captain John A. Bradt's company of State Rangers, and on March 26 enlisted for the war and was assigned to Captain Leonard Bleecker's company, 3d New York Line.

WAGGERMAN, MICHAEL: His name appears on the rolls of the 2d Albany County Militia.

WAGNER, ANDREW: His name appears on the rolls of the 2d Albany County Militia.

WAGNER, MICHAEL: His name appears on the rolls of the 2d Albany County Militia.

WAGNER, NICHOLAS: His name appears on the rolls of the 2d Albany County Militia.

WARD, CHRISTOPHER: Born at Stone Arabia, July 18, 1757; died November 13, 1838. Buried in Vale Cemetery. He lived in Schenectady during and after the war. In January, 1776, he was enrolled in Captain Abraham Oothout's company, 2d Albany County Militia. He took part in the expedition to Johnstown, and in the fall of the same year was on guard at Johnstown and Switzerbergh. In the spring of 1777 he was drafted under Captain Jesse Van Slyck and marched to Jessup's Patent. This same year he served during Schuyler's retreat, at Saratoga, Stillwater and Bemis Heights, part of the time as a substitute for Harmon Peters. From March to July 18, 1778, he served as a blacksmith in the Continental Army; he then enlisted and served three months in Captain Thomas Patten's company of artificers. With this company he went to Albany, Fishkill, Fredericksburg, White Plains and Dover. In the fall of this same year he went with a detachment from Colonel Wemple's regiment towards Cherry Valley. From January to May 1, 1779, he served in a company of artificers under Captain John Clute, and in the spring of 1780 performed three weeks' duty at Schoharie. In the summer of this same year he enlisted in Captain James McGee's company, Colonel Morris Graham's Levies. When Stone Arabia was raided by Sir John Johnson (August, 1780) he was on duty at Fort Herkimer. A pensioner under the Act of June 7, 1832.

WARN, RICHARD: His name appears on the rolls of the 2d Albany County Militia, Land Bounty Rights.

WARN, SAMUEL: On March 1, 1776, he signed an agreement with Philip Schuyler for service at Lake George and Ticonderoga. His name appears on the rolls of the 2d Albany County Militia, Land Bounty Rights.

WASSON, JAMES: In May, 1782, he enlisted in Captain Guy Young's company, Colonel Marinus Willett's Levies.

WASSON, JOHN: Born in the Schenectady Township, January 6, 1764. He was living in Princetown when, about July 25, 1780, he enlisted under Captain Jacob John Lansing, Colonel Morris Graham's Levies. He marched to West Point and there performed garrison duty about three weeks, then to Dobbs Ferry, where he remained one week, then to Albany, where the regiment was divided. His detachment marched to the Middle Fort, Schoharie. He was in the fort when Sir John Johnson attacked it and was with the troops that subsequently pursued the enemy. From April, 1781, to January, 1782, he served under Captain Stephen White, Colonel Willett's Levies. He volunteered with a party of twenty-eight Indians and white men for scout duty to Crown Point. From March to October, 1782, he served under Captain Guy Young, and then enlisted under Captain Jellis A. Fonda, Colonel Willett's Levies, and served three months when he was discharged from the service. He was in the battle of Johnstown and in an engagement with the enemy at Lake Schuyler in 1782. A pensioner under the Act of June 7, 1832.

WASSON, THOMAS: Lived in Princetown. On September 7, 1775, the Committee of Safety applied to the Albany Committee to assign him a commission as captain of militia, and on October 20 he was commissioned captain of the 5th Company, 2d Albany County Militia. He was reappointed on June 20, 1778.

WASSON, THOMAS J.: His name appears on the rolls of the 2d Albany County Militia, Land Bounty Rights.

WATSON, ALEXANDER: His name appears on the rolls of the 2d Albany County Militia.

WELLER, FREDERICK: Born at Walkill, December 5, 1757. In the fall of 1775, when he enrolled under Captain Abraham Oothout, 2d Albany County Militia, as a sergeant, he was living in Princetown and here he continued to live for about five years after the war. He was drafted for the Canadian expedition. He marched to Fort Edward and Skenesborough but was ordered home after eight weeks' service on the news of the death of General Montgomery. In the spring of 1777 he went with a body of Vermont militia to destroy a blockhouse at Jessup's Patent. When Burgoyne invested Ticonderoga he was again called to Fort Edward. He was in General Schuyler's retreat but a few days before the battle of Bemis Heights was taken with measles and obliged to return home. When he recovered his health he performed fatigue duty under Henry Glen in transporting effects for the army from Schenectady to Albany. He served on various occasions at the Schoharie Forts and Fort Plain. On July 23, 1780, he was sent to Albany under arrest as being concerned in a plot to join the enemy or of supplying them with provisions. He was, however, on August 10 released on bail. He served when Ballston was attacked and with the troops in pursuit of Sir John Johnson, following the destruction of the Mohawk settlements. In the fall of 1781 he was at Fort Hunter during the battle of Johnstown, where the troops with which he served were detailed to guard prisoners. A pensioner.

WELLER, ROBERT: He served as a private and as a sergeant in the 2d Albany County Militia.

WELSH, JOHN: On May 31, 1775, some of the soldiers of Captain Cornelius Van Dyck's company were boarded at his house while the company was being recruited and drilled.

WEMPLE, ABRAHAM: Born about 1728; died near Albany in 1799. On September 7, 1775, the Committee of Safety applied to the Albany Committee to assign him a commission as captain of militia. On October 5 he was recommended to the Provincial Congress for the office of colonel among the field officers to be assigned to the 2d Albany County Militia, and on October 20 he was commissioned colonel, being reappointed on June 20, 1778, and serving in this capacity until near the end of the war, when he resigned from the service. On November 7, 1775, he was elected a member of the second Committee of Safety and on December 29 was appointed deputy chairman of the Board. On July 26, 1779, he was again elected a member of the Committee. Colonel Wemple served with his regiment on the various occasions when called out and was throughout the war a zealous and active adherent of the American cause.

WEMPLE, BARENT (WEMP, BARNABAS): Baptized in Schenectady September 3, 1738; buried December 27, 1843. On April 11, 1776, he enlisted under Captain Gerrit S. Veeder, Colonel Cornelius D. Wynkoop's regiment. On December 28 (probably 1776) he enlisted for the war under Captain John Copp, 1st New York Line. In June, 1778, he was reported as "absent without leave and supposed to be sick." On his company roll covering the period from July to December, 1778, he was reported as "sick at Prince Town." The roll for January and February, 1780, reported him "transferred to Corps of Invalids."

During the latter part of the war he became a Loyalist and fled from the Mohawk Valley to Canada leaving behind land and other property.

WEMPLE, JOHN: Born at Fort Hunter, October 15, 1749. He was living in Schenectady in 1775 when he enrolled under Captain John Mynderse, 2d Albany County Militia. In January, 1776, he took part in the expedition to Johnstown. In the fall of 1776 he served at Skenesborough and Fort Ann for the purpose of guarding boats. In the spring of 1777 he went to Jessup's Patent in pursuit of Tories. He served five months during the campaign against Burgoyne, taking part in the battle of Snookkill. He was at Ballston in 1780 when it was burned and at Warren's Bush in 1781 under Colonel Willett. He performed considerable guard and garrison duty at Fort Plain, Fort Plank, Fort Paris and at the Schoharie Forts. A pensioner under the Act of June 7, 1832.

WEMPLE, JOHN J.: He served as a sergeant under Captain Thomas Brower Banker, 2d Albany County Militia.

WEMPLE, JOHN R.: Born April 18, 1732; died September 14, 1814. He served as a private and as a sergeant in the 2d Albany County Militia. On May 20, 1777, he testified before the Committee of Safety that his shoulder had been put out of joint and that he was therefore unfit for military duty.

WEMPLE, JOHN T.: His name appears on the rolls of the 2d Albany County Militia.

WEMPLE, MYNDERT: Born December 26, 1737; died December 18, 1821. His name appears on the rolls of the 2d Albany County Militia.

WEMPLE, MYNDERT A.: Baptized February 9, 1753; died November 10, 1804. On May 27, 1775, he was appointed second lieutenant in Captain Jellis J. Fonda's company, 2d Albany County Militia. On July 10 he refused an offer of a recruiting warrant from the Provincial Congress, and on June 20, 1778, was reappointed second lieutenant. On February 25, 1780, he was promoted to the rank of first lieutenant and assigned to the company of Captain John Mynderse.

WEMPLE, MYNDERT M.: Baptized November 20, 1738; died in 1789. On May 15, 1776, he was delegated to collect wagons to carry provisions from Albany to Lake George. On April 25, 1777, he was appointed chairman *pro tempore* of the Committee of Safety. On June 20, 1778, he was commissioned second major of the 2d Albany County Militia to succeed Nicholas Veeder. In September or October, 1779, he commanded a detachment to Fort Plank and Stone Arabia.

WEMPLE, MYNDERT R.: Born September 30, 1742. He served as an ensign in the 2d Albany County Militia. In 1777 he is mentioned as captain of a company of batteaumen performing service in transporting provisions and stores for the troops on the Hudson and Mohawk Rivers.

WEMPLE, RYER: Baptized October 17, 1703; died in 1796. His name appears on the rolls of the 2d Albany County Militia, Land Bounty Rights.

WENDELL, HARMANUS H.: Died previous to March 2, 1777. A merchant. He was a member of the fourth Committee of Safety.

WENDELL, JOHN BAPTIST: Born March 6, 1732. On March 1, 1776, he signed an agreement with Philip Schuyler for service at Lake George and Ticonderoga. His name appears on the rolls of the 2d Albany County Militia as serving under Captain John Van Patten.

WENDLE, AHASUERAS: Born in Schenectady, December 21, 1755; died February 22, 1848. On May 6, 1775, he was chosen a member of the first Committee of Safety. He served also on the second and third Committees. On May 27, together with Henry Glen, he was delegated by the Committee to go to Johnstown to inquire into the cause of the disturbances arising over the Sheriff White incident. On July 10, 1775, he was recommended to the Provincial Congress for the position of second lieutenant in the recruiting service. In the fall of 1775 he was enrolled in the company of Captain John Van Patten and in this company he served to the end of the war. In January, 1776, he took part in the expedition to Johnstown. On February 28, 1776, he refused to accept from General Schuyler a recruiting warrant with rank of ensign. On May 13, 1776, General Schuyler was requested to send him back from Lake George for the reason that he was employed in the Continental service without having signed the General Association. From June to October, 1777, he was on duty at Fort Edward and other forts in the vicinity. He was in command of a detachment at the battle of Bemis Heights, two of the officers being unfit for duty. In the fall of 1780 he marched with the militia under General Van Rensselaer in pursuit of Sir John Johnson, and in the fall of 1781 was with the troops under Colonel Willett in pursuit of Major Ross and Butler. A pensioner under the Act of June 7, 1832.

WESSEL, ARENT: Baptized June 17, 1752. His name appears on the rolls of the 2d Albany County Militia.

WESSEL, HARMANUS: Born in 1754; died March 10, 1813. Buried in Vale Cemetery. His name appears on the rolls of the 2d Albany County Militia.

WHEATON, REUBEN: Born in the Schenectady Township in September, 1763. In the spring of 1778 he was enrolled under Captain Jesse Van Slyck, 2d Albany County Militia. He served to the end of the war, performing considerable guard and scout duty. In August, 1780, he served at Fort Plank and Fort Plain, and in 1781 was on duty when

Major Ross and Butler descended on the settlements. A pensioner under the Act of June 7, 1832.

WHEATON, THOMAS: He served as a sergeant under Captain Jesse Van Slyck, 2d Albany County Militia. In May, 1779, he was in command of a detail for scout duty to Sacandaga, Fish House and Mayfield, and in September to Sacandaga and Johnstown. In June, 1780, he was second in command of a detail to Beaverdam and Harpersfield, and in September in command of a detail for scout duty to Sacandaga and Mayfield. In May, 1781, he went on scout duty to Glens Falls.

WHITE, WILLIAM: He lived on Church Street. At his house on May 9, 1775, was held the first meeting of the Committee of Safety, as well as several subsequent meetings and the election of members for the third Committee on May 7, 1776. On June 27, 1775, in order to show the friendly disposition of the Board, five Oneida Indians were ordered entertained at his house during their stay in town. On July 26, 1779, he was elected a member of the Committee of Safety. His name appears on the rolls of the 2d Albany County Militia.

WIEST, CONRAD: His name appears on the rolls of the 2d Albany County Militia.

WILEY, JOHN: His name appears on the rolls of the 2d Albany County Militia and the 2d Albany County Militia, Land Bounty Rights.

WILLIAMS, CORNELIUS: His name appears on the rolls of the 2d Albany County Militia. In 1778 he was enrolled under Captain Jesse Van Slyck. In August, 1782, he was on garrison duty at the Upper Fort, Schoharie.

WILLIAMS, JACOB: In 1778 he was serving as a sergeant under Captain Jesse Van Slyck, 2d Albany County Militia. In June he commanded a detail to Cobleskill, and in

August, 1782, was on garrison duty at the Upper Fort, Schoharie.

WILLIAMS, WILLIAM, 2D: He served as a private in the New York Line. A pensioner under the Act of March 18, 1818.

WILSON, JAMES: A merchant. On May 6, 1775, he was elected a member of the first Committee of Safety. He served also on the second Committee, on the Committee taking office June 2, 1777, and as clerk of the Committee taking office January 5, 1778. He was a deputy for the election of representatives to the first Provincial Congress.

WINNE, ANTHONY: On August 12, 1777, he was arrested and sent to Albany as implicated in a Tory plot. He was, however, at once released by the Albany Committee.

WOOD, JAMES: Born in 1760; died February 11, 1827. On June 8, 1780, he enlisted for the war under Captain Philip de Bevier, 5th New York Line. He was subsequently selected from his company to serve in the Light Infantry under the Marquis de Lafayette and was attached to Captain Aaron Austin's company, 3d New York Line. Later in the year he was transferred to a company under Captain Leonard Bleecker. In the fall of 1780 he returned to go into winter quarters and was attached to the company of Captain John F. Hamtramck, 2d New York Line. In 1782 "when the infantry went south" he was left sick in Albany. On his recovery he was attached to the company of Captain Henry Du Bois, 2d New York Line, and in this company he remained until peace was declared. On his discharge he was honored with the badge of merit. A pensioner under the Act of March 18, 1818.

WOOD, JOHN: His name appears on the rolls of the 2d Albany County Militia.

WRIGHT, JOHN: He lived in Schenectady at the time of the Revolution and died here. He served as a private in the

2d Dutchess County Militia under Colonel Abraham Brinckerhoff in the company commanded by Captain Nicholas Brower.

YATES, ABRAHAM: Born in Schenectady, February 27, 1757. He served as a private and as a corporal in the 2d Albany County Militia.

YATES, CHRISTOPHER: Born July 8, 1737, at the old homestead in Alplaus; died September 1, 1785. Buried in Vale Cemetery. During the Revolution he lived in the house built by himself now No. 26 Front Street. In this house was born his son, Joseph C., first mayor of Schenectady (1798) and governor of New York State (1823-1824). Christopher Yates was a surveyor by profession and "one of the best informed and most efficient patriots in the Mohawk Valley." On May 6, 1775, he was elected a member of the first Committee of Safety and at the first meeting on the ninth was chosen chairman of the Board. On May 24 he was appointed one of a committee to go to Guy Park to deliver an answer to a speech made by the Mohawk Indians. On June 30 he was appointed by the Provincial Congress one of a committee to determine the ranks of the various officers serving in the New York regiments. On July 26 a letter was addressed to him by the Committee asking whether or not he had resigned from the Board, and on August 9 he tendered his resignation. On November 7 he was elected a member of the second Committee of Safety, and on December 29, was appointed deputy clerk of the Board. On January 13, 1776, he was appointed lieutenant-colonel of the 2d Albany County Militia, and on March 5 Henry Glen was instructed to apply to Congress for his commission. On May 7, 1776, he was elected a member of the third Committee of Safety. From the fall of 1776 to July 8, 1777, he was in command when detachments of the regiment were on duty at Fort Ann. It is claimed that about this time Yates served on the staff of General Schuyler as a deputy quartermaster-general and that he was afterwards promoted to the rank of colonel. The evidence to support this claim is contained in letters from General Schuyler, Benedict Arnold, Governor Morgan Lewis, etc., which were at one time in the possession of Judge A. A. Yates of this city. No evidence of this detail and appointment is to be found on the regimental rolls. After the evacuation of Fort Ann (July 8) he had command of a body of Schenectady militia engaged in felling trees to stop the progress of General Burgoyne's army. He served throughout the campaign and with General Arnold selected the American position at Bemis Heights. On October 19 he was appointed by the State Committee of Safety one of a committee to repair to Albany to confer with General Philip Schuyler regarding means for checking the advance of the enemy on the northern and western frontiers. He served during the rest of the war in the Quartermaster's Department as a deputy, for the most part of the time stationed at Saratoga. In June, 1779, he was engaged in forwarding the baggage of General Clinton's brigade.

YATES, JELLIS: Born March 27, 1744; died in Glenville, November 13, 1812. On June 20, 1778, he was commissioned first lieutenant in Captain Abraham Van Eps's company, 2d Albany County Militia. In August, 1778, and again in October, 1779, he was on garrison duty at Fort Plank, and in the fall of 1780 at Caughnawaga.

YATES, JOHN: Born June 12, 1760; died December 19, 1826. Buried in Vale Cemetery. His name appears on the rolls of the 2d Albany County Militia.

YATES, NICHOLAS: On October 20, 1775, he was commissioned ensign in Captain Jellis J. Fonda's company, 2d Albany County Militia, and was reappointed June 20, 1778. On February 25, 1780, he was promoted to the rank of first lieutenant and served as such to the end of the war. In July, 1778, he was in command of a scout to Ballston and Galway, on which occasion he took four prisoners. During the year 1780 he was twice on duty at Fort Hunter.

YOUNG, BENJAMIN: On February 10, 1776, he was elected ensign in Captain Thomas Brower Banker's company, 2d Albany County Militia. On July 11 he was elected a member of the Committee of Safety and on July 14, 1777, appointed to command a body of militia to assist in impressing wagons for the service. He is also spoken of as having served as a lieutenant under Captain Banker.

YOUNG, CALVIN: On December 27, 1777, he was fined for buying clothes of a soldier. His name appears on the rolls of the 2d Albany County Militia.

YOUNG, FREDERIC: His name appears on the rolls of the 2d Albany County Militia.

YOUNG, GUY: On June 28, 1775, he was appointed a second lieutenant in the 2d New York Line and was promoted to the rank of first lieutenant on February 16, 1776. He was subsequently transferred to the 1st New York Line, and on March 26, 1777, was serving as a captain lieutenant. From July 14, 1779, to January 1, 1781, when he was retired, he held the rank of captain. He subsequently served as a captain in the Levies under Colonel Marinus Willett.

YOUNG, SETH: His name appears on the rolls of the 2d Albany County Militia.

MANUSCRIPT SOURCES

Documents, muster rolls, letters, etc., in the possession of the author.

Journal of Jabez Maud Fisher, a copy of which is to be found in the Herkimer County Historical Society.

Letter Books of Colonel Hugh Hughes. The New York Historical Society.

Journal of the expedition to Canada in 1775, kept by Colonel Henry B. Livingston.

Minutes of the Proceedings of the Committee for the City and County of Albany. New York State Library, Albany, N. Y.

Minutes of the Schenectady Committee of Safety from January 15, 1777, to February 17, 1778. Force Collection, Manuscript Division, Library of Congress, Washington, D. C.

Minutes of the Schenectady Committee of Safety from June 15, 1779, to August 15, 1779. From a copy in the possession of Mr. E. Z. Carpenter.

Papers of the Continental Congress. Library of Congress, Washington, D. C.

Pension Office Records.

Records of the Daughters of the American Revolution, Washington, D. C.

Records of St. George's Lodge as contained in a paper entitled, "St. George's Lodge in the Revolution," written by Mr. Hanford Robison.

Transcripts of the Loyalist Papers in the British Museum. New York Public Library, New York City.

Trumbull Papers. Massachusetts Historical Society.

Washington Papers. Manuscript Division, Library of Congress, Washington, D. C.

BIBLIOGRAPHY

Bloodgood, S. de Witt. The Sexagenary: or Reminiscences of the American Revolution. 1866.

Campbell, Douglas. Central New York in the Revolution. New York, 1878.

Campbell, William W. Annals of Tryon County. New York, 1831.

Chastellux, Francis Jean. Travels in North America in the years 1780, 1781 and 1782. London, 1787.

Cook, Frederick. Journals of the Military Expedition of Major John Sullivan against the Six Nations of Indians in 1779. Auburn, 1887.

Flick, Alexander C. Loyalism in New York during the American Revolution. 1901.

Gardner, Asa Bird. The New York Continental Line of the Army of the Revolution. Magazine of American History, December, 1881.

Halsey, Francis Whiting. The Old New York Frontier. 1901.

Hanson, James Howard. The Minute Book of the Committee of Safety of Tryon County. New York, 1905.

Heitman, Francis B. Historical Register of Officers of the Continental Army during the War of the Revolution. Washington, D. C., 1914.

Hough, Franklin B. The Northern Invasion of October, 1780. Bradford Club Series. 1866.

Howell and Tenney. History of Albany and Schenectady Counties. New York, 1886.

Jones, Charles Henry. History of the Campaign for the Conquest of Canada in 1776. Philadelphia, 1882.

Mahan, A. T. The Major Operations of the Navies in the War of American Independence. 1913.

Morgan, Lewis H. League of the Ho-de-no-sau-nee or Iroquois. New York, 1901.

Pearson, Professor Jonathan. Contributions for the Genealogies of the Descendants of the First Settlers of the Patent and City of Schenectady. Albany, 1873.

Pearson, Professor Jonathan. A History of the Schenectady Patent. Albany, 1883.

Roberts, James. New York in the Revolution. Albany, 1898.

Sanders, Honorable John. Centennial Address relating to the Early History of Schenectady and its First Settlers. Albany, 1879.

Schermerhorn, Richard, Jr. Schermerhorn Genealogy and Family Chronicles. New York, 1914.

Simms, Jeptha R. The Frontiersmen of New York. Albany, 1882.

Smith, Richard. A Tour of Four Great Rivers. Being the Journal of Richard Smith. New York, 1906.

Stone, William L. Life of Joseph Brant. Albany, 1864.

Stone, William L. The Life and Times of Sir William Johnson, Bart. Albany, 1865.

Stone, William L. Orderly Book of Sir John Johnson during the Oriskany Campaign. Albany, 1882.

Yates, Austin A. Schenectady County, New York. Its History to the Close of the Nineteenth Century. 1902.

American Archives, 4th Series.

The American Historian and Quarterly Genealogical Record. Edited by the Historical Society. Schenectady, 1875-1876. Vol. I, Nos. 1-4 (all published).

The American Monthly Magazine. April, 1902.

Calendar of Historical Manuscripts, relating to the War of the Revolution in the office of the Secretary of State. Albany, 1868.

Census of Pensioners for Revolutionary or Military Services as returned under the Act for taking the 6th Census in 1840. Washington, 1841.

Documents Relating to the Colonial History of New York. Vols. VIII and X. Albany, 1857.

Journals of the American Congress. Washington, 1823.

Documents Relating to the Colonial History of the State of New York. Edited by Berthold Fernow. Vol. XV. State Archives, Vol. I. Albany, 1887.

Early Schenectady Cemetery Records. Being a corrected list of inscriptions on tombstones taken from the burial ground between Front and Green Streets in 1879. Compiled by Charlotte T. Luckhurst.

Minutes of the Commissioners for Detecting and Defeating Conspiracies in the State of New York. Published by the State. 1909.

The New York Genealogical and Biographical Record.

Orderly Book of the Northern Army at Ticonderoga and Mt. Independence. Albany, 1859.

Public Papers of George Clinton, First Governor of New York. Published by the State. 1899.

Records from Family Cemeteries near Schenectady. Collected by William A. Brinkman and arranged by Charlotte T. Luckhurst.

Report of the Secretary of War in Relation to the Pensions Establishment of the United States. Washington, 1835.

A true copy of all the Members recorded in the First Reformed Dutch Church of Schenectady, N. Y., from April 11, 1694, to September 22, 1839. Compiled by Charlotte T. Luckhurst.

United States Census. 1890.

INDEX

INDEX

Aalplaats, the: 61.
Academy built by Dutch Reformed Church: 125.
Adams, William: 129.
Albany: sends troops to Ticonderoga and Crown Point, 23; council with Indians held at, 44; concentration center for accused Loyalists, 59; British forces to converge upon, 64; watch established, 66; in panic, 72, 108, 119; aid solicited for victims of fire in Schenectady, 78; complaint of partiality shown to citizens of, 81; alarmed by news of attack on Cobleskill, 85; threatened from Ticonderoga, 116; rumors of attack continue after Yorktown, 121.
Albany County: just treatment of Loyalists, 59; their obnoxious attitude after failure of Canadian expedition, 61; Tories go over to enemy, 97.
Albany Sons of Liberty: 11.
Alexander, Alexander: 129.
Alexander, Robert: 129.
Alexander, Sandy: 129.
Allen, Ethan: takes Fort Ticonderoga, 23.
Ament, Eldert: 129.
American Historian and Quarterly Genealogical Record: 18.
American flotilla on Lake Champlain: 55.
Andrews, Reverend William: 7.
Andrustown: 87.
Arnold, Benedict: retreat from Canada, 55; siege of Fort Stanwix raised at approach of, 75; deprives Burgoyne of reinforcements, 76; plot to surrender West Point, 103; burned in effigy at Schenectady, 123.
Articles of Association: signed by Continental Congress, 17; paper reopened for signature, 57; refusal to sign cause for seizure, 58; Loyalists forced to sign, 60; certificates of character refused those who had not signed, 60.
"Associated Exempts": 87, 94.
Association, General: see Articles of Association.

Ballston: 66, 107; raid on, 102.
Banker, Thomas Brower: 31, 33, 129.
Barclay, James: 130.
Barhydt, Cornelius: 131.
Barhydt, Jacob: 131.
Barhydt, James: 131.
Barhydt, Jerone: 131.
Barhydt, John: 132.
Barhydt, Lewis: 132.
Barhydt, Nicholas: 33, 132.
Barhydt, Teunis: 133.
Barracks at Schenectady: erected, 62; site of, 63; converted into hospital, 80; Oneida Indians quartered in, 110.
Bartley, Daniel: 133.
Bartley, Michael: 133.
Bastian, John: 133.
Bates, David: 53, 133.
Batteaux: description of, 6; difficulty of building, 117.
Bearup, Andrew: 133.

Bearup, John: 134.
Bearup, Thomas: 134.
Beaverdam: expedition to apprehend Tories at, 84; many Tories assembled at, 97.
Becker, Gerrit: 134.
Becker, John: 104.
Beekman, Jacob: 134.
Bellinger, Frederick: 43.
Bemis Heights: battle of, 72.
Bennington, Vermont: defeat of Colonel Baum at, 76.
Berkin, William: 134.
Bestedo, Clara: 134.
Beth, Jellis: 134.
Beth, Robert: 134.
Beth, Thomas: 135.
"Blues," The: 32.
Board of War, Philadelphia: discontinues Schenectady as army post, 102.
Boat building: important industry, 6; on Lake George and Lake Champlain, 51.
Boice (Buys), Abraham: 135.
Boice (Buys), James: 135.
Bond, Richard: 135.
Bonny, Ichabod: 135.
Bonny, John: 135.
Bovie, Abraham: 135.
Bovie, Isaac: 135.
Bovie, Israel: 135.
Bovie, Jacob: 135.
Bovie, Nicholas P.: 136.
Bovie, Nicholas R.: 136.
Bowman, Frederick: 136.
Bradford, James: 136.
Bradt, Andries: 136.
Bradt, Anthony D.: 136.
Bradt, Arent A.: 137.
Bradt, Arent S.: 137.
Bradt, Charles: 137.
Bradt, Cornelius: 75, 137.
Bradt, Elias: 137.

Bradt, Ephraim: 137.
Bradt, Frederick: 137.
Bradt, Gerrit: 138.
Bradt, Jacobus: 138.
Bradt, Jacobus S.: 138.
Bradt, John A.: 53, 58, 61, 138.
Bradt, John S.: 139.
Bradt, Mindert: 139.
Bradt, Samuel: 139.
Bradt, Samuel S.: 139.
Bradt's Rangers: 34, 61.
Bragham, John: 139.
Bragham, Joseph: 139.
Bragham, Simon: 139.
Brakeabean: 85.
Brant, Joseph: 40; joins Indians at Oghwaga, 65; attack upon Cobleskill, 84; raids on Springfield, Andrustown and German Flats, 87; raid on Harpersfield, 95; feint before Fort Schuyler and attack on Canajoharie, 98, 99; attack on Schoharie, 99; raid on Schoharie settlements, 102.
Brant, Molly: 40.
British, the: success around New York, 61; Indians cast their lot with, 83; emissaries stir up mutinies in American ranks, 97; pardon for those assisting, 117.
British Secret Service: document intercepted, 117.
Broachim, John: 139.
Brower, Hendric: 140.
Brower, Richard: 140.
Brown, Abraham: 140.
Brown, Colonel: 105, 106.
Brown, John: 140.
Burgoyne, General John: 56; submits plan of campaign to British Ministry, 64; arrives at Crown Point and Ticonderoga,

INDEX

71; advances to Fort Edward, 72; surrender of, 77.
Burnham, William: 140.
Burns, Arent: 140.
Burns, David: 140.
Burying ground: remains of American soldiers exhumed from, 80.
Butler, Captain Walter: 40, 102; attack on Cherry Valley, 88; killed at West Canada Creek and news of death received with rejoicing at Schenectady, 120.

Cahill, John: 140.
Cain, Barent: 140.
Cain, Peter Warren: 140.
Campbell, Alexander: 4, 58, 59, 60, 141.
Campbell, Daniel: 4, 21, 58, 60, 142.
Campbell, Kenneth: 143.
Canajoharie: no proper storehouses at, 91; Brant's attack upon, 98, 99.
Canoot, John: 143.
Carley, Joseph: 143.
Carleton, General Sir Guy: campaign against Crown Point and Ticonderoga, 56; returns to winter quarters in Canada, 56; General Burgoyne serving under, 64.
Carleton, Major Christopher: 79, 108; takes possession of Fort Ann, 102.
Cartwright, Henry: 143.
Cartwright, John: 143.
Cassada (or Cassety), John: 143.
Catlet, Thomas: 144.
Caughnawaga: 96, 98; Indians, 110.
Celder, Abraham: 144.
Ceron, Christopher: 144.

Cessler, Thomas: 144.
Chamblee: Schenectady troops assist in reduction of, 52.
Channel, John: 144.
Channel, Thomas: 144.
Charles, Hendrick: 144.
Chastelleux, Marquis de: description of Indian encampment at Schenectady by, 112, 113.
Cherry Valley: alarm of Indian and Tory raids, 65; attacks upon, 88, 116.
Childs, Captain: Continental troops at Schenectady under, 76.
Christiannse, Ahasueras: 144.
Christiannse, Isaac: 144.
Cilker, William: 145.
Clark, Henry A.: 145.
Clark, Matthis: 145.
Clark, William: 145.
Clement, Arent: 145.
Clement, Eldert: 145.
Clement, Johannes: 145.
Clement, Peter: 145.
Clench, Ralph: 146.
Clench, Robert: 122, 146.
Clinton, General James: in Sullivan's Campaign, 91, 92.
Clinton, Governor George: answers Schenectady petition for redress of grievances, 82; plea from Schenectady Committee for help in raids of 1778, 86; petitioned not to reduce forces guarding Schenectady, 107; visits Schenectady and arranges to provide stronger defenses, 115.
Clute, Bartholomew: 146.
Clute, Daniel Toll: 147.
Clute, Frederick: 147.
Clute, Isaac: 147.
Clute, Jacob: 148.
Clute, Jacob P.: 148.
Clute, Jellis: 148.

Clute, John: 54, 148.
Clute, John Baptist: 149.
Clute, John Curtiss: 149.
Clute, John F.: 149.
Clute, Peter: 149.
Cobleskill: raids on, 84, 85.
Combes, John: 149.
Commissioners for the Detecting and Defeating of Conspiracies: 20; acceptance of bonds by, 60.
Committee of Correspondence, Albany County: organized, 17; calls meeting of citizens and elects Committee of Safety, 18.
Committee of Correspondence, Schenectady: formation of, suggested by Albany Sons of Liberty, 12.
Committee of Safety, Albany: calls on Schenectady for troops for Ticonderoga, 23; counsels moderation toward Sir John Johnson, 47; calls on Schenectady for assistance in Canadian expedition, 53; applies to Schenectady Board for troops to check British advance from the south, 76.
Committee of Safety, Schenectady: organization, personnel and duties of, 19; relief to poor of Boston, 20; petty annoyances to members of, 20; first measures for defense, 21; votes to raise a company for service at Fort Ticonderoga, 23; entertains band of Oneida Indians, 35; difficulty with Sir John Johnson, 46; measures for assistance in Canadian expedition, 53; requisitions wagons to carry stores to Lake George, 55; difficulty with Tories in outlying districts, 61; Tories watched more closely, 62; guard placed upon Mohawk River, stockade strengthened and barracks built, 62; watch established, 66; difficulty of obtaining wagons and men, 67; letter to General Schuyler describing gloomy situation, and requesting reinforcements, 73; preparation against Tory raid, 75; settling of disputes, hearing of charges and relief of distress, 78; petitioned for redress of grievances, 80; petition transmitted to Governor Clinton, 82; plea to governor for assistance during raids of 1778, 86.
Committee of Safety, Tryon County: calls for aid against Indians, 41; letter reporting arrest and release of John Fonda, 46; Major John Frey prime mover in organizing, 46.
Conan, Daniel: 149.
Conde, Adam: 149.
Conner, Lancaster: 150.
Conner, Simon: 150.
Conover, Samuel: 150.
Consaul, David: 150.
Consaul, Manuel: 150.
Conspiracies, Commissioners for the Detecting and Defeating of: 20, 60.
Continental Army: force protecting frontier to receive same pay as, 90.
Continental Currency: penalty for rejecting, 58; depreciation in, 95.
Continental Troops: pleas for forces to protect frontier ineffectual, 86.
Corl, Henry: 151.
Corl, John: 151.
Corl, William: 151.

INDEX

Cornu, Daniel: 152.
Cornu, Wessel: 152.
Cotton Factory Hollow: 112.
Covel, William: 153.
Crawford, Alexander: 32, 153.
Crawford, John: 153.
Crawford, Joseph: 153.
Crousehorn, John: 115, 153.
Crown Point: occupied by Seth Warner, 23; a Schenectady company stationed at, 52; plan for final stand at, 55; abandoned, 56; Burgoyne arrives at, 71.
Cummings, John: 153.
Currybush: 32, 59.
Cuyler, Cornelius: 19, 20, 153.
Cuyler, John: 154.

Davis, Abraham: 154.
Davis, John: 154.
Dayton, Colonel Elias: 40, 50.
De Garmo, Matthew: 154.
Degolyer, James: 155.
Degolyer, Joseph: 155.
De Graff, Abraham: 155.
De Graff, Andreas: 155.
De Graff, Cornelius: 155.
De Graff, Daniel: 155.
De Graff, Isaac: 155.
De Graff, Jesse: 156.
De Graff, John: 156.
De Graff, John N.: 157.
De Graff, Nicholas: 157.
De Graff, Simon: 157.
De Graff, William: 157.
De La Grange, Myndert: 157.
Dellamont, Abraham: 157.
Dellamont, Hendrick: 157.
Denny, John: 157.
De Spitzer, Aaron: 157.
De Spitzer, Gerrit: 158.
Dilleno, Hendric: 158.
Dorn, Abraham: 158.
Dorn, John: 158.

Doty, Rev. John: 60, 124, 158.
Douw, Abraham: 159.
Duane, James: 106.
Duncan, John: 4, 58, 60, 80, 159.
Duncan, Richard: 160.
Dunlap, James: 161.
Durham boats: 6.
Dutch Reformed Church: 6, 30, 67, 125.

Earley, Edward: 161.
Ellice, Alexander: 162.
Ellice, James: 60, 162.
Ellice, Robert: 163.
Empie, John: 163.
Exempts: see "Associated Exempts."

Fairly, Caleb: 163.
Fairly, John: 163.
Felthousen, Christoffel: 163.
Felthousen, John: 163.
Ferguson, Jane: 120.
Fetherly, John: 164.
Fish, Major Nicholas: stationed at Schenectady, 115.
Fisher, Jabez Maud: description of Schenectady by, 7.
Flansburgh, William F.: 164.
Fletcher, ——: 164.
Folger, Benjamin: 164.
Folger, Thomas: 164.
Fonda, Abraham: 165.
Fonda, Douw: 96.
Fonda, Jacob G.: 165.
Fonda, Jellis Abraham: 34, 120, 165.
Fonda, Jellis J.: 22, 30, 166.
Fonda, John: imprisonment, and release by mob, 45.
Fonda, N. Y.: see Caughnawaga.
Forseth, George: 167.
Fort Ann: taken by Major Carleton, 102.

Fort Edward: 52, 69, 71.
Fort George: threatened, 102.
Fort Hunter: 60, 97.
Fort, John: 167.
Fort, John D.: 167.
Fort Johnson: 3.
Fort Kayser: 105.
Fort Plank: 98.
Fort Rensselaer: 101, 107, 118.
Fort St. John's: Schenectady troops at siege of, 52.
Fort Schuyler: 40, 102, 105; Brant's feint before, 98, 99; Oneidas seek shelter in, 109.
Fort Squash: 116.
Fort Stanwix: 7, 39, 117; investment of, 74.
Fort Ticonderoga: 51; occupied by Ethan Allen with "Green Mountain Boys," 23; Americans fall back upon, 56; abandoned to Burgoyne, 71; Albany and Schenectady threatened from, 116.
Fort Volunteer: 116.
Frank, David: 167.
Freeman, Richard: 167.
French, David: 168.
Frey, Major John: 46.
Freys, Hendrick: 168.
Frontier: forces raised to protect, 90, 118; Schenectady becomes, 92, 93, 95, 107, 114; Massachusetts State Levies detailed to defend, 102; minor raids on, following surrender at Yorktown, 121; return of peace to, 123.
Furman, John: 168.

Galloway Settlement: 107.
Gansevoort, Colonel Peter: 92.
Gardinier, James: 168.
Gardner, William: 168.

German Flats: 74, 83; raids on, 87, 95.
Glen, Henry: 19, 33, 47, 81, 91, 105, 117, 168.
Glen, Isaac: 87, 169.
Glen, Jacob: 169.
Glen, John: 169.
Glen, John Sanders: 169.
Goff, Isaac: 169.
Gordon, Charles: 170.
Gordon, Joseph: 170.
Gordon, Robert: 170.
Gordon, William: 170.
Gravenberg, John: 170.
"Greens," The: 32.
Gregg, Andrew: 170.
Gregg, James: 170.
Gregg, John: 58, 170.
Groot, Abraham C.: 170.
Groot, Amos: 171.
Groot, Andrew: 171.
Groot, Cornelius: 171.
Groot, Elias: 171.
Groot, Philip: 171.
Groot, Simon: 171.
Groot, Simon A.: 171.
Groot, Simon C.: 171.
Guthrie, Abraham: 172.
Guy Park: 15, conference with Indians at, 39.

Hackney, George: 172.
Hagedorn, Harmanus: 172.
Hall, John: 172.
Hall, John W.: 172.
Hall, Nicholas: 172.
Hall, William: 172.
Hand, General: 88; appealed to from Schenectady for relief of Cherry Valley refugees, 89.
Hanna, Alexander: 172.
Hare, Peter: 173.
Harnel (Harner), Samuel: 173.
Harper, Colonel John: 96, 97.

INDEX 293

Harpersfield: raid on, 95.
Harsey, William: 173.
Hedget, Abraham: 173.
Hellebergh (Heldeberg): 107.
Helmer, Henyost: 173.
Hendrick, Peter: 173.
Henry, John: 173.
Herkimer: Schenectady Militia march as far as, in effort to overtake enemy, 106.
Herkimer, Nicholas: presides at meeting with Oneida and Tuscarora Indians, 43; commands militia at German Flats, 74; defeated at Oriskany, 74.
Hetherington, Joseph: 173.
Hilton, Benjamin: 24, 58, 173.
Hoogteling, Jacobus: 174.
Hoople, George or Jerry: 174.
Horsford, John: 174.
Horsford, Reuben: 174.
House, John George: 174.
House, Peter: 174.
Howe, General: 56; unjustly criticized for failure to co-operate with Burgoyne, 77.
Hughan, John: 174.
Hydenburgh, Sybrant: 174.

Indian Department: established, with three subdivisions, 44.
Indians: trade with, 7; contention for friendship of, 35; efforts to incite them against colonists, 37; appeal by Little Abram, 37; Guy Park conference, 39; alarming reports of uprising to be led by Colonel Guy Johnson, 40; colonists try to keep them neutral, 43; Indian Department established, 44; at Albany conference agree not to take up arms, 45; reassured regarding expedition to take Sir John Johnson, 48; effect upon, of withdrawal of American forces from Canada, 64; council at German Flats ineffectual, 65; assemble with Brant at Oghwaga, 65; council at Johnstown, 83; cast their lot with British, 83, 109; raids of 1778 by, 83; Sullivan's Campaign against, 90; only incites retaliation, 93, 109; raid Ballston and the Schoharie settlements, 102; Oneidas at Schenectady, 109; raids of 1781 by, 114; assembled at Ticonderoga, 116; at the burning of Warren's Bush, 119; deprived of British support, 123.
"Injin" (or "Engine") Hill: 112.
Inland Lock Navigation Company: 6, 124.
Iroquois Confederacy: military supremacy of, 1; liberal policy adopted towards, 123.
Iroquois Trail, Old: 2.
Isle Aux Noix: 52.
Jacquish, John: 174.
James, William: 174.
Jessups Patent: 69.
Johnson, Colonel Guy: succeeds Sir William Johnson as Superintendent of Indian Affairs, 15; antagonistic to colonists, 15; opposes Kirkland's influence with Indians, 35; reported abuse of office to promote Indian uprising, 36; his denial to Schenectady Committee, 36; reports of plots against him denied, 39; withdraws to Ontario, 40; after return to Oswego retires to Canada, 42; efforts to counteract his influence with Indians, 43.

Johnson, Sir John: succeeds to estates of Sir William Johnson, 15; refuses office of Superintendent of Indian Affairs, 15; antagonistic to colonists, 15; fortifies himself in Johnstown, 46; dispute settled, but trouble continues with, 48; expedition to apprehend, 48, 62; surrenders and is released on parole, 50; departs for Canada, 50; warned of danger, 58, 59; appearing at Tribes Hill conducts raids, 96; again escapes to Canada, 97; threatens Stone Arabia and Fort Schuyler, 101, 102; probable connection with Arnold's treason, 103; surprises Colonel John Brown, 105; defeated at Klock's Field but escapes with his command, 106.

Johnson, Sir William: settles in Mohawk Valley, 3; his restraining influence on revolutionary element, 14; death, 15; brother-in-law of Joseph Brant, 40.

Johnstown: expedition to take Sir John Johnson at, 49, 62; council with Indians at, 83; failure to intercept Sir John Johnson at, 97; defeat of Major Ross at, 120.

Kees, John: 175.
Kennedy, Alexander: 175.
Kennedy, John: 175.
Kennedy, Samuel: 175.
King George III: drinking health of, penalized, 58.
Kingsley, Joseph: 58, 60, 175.
Kinsela, Joseph: 176.
Kirkland, Reverend Samuel: undertakes to win over Oneida Indians, 35.

Kittle, Adam: 176.
Kittle, Daniel: 176.
Kittle, David: 176.
Kittle, Ezra: 176.
Kittle, John: 176.
Klock's Field: battle of, 106.

Lafayette, Marquis de: makes personal investigation of conspiracy at Schenectady, 79.
Lake Champlain: Schenectady artisans serve at, 51; General Burgoyne's army to move southward on, 64.
Lake George: Schenectady company ordered to, 26; Schenectady artisans serve at, 51.
Lambert, John: 176.
Lansing, Abraham G.: 176.
Lansing, Alexander C.: 177.
Lansing, Cornelius: 177.
Lansing, Gerrit G.: 177.
Lansing, John G.: 21, 24, 26, 177.
Lansing, John S.: 177.
Laraway, Isaac: 178.
Latta, William: 178.
Lewis, Henry: 178.
Lewis, John: 178.
Lewis, William: 178.
"Liberty or Death": motto of Schenectady minute men, 32.
Liddle, Andrew: 178.
Lighthall, Abraham (Abraham J. or W.): 178.
Lighthall, George: 179.
Lighthall, James N.: 179.
Lighthall, John: 179.
Lighthall, Lancaster: 180.
Lighthall, Nicholas: 180.
Lighthall, William: 180.
Little Abram: appeals to Magistrates and Committees of Albany and Schenectady, 37; meets General Schuyler at Schenectady, 49.

Little, David: 181.
Little, John: 31, 181.
Little, Thomas: 181.
Littlejohn, Duncan: 181.
Lower Fort, Schoharie: 104.
Loyalist Party: well defined by 1770, 13; helps to call Continental Congress but soon opposes its acts, 13.
Loyalists: activities of, 57; treatment of, fair in the main, 59; expense of trials charged to, 60; must sign Association or take Oath of Allegiance, 60; exceptionally strong in New York State, 61.
Lyne, Matthew: 181.
Lyport, David: 181.
Lyport, Jacob: 181.

McBeen, John: 182.
McCallum, James: 182.
McCarty, John: 182.
McCarty, William: 182.
McCue, James: 182.
McDonald, James: 182.
McDougal, Duncan: 182.
McDougal, John: 182.
McFarlan, Andrew: 182.
McFarlin, John: 183.
McGinnis, Robert: 183.
McIntosh, John: 183.
McIntyre, William: 183.
McKellop, Archibald: 183.
McKinney, Andrew: 183.
McMartin, William: 184.
McMichael, Alexander: 184.
McMichael, Daniel: 184.
McMichael, James: 185.
McMichael, Robert: 185.
McNutt, Samuel: 185.
McQueen, James: 185.
Mabb, John: 185.
Mabb, Robert: 185.

Main, William: 185.
Manning, Edward: 185.
Manning, John: 185.
Markle, Dirk: 185.
Markle, Matthew: 185.
Markle, William: 186.
Marselis, Ahasueras: 34, 186.
Marselis, Alexander: 186.
Marselis, Arent: 186.
Marselis, Gysbert: 186.
Marselis, Henry A.: 186.
Marselis, John Baptist: 33, 187.
Marselis, John J.: 187.
Marselis, John N.: 187.
Marselis, Richard: 188.
Martin, Charles: 188.
Martin, John: 188.
Martin, Robert: 24, 188.
Massachusetts State Levies: detailed to defend New York frontier, 102.
Mead, William: 188.
Meal, Carel: 189.
Mebie, Albert: 189.
Mebie, Arent: 189.
Mebie, Cornelius: 30, 189.
Mebie, John: 189.
Mebie, Juiter: 189.
Mebie, Patrick: 189.
Mebie, Peter: 189.
Mercer, Alexander: 190.
Mercker, William: 190.
Middle Fort, Schoharie: 104.
Militia, Schenectady: for service at Ticonderoga, 23; scale of pay, 23; uniforms, 24, 32; difficulty in obtaining men, 25, 68; dissatisfaction with officers appointed, 26, 53; recruiting and provisioning, 28; duties and term of enlistment, 29; unreliability of average, 29; poorly paid and equipped, 30, 114; reorganization of three companies

of, 30; minute men incorporated with regular militia, 32; three more companies formed, 33; for relief of Tryon County, 41; assist in Canadian expedition, 52; company of fatigue men enlisted, 54; to apprehend those accused of enmity to country, 57; strengthen stockades, 62; for Wilson's Mill, Ballston, 66; disperse Tories at Jessups Patent, 69; ordered to Fort Edward, 71; retard Burgoyne's advance, 72; refusal to join expedition to relieve Fort Stanwix, 74; ordered to main army but remain to protect Schenectady, 75; join army at Van Schaick's Island, 76; as escort to General Poor's brigade, 77; guard duty at Schenectady, 78; on duty during Indian and Tory raids of 1778, 85, 87, 88; their part in Sullivan's Campaign, 92; pursue Brant after attack on Canajoharie, 99; on duty during Indian and Tory raids at Ballston and the Schoharie settlements, 101, 107, 108; details on garrison duty, 118.

"Militia, Land Bounty Rights": 121.

Mils, Chris: 190.

Minute Men, Schenectady: meeting to organize companies, 21; motto of, 32; ordered to join in apprehending Sir John Johnson, 48.

Mitchell, Hugh: 19, 43, 190.

Mohawk Indians: 49; colonists endeavor to secure sympathy of, 35; Little Abram, chief of Lower Castle of, 37; at Guy Park conference, 39; from Upper Castle follow Colonel Johnson, 40.

Mohawk River: navigable at Schenectady, 5; to be kept open for trade, 49; guarded to prevent passage of enemies, 62; St. Leger's forces move down, 64; fear of enemy's troops appearing on, 72; General Clinton's forces to proceed up, 91, 93; superseded in commercial importance by Erie Canal, 124.

Mohawk Valley: number and nationality of settlers on eve of Revolution, 2; laid waste, 95.

Moneer, John: summoned before Committee of Safety, 60.

Moore, John: 190.

Moore, William: 32, 58, 191.

Morrell, John: Schenectady Militia take part in expedition to capture, 69.

Morrel, Thomas: 191.

Moyston, Robert: 191.

Muller, Jacob, Jr.: 191.

Munro, Major John: 103, 191.

Munroe, Alexander: 192.

Murphy, Timothy: 104.

Murray, Alexander: 192.

Murray, John: 192.

Murray, William: 58, 192.

Mynderse, Harmen: 192.

Mynderse, John: 22, 31, 192.

Mynderse, John R.: 193.

Mynderse, Lawrence: 31, 193.

Mynderse, Reinier: 19, 73, 193.

Navy, first American: 56.

Neally, Matthew: 194.

Neard, Christopher: 194.

Negroes: to be arrested by watch after ten o'clock, 67.

Neiger, John: 194.

Nesbit, Joseph: 194.

INDEX 297

Nestle, George: 194.
New Year's Day: firing of guns on, 62.
Nixon, Joshua: 194.
Northern Army: detachments of Schenectady militia remain with, 72.

Oath of Allegiance: Loyalists forced to take, 60.
Ogden, John: 194.
Ohlen, Henry George: 194.
Old Fort, Scotia: 31.
Oneida: Sir John Johnson, Butler and Brant at, 102.
Oneida Indians: Reverend Samuel Kirkland to win over, 35; meeting with Tryon County Committee, 43; do not join forces with British, 83; at Schenectady, 109; attacked for favoring colonists, 109; supported in Schenectady at expense of Government, 110; lands granted to, 123.
Oothout, Abraham: 19, 32, 33, 43, 194.
Oriskany: battle of, 74; Indian loss at, 83.
Ouderkirk, Arent: 195.
Ouderkirk, John: 195.

Passage, George: 196.
Passage, George, Jr.: 196.
Patterson, Oliver: 196.
Patterson, Thomas: 196.
Peace, declaration of: received in Schenectady amid rejoicing, 123.
Peek, Arent: 197.
Peek, Christopher: 53, 197.
Peek, Cornelius: 197.
Peek, Cornelius, Jr.: 197.
Peek, Daniel: 197.
Peek, Harmanus: 198.

Peek, Henry H.: 198.
Peek, Jacobus C.: 198.
Peek, Jacobus Vedder: 198.
Peek, James: 198.
Peek, James H. (or Jacobus): 31, 198.
Peek, Jesse: 199.
Peek, John: 33, 199.
Peek, Joseph: 199.
Peek, Lewis D.: 200.
Pendelton, Solomon: 31, 53, 200.
Peters, Harmon: 116, 201.
Peters, William: 201.
Peterson, Charles: 202.
Peterson, Harmanus: 202.
Philips, Thomas: 202.
Phyn, James: 202.
Phyn & Ellice: 4.
Post, Elias: 202.
Post, John: 21, 33, 202.
Presbyterian Meeting House: 6; congregation, 124.
Prices: regulated by Committee of Safety, 20.
Putman, Arent J.: 203.
Putman, Arent L.: 203.
Putman, Cornelius: 203.
Putman, John: 203.
Putman, Teunis: 203.
Putnam, Arent: 203.

Quackenbush, Garardus: 203.
Quackenbush, John: 203.

Raids, Indian and Tory: Cobleskill, 84; Springfield, 87; Andrustown, 87; German Flats, 87, 95; Cherry Valley, 88, 116; Harpersfield, 95; Tribes Hill, 96; Canajoharie, 98; Schoharie, 99; Ballston and Schoharie settlements, 102.
Rangers, State: company of, formed in Schenectady, 61.

298 INDEX

Ramsey, George: 20, 58, 60, 204.
Recruiting: general plan of, 28, 33.
Reis, John: 204.
Revolutionary movement: rise of, 11; gains adherents in Mohawk Valley, 15.
Righter, Michael: 204.
Robison, John: 205.
Romeyn, Doctor: 125.
Rosa, Elias: 205.
Rosa, Isaac: 205.
Rose, John: 205.
Roseboom, John: 19, 24, 34, 35, 39, 206.
Ross, Major: attacks Warren's Bush, 119; defeated at Johnstown, 120.
Rykman, Cornelius: 206.
Rykman, John: 207.
Ryley, Jacobus: 207.
Ryley, James Van Slyck: 207.
Ryley, John: 207.
Ryley, Philip: 207.
Ryley, William: 207.
Rynex, Andrew: 207.
Rynex, John: 207.
Rynex, Richard: 208.

Sacia, David: 208.
St. George's Church: attendance in 1771, 4; erected, 6; John Doty, rector, sent to Canada, 60; building and parochial activities restored, 124.
St. John, Thaddeus: 208.
St. Leger, Lieutenant-Colonel Barry: 64, 74, 75.
Salt, scarcity of: 78.
Sanders, John: 19, 58, 208.
Sawyer, James: 209.
Schenectady: description of town and inhabitants prior to Revolution, 4, 5, 6; forts and other defenses of, 7, 8, 9, 31, 62, 123; Committee of Safety and first militia companies, 17; company raised to defend Ticonderoga, 23; militia meets to form companies, 30; troubled by Tories in outlying districts, 61; town watch, 66; dejection at, after loss of Ticonderoga, 73; rumors of investment of Fort Stanwix reach, 74; disastrous fire, 78; list of grievances submitted to Committee of Safety, 80; distress and dangers due to Indian and Tory raids of 1778, 86, 88, 89; supplies for Sullivan's Campaign concentrated at, 91; as frontier of State, 92, 93, 95, 107, 114; retirement of citizens to Albany, 100; discontinued as army post, 102; memorial to Governor Clinton not to reduce forces guarding, 107; Oneida Indians at, 109; threatened from Ticonderoga, 116; rejoicing at death of Butler, 120; rumors of attack after Yorktown, 121; General Washington's visit, 122.
Schermerhorn, Aaron: 209.
Schermerhorn, Abraham: 209.
Schermerhorn, Andrew (Andreas): 209.
Schermerhorn, Barnhardus Freeman: 33, 209.
Schermerhorn, Bartholomew: 209.
Schermerhorn, Gerrit: 210.
Schermerhorn, Henry J.: 210.
Schermerhorn, Jacob: 32, 33, 75, 87, 210.
Schermerhorn, Jacob: 211.
Schermerhorn, Jacob J.: 211.
Schermerhorn, Jacobus: 211.
Schermerhorn, John J.: 211.

INDEX

Schermerhorn, Lawrence: 211.
Schermerhorn, Maus: 212.
Schermerhorn, Nicholas W.: 212.
Schermerhorn, Richard: 212.
Schermerhorn, Ryer: 212.
Schermerhorn, Simon: 213.
Schermerhorn, William: 213.
Schoharie: 2, 74, 84, 85, 86, 98; forts in vicinity of, 104.
Schoharie settlements: Indian and Tory raids on, 101, 103.
Scotia, old fort: 31.
Schuyler, Major-General Philip: advised concerning delay in sending militia to Ticonderoga, 26; orders relief to Tryon County, 41; appointed Indian Commissioner, 44; sent to apprehend Tories, 48; expedition to Johnstown, 49; advocates erection of barracks at Schenectady, 62; calls council at German Flats to hold Indians to neutrality, 65; his house at Saratoga rebuilt, 84; investigates condition of Oneida Indians at Schenectady and personally advances funds for their support, 110; visits Schenectady with General Washington, 122.
Schuyler, Reuben: 213.
Seneca Indians: 83.
Shannon, Alexander: 213.
Shannon, George: 213.
Shannon, John: 214.
Shannon, Robert: 214.
Shannon, Thomas: 214.
Shannon, William: 214.
Shearer (alias Sherwood), James: 214.
Shelling, Alexander: 214.
Shelly, Samuel: 214.
Shields, Daniel: 215.
Simonds, Reuben: 215.

Six Nations, Confederacy of: British and colonists contend for friendship of, 35; numbers in 1773, 35; to be asked to unite in measures of peace, 43; Oneidas alone favor colonists, 83, 109.
Skenesborough: 52, 56, 72.
Smilie, John: 216.
Smith, Adam: 216.
Smith, John: 216.
Smith, Robert: 216.
Snell, Major: 216.
Snow, Ephraim: 53, 216.
Speck, Abraham: 217.
Speck, Tobias: 217.
Sons of Liberty: first tendencies not revolutionary, 11; Albany organization formed, 11; favored originally by both Whigs and Tories, 11, 13; letter from Albany organization to Schenectady urging organization of Committee for Regulations and Correspondence, 12; no evidence of organization in Schenectady, 13; proposed First Continental Congress, 13.
Staley, George: 217.
Staley, Jacob: 217.
Staley, Matthias: 217.
Stanley, John: 218.
State Rangers: company of, formed in Schenectady, 61.
Steeley, Henry: 218.
Steers, John: 218.
Steers, Peter: 218.
Stevens, John: 218.
Stevens, Nicholas: 218.
Stevens, William: 34, 219.
Stewart, Daniel: 219.
Stewart, David: 219.
Stone Arabia: 3, 101, 102.
Stuart, George: 219.

Stuart, James: 219.
Stuart, John: 219.
Stuart, John: 60, 220.
Sullivan, Charles: 221.
Sullivan, Jacob: 32, 221.
Sullivan's Campaign: 90; plan of, 91; only incites Indians to retaliation, 93, 109.
Swart, Jacobus: 221.
Swart, James: 221.
Swart, Nicholas: 221.
Swart, Teunis: 30, 31, 221.
Sweet, Caleb: 222.
Swits, Abraham: 31, 32, 71, 76, 222.
Swits, Hendrick: 223.
Swits, Isaac: 223.
Swits, Jacob: 223.
Swits, Jacob A.: 223.
Swits, Walter: 116, 223.
Swords, Thomas: 223.

Taws, David: 224.
Taylor, Solomon: 224.
Taylor, Walter: 224.
Teller, Jacobus: 19, 224.
Teller, John, Jr.: 225.
Teller, William: 225.
Ten Broeck, General Abraham: 71, 76, 85, 87, 99.
Ten Eyck, Henry: 225.
Ten Eyck, Jacob T.: 225.
Ten Eyck, Myndert: 225.
Ten Eyck, Tobias: 19, 226.
Terwilliger, Isaac: 226.
Terwilliger, Jacobus: 226.
Terwilliger, Solomon: 226.
Thompson, John: 226.
Thomson, Peter: 226.
Thorn, Samuel: 226.
Thornton, James: 226.
Thornton, John: 31, 32, 227.
Thornton, Thomas: 228.

Ticonderoga: see Fort Ticonderoga.
Toll, Charles: 228.
Toll, Daniel: 30, 228.
Toll, John: 228.
Tories: from what nationalities recruited, 3; unite with Whigs in forming Sons of Liberty, 11; penalty for associating or corresponding with, 58; plots of, unearthed everywhere throughout New York, 61; close watch upon, 62; dispersed at Jessups Patent, 70; renewing activities, disarm opponents, 75; attitude less threatening after Burgoyne's reverses, 76; conspiracy at Schenectady investigated by Lafayette, 79; raids of 1778 by, 83; Sullivan's Campaign against, 90; join Sir John Johnson, 97; raids by, on Ballston and Schoharie settlements, 101; second invasion of Ballston threatened by, 108; raids of 1781 by, 114; everywhere increasing in numbers, 114; second raid on Cherry Valley by, 116; assemble at Ticonderoga, 116; burn Warren's Bush, 119.
Treason: persons charged with, 20; of Benedict Arnold, 103.
Truax, Abraham I.: 228.
Truax, Abraham J.: 31, 228.
Truax, Abraham P.: 228.
Truax, Andries: 228.
Truax, Caleb: 229.
Truax, Isaac: 229.
Truax, Isaac I.: 229.
Truax, Jacob J.: 229.
Truax, John: 229.
Truax, John P.: 230.
Truax, Peter: 230.
Trumbull, John: 230.

Tryon County: settlement of, 2; taken from Albany County, 39; districts composing, 39; appeals for aid against Indians, 41; friction with Alexander White, sheriff of, 45; General Schuyler leads expedition to, 48; militia assembles at German Flats, 74; aid solicited for victims of Schenectady fire, 78; critical situation due to raids of 1778, 86; many Tories join enemy, 97.
Tuscarora Indians: 43, 83; lands granted to, 123.
Tuttle, Ezra: 230.
Tuttle, Solomon: 230.
Tyms, Michael: 230.

Unadilla: 84, 88, 98.
Union College: 125.
Upper Fort, Schoharie: 104.

Van Antwerp, Arent J.: 34, 230.
Van Antwerp, Gerrit: 230.
Van Antwerp, John: 230.
Van Antwerp, Peter: 231.
Van Antwerp, Peter A.: 231.
Van Antwerp, Simon J.: 231.
Van Bentheuysen, Martin: 231.
Van Benthuysen, Peter: 232.
Van der Bogart, Joseph: 232.
Van der Bogart, Nicholas: 232.
Van der Bogart, Tacarus: 51, 232.
Van Derheyden, Daniel: 232.
Van Derheyden, David: 232.
Van der Volgen, Cornelius: 233.
Van der Volgen, Nicholas: 233.
Van der Volgen, Peter: 233.
Van der Werken, Martin: 234.
Van Driesen, Henry: 234.
Van Driesen, John: 33, 234.
Van Driesen, Peter: 234.
Van Dyck, Cornelius: 22, 24, 26, 52, 93, 109, 234.

Van Dyck, Cornelius H.: 235.
Van Dyck, Cornelius N.: 235.
Van Dyck, Henry: 235.
Van Dyck, Henry H.: 235.
Van Dyck, Henry I.: 235.
Van Eps, Abraham: 34, 235.
Van Eps, Abraham I.: 75.
Van Eps, Alexander: 236.
Van Eps, Gerrit: 236.
Van Eps, James: 236.
Van Eps, John: 237.
Van Eps, John Baptist: 237.
Van Eps, John J.: 238.
Van Ess, Gerrit: 238.
Van Etten, Benjamin: 238.
Van Guysling, Cornelius: 238.
Van Guysling, Elias: 238.
Van Guysling, Jacob: 239.
Van Guysling, Peter: 239.
Van Ingen, Dr. Dirk: 106, 239.
Van Ingen, John: 239.
Van Ingen, John Visscher: 240.
Van Ingen, Joseph: 240.
Van Patten, Aaron N.: 33, 240.
Van Patten, Adam: 241.
Van Patten, Andrew: 22, 30, 241.
Van Patten, Dirk: 241.
Van Patten, Frederick: 241.
Van Patten, Frederick D.: 242.
Van Patten, Frederick S.: 242.
Van Patten, Henry: 242.
Van Patten, John: 22, 30, 242.
Van Patten, Nicholas: 243.
Van Patten, Nicholas A.: 243.
Van Patten, Nicholas H.: 243.
Van Patten, Nicholas R.: 243.
Van Patten, Nicholas S.: 243.
Van Patten, Peter: 244.
Van Patten, Philip: 244.
Van Patten, Simon F.: 30, 244.
Van Rensselaer, General Robert: 101; pursues Sir John Johnson, 104, 105; defeats him at Klock's Field, permits his escape, but is

exonerated by Court of Inquiry, 106.
Van Santvoord, Cornelius Z.: 33, 244.
Van Santvoord, Zeger: 245.
Van Schaick, Gerrit: 245.
Van Schaick, Colonel Goose: 74, 95, 99.
Van Schaick's Island: 76.
Van Sice, Abraham: 245.
Van Sice, Cornelius: 245.
Van Sice, Gysbert: 245.
Van Sice, Isaac: 245.
Van Sice, Jacobus: 246.
Van Sice, John: 246.
Van Sice, Joseph: 246.
Van Slyck, Adrian: 246.
Van Slyck, Andrew: 246.
Van Slyck, Anthony: 246.
Van Slyck, Arent: 246.
Van Slyck, Cornelius A.: 87, 246.
Van Slyck, Cornelius P.: 22, 24, 26, 69, 246.
Van Slyck, Harmanus: 247.
Van Slyck, Harmanus A.: 247.
Van Slyck, Jesse: 34, 247.
Van Slyck, Martin: 248.
Van Slyck, Peter: 248.
Van Slyck, Samuel: 248.
Van Veghten, Anthony: 46.
Van Vleck, Benjamin: 248.
Van Vorst, Abraham: 249.
Van Vorst, Ahasueras: 249.
Van Vorst, James: 249.
Van Vorst, James J.: 249.
Van Vorst, Jellis: 249.
Van Vorst, John B.: 250.
Van Vorst, John Jacob: 250.
Van Vorst, Peter: 251.
Van Vorst, Philip D.: 34, 251.
Van Vranken, Derick: 251.
Van Vranken, Gerrit: 251.
Van Vranken, Maus: 251.
Van Vranken, Nicholas: 252.

Van Vranken, Nicholas N.: 252.
Van Vranken, Richard: 252.
Van Vranken, Ryckert: 253.
Vedder, Albert A.: 253.
Vedder, Albert H.: 253.
Vedder, Albert L.: 253.
Vedder, Alexander: 253.
Vedder, Arent A.: 254.
Vedder, Arent S.: 33, 254.
Vedder, Francis: 34, 254.
Vedder, Frederick: 254.
Vedder, Harmanus: 255.
Vedder, John: 255.
Vedder, John: 34, 255.
Vedder, Nicholas Alexander: 255.
Vedder, Philip: 30, 255.
Vedder, Simon: 59.
Vedder, Simon H.: 256.
Vedder, Colonel Volkert: 97.
Veeder, Barent: 256.
Veeder, Claus: (see Veeder, Michael).
Veeder, Cornelius: 256.
Veeder, Gerrit (S. or N.): 22, 31, 53, 256.
Veeder, Helmar S.: 256.
Veeder, Hendrick: 257.
Veeder, John B.: 257.
Veeder, John H.: 257.
Veeder, Michael: 51.
Veeder, Nicholas G.: 257.
Veeder, Nicholas P.: 32, 258.
Veeder, Peter S.: 258.
Veeder, Simon: 258.
Veeder, Simon B.: 259.
Veeder, Simon H.: 259.
Veeder, Wilhelmus: 259.
Viele, Philip: 259.
Visscher, Colonel Frederick: 96, 122.
Visscher, Harman: 96.
Visscher, John: 96.
Visscher, John: 260.
Visscher, John, Jr.: 260.

INDEX

Vrooman, Abraham: 260.
Vrooman, Adam: 261.
Vrooman, Adam S.: 261.
Vrooman, Arent: 261.
Vrooman, Barent: 261.
Vrooman, Cornelius: 261.
Vrooman, David: 262.
Vrooman, Hendrick: 262.
Vrooman, Isaac: 262.
Vrooman, Jacob A.: 262.
Vrooman, Jacob I.: 262.
Vrooman, Jacob J.: 262.
Vrooman, Jacob S.: 51, 84, 262.
Vrooman, John B.: 31, 33, 263.
Vrooman, John J.: 263.
Vrooman, John T.: 263.
Vrooman, Lawrence: 30, 263.
Vrooman, Nicholas: 264.
Vrooman, Colonel Peter: 98.
Vrooman, Simon J.: 264.
Vrooman, Walter: 34, 265.

Waggerman, George: 266.
Waggerman, Michael: 266.
Wagner, Andrew: 266.
Wagner, Michael: 266.
Wagner, Nicholas: 266.
Ward, Christopher: 266.
Warn, Richard: 267.
Warn, Samuel: 267.
Warner, Colonel Seth: 23, 69.
Warren's Bush: 3; attack upon, 119.
Washington, General George: 62; directs Sullivan's Campaign, 90; informed of Brant's attack on Canajoharie, 99; visits Albany and Schenectady, 121, 122.
Wasson, James: 267.
Wasson, John: 267.
Wasson, Thomas: 31, 268.
Wasson, Thomas J.: 268.
Watch: establishment and regula-

tions of, 66; militia to guard town, 75, 78.
Watson, Alexander: 268.
Weller, Frederick: 268.
Weller, Robert: 269.
Welsh, John: 24, 269.
Wemple, Abraham: 31, 32, 53, 65, 68, 77, 84, 85, 99, 107, 269.
Wemple, Barent (Wemp, Barnabas): 269.
Wemple, John: 270.
Wemple, John J.: 270.
Wemple, John R.: 270.
Wemple, John T.: 270.
Wemple, Myndert: 270.
Wemple, Myndert A.: 22, 30, 31, 270.
Wemple, Myndert M.: 32, 55, 271.
Wemple, Myndert R.: 22, 271.
Wemple, Ryer: 271.
Wendel, Ahasueras: 271.
Wendell, Harmanus H.: 19, 47, 52, 271.
Wendell, John Baptist: 271.
Wessel, Arent: 272.
Wessel, Harmanus: 272.
West Canada Creek: engagement at, 120.
Westina, the: 21, 30, 61.
Wheaton, Reuben: 272.
Wheaton, Thomas: 273.
Whig Party: well defined by 1770, 13.
White, Alexander: sheriff of Tryon County, arrests John Fonda, 45; leaves Johnstown, 47.
White, William: 19, 35, 273.
Wiest, Conrad: 273.
Wiley, John: 273.
Willet, Colonel Marinus: 118, 119, 120.
Williams, Cornelius: 273.
Williams, Jacob: 273.
Williams, William, 2d: 274.

Wilson, James: 19, 274.
Winne, Anthony: 274.
Woestyne: see Westina.
Wood, James: 274.
Wood, John: 274.
Wright, John: 274.
Wynkoop, Colonel Cornelius D.: 54.
Wyoming massacre: 87.

Yates, Abraham: 275.
Yates, Christopher: 19, 32, 39, 72, 84, 85, 92, 275.

Yates, Christopher P.: 45, 46.
Yates, Jellis: 34, 276.
Yates, John: 276.
Yates, Nicholas: 30, 276.
Yorktown: surrender of Lord Cornwallis at, 120; period following, 121.
Young, Benjamin: 33, 277.
Young, Calvin: 277.
Young, Frederic: 277.
Young, Guy: 277.
Young, Seth: 277.

www.ingramcontent.com/pod-product-compliance
Lightning Source LLC
Chambersburg PA
CBHW071957220426
43662CB00009B/1165